Rules, Rubrics and Riches

Rules, Rubrics and Riches highlights the limitations of existing approaches to understanding the relationship of the law to the process of development. It interrogates neoclassical economic thinking that draws on the narrow rubric of self-interest to understand the acquisition of riches. It takes issue with both the traditional 'law and development' movement, that was unable to shake colonial overtones, and the more recent 'law and economics' school that continues to emphasise the centrality of rational man at the micro level and the superiority of linear models of economic progress at the macro level.

Written as an analysis of and commentary on the contribution of the law to international development, using legal cases and development trajectories in China, India and Malaysia, the book makes the case that individuals do not operate in a vacuum but rather within the social contexts of larger human structures such as family, community and nation. *Rules, Rubrics and Riches* is distinctive in the view that demanding equality for the individual is inappropriate if this occurs without looking at the broader context of the need for equity: within families, communities and nations. The book offers a new frame for 'law and development' thinking that points to a new set of rules, using a broader rubric to ensure a sustainable accumulation of riches. It will be of interest to students and scholars working in the fields of law and development, development studies and international and comparative law.

Shailaja Fennell is University Lecturer in Development Studies at the University of Cambridge. Her research interests include institutional reform; provision of education; and gender, kinship and ethnicity. Her recent publications include *Gender Education and Development: Conceptual Frameworks, Engagements and Agendas* (2007), edited with M. Arnot.

Rules, Rubrics and Riches

The Interrelations between Legal Reform and International Development

Shailaja Fennell

Routledge
Taylor & Francis Group
a GlassHouse book

First published 2010
by Routledge
2 Park Square, Milton Park, Abingdon, Oxon, OX14 4RN

Simultaneously published in the USA and Canada
by Routledge
270 Madison Avenue, New York, NY 10016

A GlassHouse book

Routledge is an imprint of the Taylor & Francis Group, an informa business

Transferred to Digital Printing 2010

Typeset in Sabon by Taylor & Francis Books

British Library Cataloguing in Publication Data
A catalogue record for this book is available from the British Library

Library of Congress Cataloguing in Publication Data
A Catalogue record for this book has been requested

ISBN10: 1-904385-29-X (hbk)
ISBN13: 978-1-904385-29-5 (hbk)

ISBN10: 0-415-42035-0 (pbk)
ISBN13: 978-0-415-42035-8 (pbk)

ISBN10: 020-3-87151-0 (ebk)
ISBN13: 978-020-3-87151-5 (ebk)

Contents

Figures

Preface

The advent of capitalism gave a very particular twist to accumulating riches whereby, over the last two centuries, it has come to be regarded as the ultimate mark of individual, corporate and national success. The attraction of wealth creation has reworked the very legal foundations of the State and it is the rules of the market that have grown to become the most important set of directives to ensure economic development at the end of the twentieth century. The older rubric of equity within communities and across nations has been replaced by a demand for individual-based equality of rights that has severed the link between the legal right of wealth accumulation and the obligation to protect the equitable distribution of wealth.

The ascendancy of self-interest as the rubric for market exchanges and the demotion of the law to a mere instrument for ensuring private contracts and protecting private property has blinded the market to inequalities and hierarchies within society. Economic development has continued to be blind to social differentiation, as technical models it adopts do not account for the gendered impact of accumulation processes on the household and families within a nation till the very end of the twentieth century. Advancing the right of the individual without ensuring there are laws to protect as well as constrain the economic decision-making power of enterprising individuals and organisations has resulted in class and group discrimination across Asia, Africa and Latin America. In this intellectually arid and restrictively technical rubric, judicial activism has emerged as the sole champion, and the mechanism of affirmative action has been drawn on to redress historical injustices even as the corporate sphere sees a further growth in the power of the firms to accumulate and direct wealth to the rich. The legal system in developing countries has, nonetheless, been reduced to an economic instrument and continues to overlook people who reside in marginal worlds, and ignores sub-national and local understandings and meanings of law. The excluding tendency of capitalism and resulting exploitation generate, as a reaction, the counter-tendencies that manifest themselves in sub-national and local spaces of society in forms of collective violence and have shown an increasing tendency to spill over national borders.

Within this dominant rubric of the market, international development continues to require the guidance of the nation-state, and it is the national government that gives the directives for reorganising and reorienting national economic production to expand domestic production and permit external trade. The guiding spirit of the United Nations system was to regard developing-economy nations as equal players in the global sphere and trade treaties were seen as an international convention akin to international law. With the advent of the World Trade Organisation (WTO) there has been a shift to a more overtly contractual system. Agreements in the WTO have skewed the realm of political statesmanship, and international trading is based on the notion that all countries have the same economic structure. The opposition of global institutions to national actions that are regarded as inimical to free trade weakens the ability of developing countries to ensure continued domestic production of goods and services and generation of employment within the nation-state. Investigating the power of the disciplinary rubrics to understand the process of capitalist development, and particularly of how interplay between economics and law provided a possible way forward to reorder how we conceptualise the relationship between riches and rules, has been a major reason for writing this book.

My explorations in international development began when I took up the study of economics in the early 1980s. I was struck then by the huge impact of historical processes on the development strategies of countries, a feature that seemed to be equally important for the early developers such as Britain and the United States as it was for the latecomers to development such as India and China. I continue to be fascinated by the manner in which social structures and institutions impact development processes in multiple ways: through the legal system, social norms and forms of collective engagement. The early attraction of studying Asia's two largest countries, China and India, so similar in size, population and economic structure and yet so different in their political systems, deepened into a doctoral dissertation of household, community and national trends in Chinese and Indian agriculture., As part of the process of travelling across Asia on my research I was fortunate enough to spend time in Malaysia, and was completely caught up by its rich diversity of language, ethnicity and its powerful historical experience. I have turned to these countries to understand their development experience, by exploring their legal systems, digging out cases that show the complexities of moving from households community to nation within an increasingly global market, and putting together the puzzle of how a particular understanding of rules, rubrics and riches affect the course of international development and the promise and opportunity provided by legal reforms to alter both direction and contours.

This book has been in the making for nearly five years. Its roots go back even further to the Michaelmas term of 1997, at the University of Cambridge, when as a recently appointed lecturer in development studies I was asked to teach topics in regulation on a lecture course on law and economics that was jointly provided by the Faculty of Law and the Department of Land Economy at the University of Cambridge. Having read the likes of Ronald Coase, Oliver Williamson, Eric Furubotn and Oliver Hart that were located within a large and heterodox framework of the political economy of labour and capital, as a graduate student taking a course on institutions, I was surprised to find that the world of law and economics was inhabited by a far more neoclassical set of views: those of Richard Tullock and Richard Posner, with much narrower views on the relationship between economic behaviour, legal rules and social structures. My disquiet about the particular contributions of the new field of law and economics grew as I read recommended texts that seem to overlay the framework of marginal economics onto the legal rules and principles that inform the discipline of the law.

As is the wont of a university lecturer, I took the opportunity to raise these questions in my graduate lectures, seminars and classes and gained hugely from the comments and criticisms of many cohorts of development-studies students, who came to the MPhil course from a range of disciplinary stables across the social sciences. They have continued to come back on my arguments, drag me out for cups of coffee to debate these points and push me to complete this work so that students beyond my university walls could participate in this conversation. I am particularly grateful to Maleeha Aslam, Yan Gao, Maria Fernanda Garcia Rincon, Jennifer Hsu, Solava Ibrahim, Nitya Mohan, Ravin Ponniah, Ezra Rosser and Cassandra Sweet for taking the time to read and comment on drafts and to draw my attention to work from their own disciplines that might push my thinking further.

The long roots that produced this book would not have survived if it had not been for the nourishment I received due to the generosity of many kindred spirits and experiences shared by numerous comrades in arms. My quest for social justice began as a student at Delhi University and it was student demonstrations there that opened my eyes to social protests and the power of collective action. If I learnt the value of action from the street marches, I came to know of the importance of argument during the many hours spent in the tea shops and coffee canteens drinking endless glasses and cups of steaming brown beverages across the city. The warmth and friendship showered on me by older and better-versed friends and academics, both within the University and outside of it, provided me intellectual sustenance from the many books they lent me off their various shelves. I owe much to Kaushik Basu, Sumanto Bannerji, Aaditya Bhattacharjea, Sukhamoy Chakravarthy, Uma Chakravarthy, Anand Chakrvarthy, Nandita Haksar, K.L. Krishna, Gautam Navlakha, C.V. Subba Rao, N. Raghunathan, Mohit Ray, K. Sundaram, Sanjay Subrahmanyam and Sudesh Vaid for the unstinting gifts of their experience and time as I tried to understand where and how economics, justice and development intersected. My search was made more companionable by the exchange of arguments I had on marches, and around tables, through the 1980s. Whether preparing for protest meetings or discussing the disconnect between academic thinking and social reality during my decade at Delhi University my experiences were enriched by the tangible sense of a collective morality that I had the joy of sharing with Saba Dewan, Harish Dhawan, Vrinda Grover, Jaspal Kaur, Joseph Mathai, Ashok Prasad and Jaivir Singh.

At the University of Cambridge I encountered concerns of social justice enunciated through intellectual argument and academic reasoning rather than participation in protest movements. My understanding of how disciplinary tools were transformed into frameworks to examine economic development benefited hugely from discussions with Ha-Joon Chang, Geoff Harcourt, Mushtaq Khan, Peter Nolan, Ugo Pagano, Bob Rowthorn and Ajit Singh. As I began to unpick the particularities of law and economics my learning was assisted by regular conversations with Simon Deakin and David Howarth, who co-taught the law and economics paper when I embarked on my teaching venture.

My family at Cambridge, Stephen, Edwin and Thea, have had to live with the slow and painful process of transforming the manuscript from an idea that originally was an afterthought in my doctoral thesis to a fully formed set of chapters. Stephen, in particular, has selflessly put his research work on the back burner and listened intently through various drafts about the difficult relationship between law and development. He never complained when I had to travel repeatedly to China, India, and Malaysia but cheerfully took to accompanying me so that the family could be together on this adventure. Without Stephen this book would never have been completed and it is his intellectual honesty, legal training and sharpness of argument that have assisted me over this long journey. Edwin, who thinks about the world in terms of mathematical problems, kept asking whether what I was writing about was a very difficult matter and that was why the task was still outstanding. I can now tell him that I was able to work through my conundrum, and what I worked out was that there was no trivial answer to the puzzle. Thea, who is enamoured of all things magical and took to calling the manuscript 'Wules, Wubwics and Witches', will be glad to know that the strange characters that I wrote about have had their ending.

My commissioning editor, Beverley Brown at GlassHouse, was a tower of strength and inspired me to convert a string of half-worked-out ideas into a set of chapter themes. Her friendship and guidance were critical in the long process of completing this manuscript. Colin Perrin and his team at Routledge-Cavendish have been incredibly patient and hugely supportive as I have moved this project to completion and I am grateful to the editorial team for their continued assistance and engagement through these five years.

My father, N. Sivasubramanian, has been the hand and mind that has steadfastly steered me along the long journey. I have learnt hugely from the wealth of knowledge that he has showered on me, benefited tremendously from our exchanges on the validity of legal and economic arguments, and I have grown both in ability and maturity from the warmth provided by his constant companionship. My mother, Vatsala, has through her life's work provided me with a role model of what can be achieved when social work and counselling are undertaken with the utmost compassion and care. She ensured that the many conversations held at the family dining table, both in Cambridge and in Delhi, were helped along by her culinary delights and her editing skills so that both our exchanges and those in the book were much improved. I dedicate this book to my parents.

Shailaja Fennell
Cambridge
December 2008

1 The market economy, the rule of law and the path of development

> This disposition to admire, and almost to worship, the rich and the powerful, and to despise, or, at least, to neglect persons of poor and mean condition, though necessary both to establish and to maintain the distinction of ranks and the order of society, is, at the same time, the great and most universal cause of the corruption of our moral sentiments. That wealth and greatness are often regarded with the respect and admiration which are due only to wisdom and virtue; and that the contempt, of which vice and folly are the only proper objects, is often most unjustly bestowed upon poverty and weakness, has been the complaint of moralists in all ages.
>
> (Adam Smith 2002: III, 94)

Introduction

Adam Smith, professor of political philosophy and economy at the University of Edinburgh, was concerned with the inordinate extent to which the creation and possession of wealth was admired and even idolised at the end of the eighteenth century. If the glamour of being rich was palpable in the late eighteenth century, it has not reduced in the two hundred years that followed: rather, it appears to be even more mesmerising today. What is more, the capitalist world that was emergent in the eighteenth century has now established itself through a set of rules that ensure wealth accumulation and reinforce the virtue of the rich.

These rules are made by capitalist institutions that operate in a rubric that publicly regards the market as the main source of growth but covertly draws on the power that is generated and maintained by social hierarchies and the value accorded to rank and status. This rubric that takes Smith as its starting point has increasingly downplayed the social dimension of the market and increasingly uses a framework that sees the market as a force to advance value creation through increasing efficiency where social forces have ceased to have any influence. What has changed dramatically between the late eighteenth and twentieth centuries is that the world of god, gold and glory that Smith saw as inimical to economic advancement has been replaced by one that regards rules, rubrics and riches as the core of capitalist accumulation. It is in the separation of the social from the economic that capitalism today[1] is far removed from the world of

Smith; for in that period of emerging capitalism the desire to truck, barter and exchange was regarded as a direct consequence of human speech and reason, yet such activities were not seen as devoid of sentiments, but rather as distinct from sentiments and often permitting a move away from the oppressive clutches of tradition and conducive to availing of rational thought and independent action (Rothschild 2001).

Rules

The particular international fascination at the end of the twentieth century is with the importance of a rule of law in creating a global market and ensuring free trade between nations (World Bank 1996, 2003). This is accompanied by a growing call for a world market that would permit 'trade without borders' on the premise that trade as a mechanism will ensure economic growth for all (Berg and Krueger 2003; Bhagwati 2002). There is also a greater demand among some national governments and various international agencies for using rules to make certain that markets can operate more independently of their social, domestic contexts, proclaiming that such policy is opening up the national economy to international competition.[2] While the emphasis of international financial institutions has been on changing the global and national rules of economic behaviour to ensure greater market access and more incentives to trade, there are other voices located in the worlds of academia, non-governmental organisations and even within some development agencies which advocate looking at the manner in which the changes in rules will modify social structures and institutions and how they will affect the everyday lives of people.[3]

The call for more rules to ensure the dominance of the market in ensuring economic development in economies around the world occurs at a time when economics as a discipline, as it is both taught in academic institutions and understood in the work of policymaking, regards the market as both supreme and infallible. This mainstream understanding of the market regards the possibility of imperfections in the market due to gaps or oddities in the economic system or excessive and undesired influence by non-economic factors as few and far between. For instance, in an auction where buyers choose to form a cartel and thereby keep down prices, the joint cartel interest is a market imperfection.

1 Karl Polanyi sets out the centrality of the social environment in determining economic development under capitalism in 1944. See Polanyi (1971 [1944]).

2 Vogel (1996) points out that freer markets emerge only when there are more rules regarding their creation and operation. National regulatory policies that accompany privatisation do not open or increase the size of infrastructure and utility markets to greater competition; rather, they make conditions to ensure more competitive rules for players within the existing market.

3 Rajagopal (2003) has a thoughtful exposition on how international agendas are being countered from below by a variety of civil society organisations, as was witnessed in the US during the anti-globalisation protests in Seattle in 1999; Appadurai (2002) sets out a model of deep governance where local institutions and networks work across platforms of alliances to create sustainable solutions.

This deviance in a perfect market is regarded as the consequence of a strong interest among market agents that has succeeded in manipulating the market. Such a strong manifestation of group interest is explicitly identified as market power. However such evidence of power in the market is seen as an exception to the perfect market where economic self-interest operates unfettered by these powerful feelings rather than acknowledging that the wielding of group power is very much part of market interactions.

Rubrics

The prevalent economic rubric that deems that the market separates the social from the economic also sees no role for the moral or the affective in the functioning of the market. That the same player who has economic self-interest might also have other feelings such as love for others is not regarded as relevant for the functioning of the market. Such concern for others is regarded as an exceptional context where individual preferences such as altruism or trust might emerge but economic theory does not comprehend of the role of such feelings in directing economic activity. Consequently the love of others, truth and honesty in dealings, care for others as oneself are deemed as 'other-regarding' in economic analysis. The very limited acknowledgement within economics, of a broader range of human motivations, prevents it from explaining why individuals are ashamed to ask for help or to sell items that they own in transition economies or to comprehend that such sale is closely tied up with emotions of shame, even forms of economic motivation that are seen as morally reprehensible.[4] It is the narrow purview of this economic rubric that has moved the focus away from Smith's concerns with the moral and replaced it by a singular focus on self-interest. The rubric consequently regards all economic activity as being guided by a single objective of self-interest and precludes any role for groups or other social bonds to operate in the marketplace. It therefore has to regard any presence of the social, moral or affective as an irregularity in the economic system. So in an ironic twist of Smith's original concern about the privileging of wealth, there is an emerging view in economics that the growing number of wealth-creating instruments has the ability to make people happier than before, even the happiest ever.[5]

Riches

While it is true that today there is more accumulated tradable wealth than ever before, these unsurpassed riches have also become the cynosure of all eyes and

4 The disappearance of moralities is not just a myth in market economies. The importance of moralities in transition economies that are reorienting themselves to regard markets as central mechanisms of allocation and distribution is the subject of Mandel and Humphrey (2002).

5 The relationship between economic growth and happiness has not been studied till rather recently. The fact that rising income may or may not make for happier people and the reasons behind this seeming paradox is of central interest in the area of the economics and happiness. See Bruni and Porta (2005) and Frey and Stutzer (2002).

the object of their desire. The power of capital has not always been regarded as benign, and today the market is seen to have the ability to wreak untold havoc on national economies. The Marxian position is that accumulation of wealth is at the heart of the capitalist system and is based on a model of expanded reproduction that uses mechanisms to ensure growing profits that are concentrated with centralisation of capital in a few hands.[6] Where there is huge concentration of tradable capital wealth, arising from expropriation resulting from unfair competition or monopolies, the inequality at global and national levels is regarded as a cause of violence and war.[7] There are even those who see national governments as subservient, if not meaningless, in the face of advancing and mighty global market players.[8] The reason for regarding national economies as subordinate to the global market players is that wealth creation is increasingly regarded as a consequence of international trade and international capital flows.[9] The seeming ability of global commodities and capital flows to generate and develop new and better instruments for creation and transfer of wealth has generated paeans of praise for global capital investment. On the other hand, the evidence of accumulation of capital and resources by rich nations, both within their economies and in international markets, has also been the subject of sharp criticisms and harsher forms of antagonisms from groups and governments in the developing world.[10]

The rising importance of the richest indicates that the growing global market and the tools of its architecture, the rules and rubrics that have come to the fore in the two centuries of economic advancement, have within them both the solutions and the problems of economic development. Whether capitalism is a two-faced Janus, a force for good or a collapsing house of cards cannot be established by an even narrower examination of the market. It requires drawing from outside the central tenets of modern economics, using perspectives that lie beyond the realm of economic theories and the traversing of the more complex

6 See Paul Baran's classic *The Political Economy of Growth* on the tendency to centralisation (Baran 1957). The original point is raised by Marx in *Capital* (Marx 1867: Vol. 1, Ch. 25).

7 The renewed concerns about the political and security consequences of inequality are evident in recent research. See Stewart (2001) for the implications of inequality in the developing world; also the work of CRISE; and Tony Atkinson has shown that rising inequality among rich countries is also problematic and not an inevitable state of affairs (Atkinson 1999).

8 The view that economic development has done away with the rationale for the nation-state is countered by authors such as Theda Skocpol and Linda Weiss. See Weiss (1998) for an explanation of why the international agendas began to discredit the nation-state.

9 The counter to the view that it is international agendas that provide the basis of growth can also be found in the work of leading mainstream economists such as Dani Rodrik. See Rodrik (2001), a paper prepared for the UNDP for an analysis of why global integration is not a solution for development of poor countries.

10 The World Social Forum began in 2001 as the basis of an alternative globalisation movement that was driven by a bottom-up approach for the exchange of knowledge to strengthen social movements with the motto 'Another world is possible'.

realm of human motivations, and the larger ethical and moral world within which realities operate. The power and ability of social norms that operate in the much larger world of human interaction, encompassing the social, political, moral and affective, to foster new rules for market operations and trade negotiations by influencing and refocusing the motivations and actions of individuals and groups in every corner of the world are no longer restricted to the predilections of a few isolated scholars of political economy. They press forward the need to reintegrate social science thinking to achieve the breadth and understanding that was evident in Smith's analysis of capitalism by drawing on rules to show how rules and rubrics have created the riches of capital accumulation.[11]

The institutionalisation of the market paradigm

Economists consider the market to be the site of exchange of goods and commodities as well as the acquisition of inputs for production, such as capital, labour and land. Economic development takes place through expanding the basket of goods and reducing the price at which these are made available to the public.[12] The modern-day mainstream economic paradigm, that focuses on equalising the forces of demand and supply in the market to ensure stable economic growth, has been built on the foundations of the marginal analysis framework that was introduced by Alfred Marshall in the last decades of the nineteenth century. Within this paradigm the market pricing of goods ensures that the production of commodities and services follows the economic rule of least cost/maximum output.[13] The place and time at which suppliers bid against demands from buyers and buyers agree to buy against offers from sellers is the site called market.

Though market exchange is regarded as an instantaneous transaction which does not have coordinates in time or space, this 'perfect' market is neither instantaneous nor able to provide complete coverage of all possible bids and offers. The imperfections that mar are said to arise through the presence of externalities of production and/or asymmetry of information between producers

[11] The push is not only from heterodox economists, but also from a much larger academic interest in the implications of international development. For instance, the lawyers Trubek and Santos focus on 'moments' in the law and development literature that have questioned the market (Trubek and Santos 2006); while sociologists such as Smelser and Swedberg (1995) have raised questions about whether sociological motivations should be regarded as opposed or mutually exclusive to those regarded as economic motivations;

[12] Adam Smith focused on the power of the market to increase the quantity and reduce the price of production while Karl Marx commended capitalism for its ability to provide more commodities than ever before at the lowest feasible prices. See Smith (1976) and Marx and Engels (1848).

[13] This is known as the dual problem in economic theory, i.e. maximising production subject to a budget constraint is identical to minimising cost subject to a production requirement.

and consumers.[14] In these cases the market is no longer able to ensure that an efficient pricing mechanism will fulfil the least cost/maximal output criteria that exist at the heart of Marshallian analysis.[15] Where the buyer and seller do not have the same set of information regarding a future transaction, the market price may not be the consequence of equal play between buyer and seller but may be closer to the price which the player with most information wants. The power of the invisible hand is considerably reduced where there are externalities and information problems, and the market is unable to fix price in the most 'efficient' manner. Such shortcomings can be overcome by repeated actions of market exchange where the habitual activity creates its own set of norms to ensure symmetry of information; and the exchange gets regarded as an infinite set of rounds in a game, and this motivates individuals to cooperate in conforming to norms of market exchange.

The analogy of the instantaneous transaction seems ill-conceived for the act of market exchange, as it seems more akin to a procedure emerging from rounds of bidding that are continually underway in a market. In each round buyers bid for what is offered for sale, with the highest accepted bid denoting the maximisation of price. The quantity of each type of product contracted for and value of exchange becomes available in the form of information available to traders in the market.[16] Markets also generate information which helps companies plan their bids against future offers by estimation of demand and supply and expected return on their purchases in the market. Thus market exchange appears to be the consequence of the working of a pricing mechanism, whereas the market is actually a site for acquiring and accumulating market-specific information.

The allocation of resources depends on information regarding the supply and demand of commodities and services and the activities of competitors in the market. The maximal output/minimum cost combination is obtained through ensuring an efficient allocation of resources where the last unit of any input is placed so that the marginal return on it would be equal to the marginal cost of using it. The ability of economics to allocate resources in relation to costs and returns in this clear-cut and direct manner is the major attraction of the economic framework.[17] There is no requirement, at this level, for bringing in the

[14] There is a large literature on externalities: see Scitovsky (1954), 'Two Concepts of External Economies', where he differentiates between technological externalities and pecuniary externalities, and points out that it is the latter that operate in developing countries and require state intervention.

[15] Marshallian analysis gets its name from the work of Alfred Marshall, a professor of political economy at Cambridge who developed and taught that the forces of supply and demand that operate within an economic market would equilibrate and thereby ensure stability in the economy.

[16] Leon Walras gave economics the entity of the auctioneer calling for bids. Malinvaud (1977) developed a general equilibrium model of the labour market based on the Walrasian auctioneer that was favoured for a decade but has not been embraced by the whole tribe of economists. (See Patinkin 1987: 864–7.)

[17] It is this simplicity and elegance that is at the core of the Marshallian solution.

larger domain of societal relations or prevailing moralities, or placing liability on the State for unmet needs.[18]

If economic exchange in the market is located within a sphere generated by the axes of location and time, the success of exchange would require the completion of three activities, namely search, negotiation and monitoring. These activities are required for (a) the identification of a potential agent with whom to exchange, (b) the decision of what price to agree on and (c) ensuring that the product delivered matches that which was offered in the bidding process.[19] The process of exchange requires the recognition of rights and liabilities of the exchanging parties, for which enforceable market rules are necessary, implying cost-effective obedience to rules through brokers, rather than costly enforcement of rules through courts of law. The ability of the players in the market to effectively ensure efficient exchange depends on a smooth operation of the separate acts, of search, negotiation and policing, that do not necessarily telescope into a moment in time and space called completion of exchange.

The importance of economic instruments to trade-risk so as to buttress economic exchange, has been at the heart of recent trading on national and international financial markets in financial derivatives.[20] The addition of these new features of capitalism such as capital derivatives, which has occurred in the last decades of the twentieth century, is regarded as the rise of new forms of capitalism. In the case of futures markets there is the need to protect against risks of loss through hedging against the future by investing in a financial instrument which is unlikely to rise or fall in value along with the futures instrument. Late twentieth-century capitalism is seen as a natural progression from the early decades of industrialisation where the market mechanism was supreme, and it may well continue to be the unvanquished hero. The financial crises of the 1990s are regarded variously as the misdemeanours of some rogue traders or some crony capitalists rather than symptoms of malaise in the capitalist system and in some quarters have given voice to calls to protect mechanisms of capitalism from the capitalists.[21]

Introducing morality into economics is an attempt to incorporate the concern for and impact of others in society that allows the possibility of delving into the self-interest of economic players might be intertwined with other social norms that operate in society. The broader notion in other social sciences, that morals arise from respect or concern for all others is absent within the economic approach to market transactions. The narrow understanding that individual motivation was driven by economic self-interest is useful in explaining the resource allocation decisions

[18] If there was to be a distinction made between self-regarding or egotistic preferences and other-regarding or altruistic preferences that come up in economics, then the role which moralities might play in a market context becomes relevant.

[19] The effectiveness of the various components of an exchange process within a hierarchical social structure is the subject of the classic text, *Economics, Politics and Welfare* by Dahl and Lindblom (1953).

[20] A critical review of financial derivatives is undertaken in Bryan and Rafferty (2005).

[21] See Rajan and Zingales (2004).

undertaken by individuals, as producers and consumers, but it has had little success in explaining the relationship between economic activity and the social context.

The Coasean contribution

The importance of structural support and instruments drawn from outside the market might seem new in economics but this is not so in other social sciences. An early advocate for bringing social structure into economics was Ronald Coase, an economist trained in the United Kingdom but who spent much of his working life in the United States, who examined the success of the market pricing through examining whether the aspects of search, negotiation and policing were adequately achieved. Coase pointed out that there was a cost associated with all three aspects of the exchange process and if any of these costs became exorbitant it would undermine the possibility of market exchange. The total cost was termed 'transaction costs' and Coase pointed out that the market was efficient as a form of exchange only so long as transaction costs were low. The costs of using the market relate to the ability to agree on a mutually acceptable price. This process requires a large number of additional structures and instruments, which are not necessarily economic in their orientation or origin. In fact, the fundamental notions of rights and liabilities arise from the laws creating them, and they form the very basis of the contracts on rights and liabilities in private wealth that individuals enter into when they undertake exchanges. Coase was one of the earliest economists to take it upon himself to explain why the market, in itself, was not a sufficient basis for economic activity.

> I found the answer by the summer of 1932. It was to realise that there were costs of using the pricing mechanism. What the prices are has to be discovered. There are negotiations to be undertaken, then contracts have to be drawn up, inspections have to be made, arrangements have to be made to settle disputes, and so on. These costs have come to be known as transaction costs. Their existence implies that methods of co-ordination, alternative to the market, which are themselves costly and in various ways imperfect, may nonetheless be preferable to relying on the pricing mechanism, the only method of co-ordination normally analysed by economists. It was avoidance of the costs of carrying out transactions through the market that could explain the existence of the firm in which the allocation of factors came about as a result of administrative decisions (and I thought it did).
>
> (Coase 1990: 35)

Coase regarded the primary pursuit of economics as that of amending and advancing the ideas of Adam Smith regarding the power of the market.[22] The Smithian proposition that the superiority of the invisible hand emerges from its

[22] Coase (1976) focuses on how Smith's view on man and morality provided the base for establishing the superiority of the market.

ability to maximise product value is corroborated by Coase, who points out that the market will continue to dominate as indicated in this Smithian proposition, so long as the transaction costs of using the market or the firm are taken into account while determining how to organise the production process. Coase showed that the extent to which the market mechanism and contracts are used by producers is influenced by the laws on property rights, by pointing out that it is the high transaction costs of readjusting legal rights that preclude the adoption of certain seemingly low-cost options.[23]

The importance of contracts is particularly relevant in the case of employment. Employees are awarded annual or longer-term contracts in a market where the alternative is to recruit labour on a daily basis at a lower cost, in order to offset the repeated payment for a brokerage service. This is the reason that a long-term 'employer–employees' firm replaces a labour gang foreman contracting labour on a daily wage basis. The essence of the firm is a contract, covering a period of time and at a fixed price for exchange. The contract helps in the planning and coordination of production, at a cost less than the cost of repeated exchange in the market for the same services.[24] The economic rationale for the firm was the central focus of Coase's early analysis and he pointed out that

> in a competitive system there would be an optimum of planning, since a firm (that little planned society) could continue to exist only if it performed its coordination function at a lower cost than would be incurred if coordination were achieved by means of market transactions, and also at a lower cost than if this same function were to be performed by another firm.
>
> (Coase 1995a: 8)

The Coasean postulate that the market and the firm are alternative institutions for undertaking production is based on the relative levels of transaction costs which determine an economic producer's preference for one institution over the other. While Coase provided a rationale for the existence of the firm and the superiority of contracts, his work also paved the way for explaining how legal instruments ensure successful exchange through the market. As contracts are increasingly used within both the market (even allowing trading in contracts) and the firm to reduce production risks, they begin to highlight the interplay between economic opportunities and legal obligations in order to ensure the continued possibility of exchange. At the same time, the manner in which legal and economic instruments support both the market and firm as institutional sites for production and affect the nature of contracting, liabilities and legal obligation has become an important starting point for the new research

[23] Coase (1960) discusses the consequences of different liability rules on which party should bear the burden of the externality.

[24] Williamson (1982) draws on the importance of the employment contract for ensuring stability in capitalism.

paradigm of 'law and economics'.[25] The consequences of bringing in the legal rules regarding the conditions within which production and labour operate permits an expanded understanding of the nature of costs associated with using the market and the firm. In particular, the ability of legal rules to reduce transaction costs and thereby enhance the deploying of resources in pursuit of wealth creation and asset accumulation is increasingly reflected in the growing complexity of economic and legal instruments used in the corporate world.[26]

Coase points out that

> in a regime of positive transaction costs, the character of the law becomes one of the main factors determining the performance of the economy. If the transaction costs were zero (as is assumed in standard economic theory) we can imagine people contracting around the law whenever it was possible to increase the value of production by a change in the legal position. But in a regime of positive transaction costs, such contracting would not occur whenever transaction costs are greater than the gain that such a redistribution of rights would bring. As a consequence, the rights which individuals possess will commonly be those established by the law, which in these circumstances can be said to control the economy.
>
> (Coase 1995b: 11)

The case where there are no transaction costs associated with exchange, later to be termed a zero transaction costs (ZTC) world, was brought in only as a hypothetical case to show the importance of legal arrangements to economic analysis of production and exchange.[27]

Bringing the law into standard economic analysis through case studies allowed Coase to illustrate how economic activity is premised on structures behind and beyond the market. Situations where imperfections in the market are evident provide a valuable opportunity to identify the impact of the law on economic activity. The very telling, yet simple, illustrations drawn upon by

[25] There are many schools with the subject of law and economics. In the United States the mainstream is represented by the Chicago school and the rise of textbooks such as *Economic Analysis of the Law* (Posner 1998) and *Law and Economics* (Cooter and Ulen 2007), while the more heterodox approaches emerge from the radical schools of critical legal studies. In Europe, law and economics has taken a more evolutionary approach under the influence of the Austrian and the German Historical schools. The works of McAuslan (2003) and Amanda Perry Kessaris and John Hatchard (see Hatchard and Kessaris 2003) have been influential in the U.K. in raising the issue of international development in a discerning manner drawing out the older tradition of law and development into the new law and economics.

[26] Oliver Williamson's book, *The Economic Institutions of Capitalism* (Williamson 1982) has now become a classic on the manner in which capitalist production and labour contracts interact to give different levels and types of capitalist relations.

[27] It was George Stigler who coined the term 'Coase Theorem', which first appeared in his textbook *The Theory of Price* (Stigler 1966). For a very useful survey of the theorem and its uses in the field of law and economics, see Medema and Zerbe (2000).

Coase show the rearrangement of legal rights by the parties themselves to maximise their product. Where smoke from a factory affects neighbouring residential properties the law of torts would indicate that the property owner can claim damages from the factory owner and also obtain an injunction from the court to have the factory shut down. The factory owner may offer to buy out the residential property at the market price (which could well be less than damages payable and loss incurred in shutting down the factory) and he may even expand the factory into this purchased property. In the case where there is no legal liability on the other, the home owner might purchase the land from the factory owner if this financial outlay was less than the legal cost of getting a court order to shut down the factory or cost of moving elsewhere. This case illustrates the implications of property, liability and inalienability rules in property disputes. The judgement in this case of Sturges v. Bridgeman was made in favour of the doctor as the area where the confectioner's and doctor's properties were located was subject to a policy for developing land for residential purposes. The precedent cited before the court in this case was of a forge in a moor being closed down when the moor was developed for residential purposes.

In cases where there is a failure in duty to care on the part of those who market goods and services used by the general public, there is a considerable role for the legal profession.[28] In the case of Industries, Inc. v. Del E. Webb Dev. Co., 494 P.2d 700 (Ariz. 1972), Del Webb, an Arizona real-estate developer that was building Sun City, a retirement community, sued for an injunction against Spur Industries, a pre-existing feedlot owner. The complainant submitted that the activities of Spur Industries were a nuisance to the expanding retirement community as the offensive smell of the feedlot was putting off sales of retirement homes. The court ruled that Spur Industries must move the premises of its activities but that Del Webb had to indemnify the business for its trouble. In passing the judgement the Arizona state Supreme Court ruled that Spur Industries' activities did create a nuisance, but Del Webb had come to the nuisance and brought its unwitting retirees along with it. The Spur Industries case has become widely read as an illustration of a successful balancing of efficiency, distributional and other justice concerns.[29] The general principle handed down by the court was that if a party entered an area that was reserved for industrial or agricultural use and experienced damages by a *nuisance*, relief would not be available, on account of the doctrine of 'coming to the nuisance'. The relief obtained by Sun City was due to Spur being a public nuisance. In the

[28] In the United States such cases have contributed to the phenomenal increase in wealth generated by the activities of the legal and judicial system, with lawyers contributing to the passing of new laws on mergers and acquisitions that shore up new corporate capital forays. The massive increase in legal activity on behalf of the corporate section has also resulted in actions against firms and a corporate clamour for legal limits on damages awardable by courts in tort cases.

[29] Spur Industries v. Del Webb is used extensively in law and economics courses in graduate schools to illustrate nuisance and planning decisions.

case of Sturges v. Bridgeman, no aspect of public nuisance was raised and the doctor who sued the confectioner was awarded relief for the loss of private income based on the principle of private nuisance, and, no doubt, on public policy.

In a regime of zero transaction costs, negotiations between the parties entering into an exchange in the market would lead to those arrangements being made which would maximise wealth irrespective of the initial assignment of property rights. It is this particular insight revealed by Coase that has become famous as proof that market exchange does not require attention to be given to legal matters, particularly the existing property rights regime. Coase's formulation of the implications of no transaction costs, later termed the 'Coase Theorem' by George Stigler, has come to be regarded as a touchstone to analyse the real world of positive transaction costs where all economies are located. The zero transaction cost (ZTC) world is called up in the economic analysis of markets to make the case that regulation and other forms of intervention are not required, as parties will make the arrangement that maximises returns (Glaeser *et al.* 2001). The legal system is regarded as having the ability to bring in the necessary rules to ensure that a ZTC world operates and therefore property rights no longer need to be considered within the market by economic agents (Medema and Zerbe 2000). This result finds its way into the popular understanding that the legal system has the power to move us towards a ZTC world, yet the theorem was devised only to show that in the very unlikely circumstances of ZTC the property rights of the parties effecting an exchange would neither be relevant nor affect exchange, since the product-maximising solution involving property rights would have a role in all cases of positive transaction costs. Also, the focus on property rights does not distinguish adequately that what is traded on the market is not physical goods but the parts (or even the whole of) the bundle of rights associated with each good.[30] It is this bundle of rights that permits the performance of certain actions and the results accrue to individuals through the legal system. Therefore, in the world of positive transaction costs the solution to exchange lies in the particular allocation of the bundles of rights that are assigned to individuals.

The importance of rights in directing and deciding the exchange process is at the core of Coase's insight, and yet this has progressively been narrowed over the last half-century to mere consideration of a hypothetical position within economics rather than an extreme case (or an intellectual straw man) against which to examine real-life examples. Consequently, the existence of transaction costs has been used to pursue inductive reasoning rather than the deductive

[30] In 'The Problem of Social Cost', while discussing the damage inflicted on the farmer by the cattle raised by a neighbouring cattle raiser, Coase points out that the options are not just the shutting down of the cattle-raising activity, but could range from changing the crop raised by the farmer to a partial reduction in the area cultivated (Coase 1960). The range of options are related to the various bundles of rights that come with the ownership of land and are far wider than that of operation or non-operation of the activities of cattle raising or farming.

approach that was favoured by Coase himself. The opportunity to use a Coasean analysis to understand the full implications of the legal system requires a historical and descriptive analysis that traces the development of both the economic and the legal systems in particular nations. This approach would encourage an inclusive rather than a marginal approach to the role of the law in economic development and return us to the original form of the problem of why the market was eschewed in favour of other forms of organisation. The additional benefit of focusing on a historical trajectory is the ability to trace the process of wealth accumulation and examine its relationship to existing patterns of legal rights.

Rules or regulation: the implications of Coase for law and economics

There is still debate about whether the legal system or regulation should be used to reduce transaction costs. If the rearrangement of legal rights is obtained through the drafting of contracts in the real world then parties would not easily change their rights and responsibilities in this world of positive transaction costs. The transaction costs that go into pricing a good are reduced by the drawing up of contracts to replace simple (barter) exchange and by the regulation of the flow of goods held in stock as per the requirements for delivery specified in the contract. The crux of the market is neither in the stalls frequented nor in the bustle of people but in the purpose which they all serve, namely ensuring that demand and supply in the market create an optimally agreed price for the product exchanged. The determination of price in a perfect market is a random event that is not under the control of any player. It is to be noted that the notion of the perfect market represents the ideal, while imperfectness is the fact and reality, not an aberration or exception.

The essence of the firm lies in the planning and coordination of economic activities over time and space vastly wider than the coverage by specific markets. Planning and coordination sets up costs of information and litigation, and the decision to produce through the firm or the market is based on setting the said costs against the costs of market transactions. The difference between contracts for exchange in the market and other contracts, such as bilateral contracts made outside of the market, is that far fewer persons are involved in determining prices in the latter. The parsimony of numbers gives economic and political power to the legal instrument of non-market contracts. Economic and legal interpretations of the contract differ, with the economic view seeing it as an instrument for assisting the parties to the contract (Williamson 1982), while the legal view will balance private interests of parties with public interest, if any (Calabresi and Melamed 1972). As the legal perspective is more ready to recognise the importance of the legal framework in facilitating the very contracting through the market or the firm, it lends itself to a broader interpretation by the State, as the authority that can fundamentally shape the working of the economic system with the ability to direct and even control its expansion and growth.

Exchanges are not restricted to those within the market or the firm, and increasingly take place within institutions at the heart of capitalism, as in the case of the stock exchange. Here individuals buy the shares of successful companies which transfer rights to them, whereby they share in the wealth-creating abilities of entrepreneurs. The regulations on trading activities, what can be traded, when trading will go on, the terms of trade settlement and so on, are all laid down in rules framed by the authorities of the exchange. The rules are in effect a private law. Without such rules and regulations, the speedy conclusion of exchanges through trading would not be possible. But such private law would be difficult to establish where dealers are scattered in space and have very divergent interests, as in retailing and wholesaling, so their activities and those within the stock market get regulated by the laws of the State. The organisational setting of the stock market within which the trading takes place also affects the incentives to produce and the costs of transacting.[31] The economic understanding is that changes in the ebullience of the market, that generate both bullish and bearish trends in the market, are based on individual expectations. But the investing public believe that their losses arise because of manipulation of the market by large financial players, while their gain is due to fair play.

The role of insiders and outsiders in the financial market has a telling impact on the rewards. The players in the market drive the price up, selling at the top of the crest, while insiders work to ensure that the exuberances do not cause the market to spiral out of control and to bring the market down again. The losses of the outsiders are equal to the gain of the insiders and the market as a whole is at a stand-off. The professional insiders have more knowledge of the reasons for the upswings and the falls, while the outsider amateurs, who buy high and sell low, are less price manipulators and more the victims of euphoria, which infects them late in the day. When they lose, they go back to their normal occupations to save up for another splurge.[32]

The economic rationality in the financial market gets lauded as the key to wealth accumulation and presumes that private behaviour does not ordinarily spill over beyond the transacting parties.[33] Notions of public interest do not appear on their economic radar screen but they do become visible on the legal screen. The economic view of a regulator for financial markets to ensure public interest is riddled with fears of his capture and the pursuance of private interest rather than public interest (Heremans 2000). Yet there is an abundance of cases, highlighted by the broadsheets, financial institutions and academic articles, which point out that banks, mutual funds, pension funds and housing

[31] The proposition that the US-type stock market-based corporate model was conducive to efficient allocation by the market was questioned by Michael Porter and a number of other Harvard-based economists in 1992. See Porter (1992).

[32] The role of professional insiders in creating asset bubbles that then lead to panics and crashes is identified by the renowned MIT economist Charles Kindleberger. See Kindleberger and Aliber (2005).

[33] Singh *et al.* (2005) point out how the stock market is seen as technology-inducing because of its efficiency and incentives for private capital investment. Shareholder value maximisation, stock market and new technology: should the US corporate model be the universal standard?

cooperatives have inflicted losses on their investors and clients in the pursuit of maximal profits and show instances of private interest in conflict with public interest. The possibility that judicial and regulatory power could be used to control the market as an integral part of market operations is shunned yet this same economic perspective embraces the uses of legal rights and rules to maximise wealth by enforcing low wages and cheap prices of inputs. The difference in economic and legal thinking regarding the impact of capitalist institutions on individual gain and its implications for the public goes beyond the traditional exchange within the market to that of life and work in the community.

Market logic and valuation of human life

An economic analysis of the market uses a *ceteris paribus* approach – that is, holding all other things constant – which permits a marginal cost- and return-based pricing of the final unit of production. This gives an analytical advantage for costing activities in terms of opportunity cost, i.e. the loss of revenue from not undertaking other possible forms of investment, production or consumption. The marginal costing rule has been increasingly extended to cover misdemeanours in the delivery of goods and services such as breakages, accidents, and is formalised in the field of law and economics to cover acts of negligence and the incidence of torts.[34] The use of marginal principles to evaluate compensation for death draws on the principle of 'foregone income' which is based on the earning capacity of the deceased individual, as the relevant cost. Basing opportunity costs on income-earning capacity links lives solely to their income-generation abilities. Given the difference in earning capacity and currencies in different countries, this would result in the compensation granted to workers in the same profession differing widely between, say, the United States and China. Compensating death by payments related to income would also result in large differences in awards to families living in two different states of the US with widely differing standards of life. This might appear fair in an economic sense, but it would be deemed immoral within a legal understanding of equality of lives and it also ignores the obligations and liabilities of the deceased individual to her family and community. In contrast, under customary law, morality is central to compensation considerations, and the deceased person's family is compensated for all future obligations of the deceased by the perpetrator of death through payment by a living member of the family of the accused.[35]

It is a curious feature of the new law-and-economics approach that it embraces self-interest as a key principle of individual behaviour and that singular pursuit

[34] The need to insure against risk and the calculation of transaction costs to cover these costs is a central feature of the teaching in law and economics. See Cooter and Ulen (2007) for a representative textbook set of analysis of this school of thinking.

[35] As indicated in the displacement of customary law by modern legal principles in 1997 in a ruling by the St Hagen National Court, Papua New Guinea, in the case of 'head payment', i.e. mortuary gifts to the deceased, that would have required the human sacrifice of 18-year-old Miriam Willingal. See Strathern (2005: 111–16).

of wealth maximisation is regarded as an appropriate framework.[36] Giving centre ground to the market, the law-and-economics analysis employs methods that regard individual motivation as identical to the creation of private wealth, thereby equating individual gain with societal benefits in a seemingly direct and uncomplicated manner. The approving nod thereby given to the de-linking of wealth accumulation from the distribution of assets reaffirms that the capitalistic mode of wealth generation is solely about the creation and protection of private property. This approach, which is oppositional to older systems of valuing the services of labour as was present from the inception of economics in the work of Adam Smith to the consequences of labour as congealed capital, later become the subject of serious debate in the Marxist and heterodox economics, early and late in the twentieth century, respectively. The desire of liberal and conservative lawyers to take neoclassical market economics at face value and to further restrict its coverage by importing marginal analysis into legal thinking has had the effect of effacing the political implications of legal rights that are awarded to individuals.[37]

Legal rights and notions of equality

The law gives rights to people and also promises that all persons will be treated equally by the State. However, the notions of justice and equality in the legal statutes and their relation to society do not follow in a straightforward manner. For instance, laws do not ensure, by their very presence, a remedy in all cases of the violation of rights of persons. Rather, the possibility and type of remedy depends on the manner in which the State intervenes. In particular, remedy can be effected either by direct intervention or indirectly through working with social norms. The importance of social laws is emphasised in the case of Shasta County in California, where cattlemen are not liable for trespass, except in a closed range.[38] The rule of strict liability (under law of torts) applies only in the closed range areas in the county and while most cattle owners in Shasta County are ignorant of the letter of the law their actions indicate that they operate on the belief that strict liability operates on a closed range and 'no liability' operates in open-range situations. Good social relationships among ranchers create informal norms and potential disputants ignore the formal law. When cattle stray from one ranch to another and a rancher finds other brands among his herd, the loss of grass is considered trivial as long as the owner removes his cattle from another's ranch within a day or two. However, the trespass rule is enforced by the ranchers in the case of trespass by

[36] Posner (1987) provides an exposition on the benefits of the law-and-economics movement or what Posner calls the 'economics of law'.

[37] The debate about whether use of formal economic models and methods is advantageous has generated longstanding arguments within economics. See Maki (1998) for an exposition on the debate between Posner and Coase on the role of formalism in the law and economics, and his conclusion that formalism is not the only way to make a theoretical contribution and that looking at specific institutions rather than general principles is not anti-theoretical.

[38] Ellickson (2005) provides a powerful exposition of the role of social norms.

goats, swine and vicious dogs. Trespass through a complete and unbroken fence is deemed intentional trespass and invites liability. Reasonable force may be used to drive off animals. Animals may be seized and their care billed to the owner, but the killing or wounding of the animals is not allowed. The law is not called upon – rather, it is within the remit of social practices that the security of legally registered rights is maintained. The State in its turn does not impound the livestock but encourages the ranchers to avoid impounding because of the high costs involved.

The adherence to social norms as the way forward to enforce appropriate behaviour has been regarded as the exception rather than the norm in the established law-and-economics literature. There is small, if any, admission that there is an appropriate place to deploy the reflexive role of the State. In contrast, there is strong preference in the early interpretations of Coase calling for expanding the realm of formal laws and formalising the informal rules to ensure the rights of individuals (Demsetz 1966) and simplify economic interaction (Epstein 1995). This is accompanied by a rising clamour for extending the arena of private property to the realm of natural resources to increase the efficiency of markets and surety of wealth creation (Libecap 2004). While trading in natural resources is conducted in the market through the use of contracted rights and liabilities, little is said regarding the manner in which tangible and intangible wealth is accounted for in society. Yet the title to wealth (or right to accumulate) and the right to utilise wealth is only as secure as the legal system, on which such a market is based and which can enforce it. If the law is unable to remedy failures in the market that violate the rights of individuals – such as defaulting on returns on financial investment – there will be a desertion of such a market and traders will move to more lucrative markets. Such threats to the functioning of a market arise from the inability of the legal system to provide remedy to violations of legal title but can also be the result of illegal and underhand operations in the market which flout the legal system and the state. The response of the economic literature has been to emphasise the need to protect assets and to keep them secure from the rapacious clutches of the State, particularly evident within the New Institutional Economics (North 1990; Alt and Shepsle 1990). On the other hand, despite the importance of the firm and market in understanding economic production in an institutional context, neither the early law-and-economics literature of the 1960s and 1970s nor the later thinking within the New Institutional Economics sought to use the interrelationship between the market and the firm to provide a new framework for analysing capitalism that focused on the importance of political hierarchy in directing and pushing forward the propensity for capital accumulation.

This oversight is particularly striking as the hierarchy of the firm provides the skeleton of the central production structure and ensures that rules set out by the employment contract are adhered to by employees/members. The need to control members is evident in the design of and adherence to such rules, and it works to prevent opposition and disruption of the production system.[39] These

[39] See Stephen Marglin for a powerful explanation of how hierarchy is not a technological requirement but a social requirement to ensure greater wealth accumulation (Marglin 1974).

rules are not restricted to the sphere of economic production but also extend to other forms of organisations or groups in the economic and social sphere. The importance of transaction costs and the reduction of such costs within the firm and its positive impact on increasing the extent and coverage of private property in a society have been identified as a historical trend in the West, with particular, sometimes exclusive, emphasis on the importance of institutions in devising rules to distance and control the rapacious power of the pre-modern and early modern State.[40] The focus of long-term historical analysis of economic development is on the ability of capitalists to bypass the rapacious State and to overcome the weaknesses of the market when faced with the problems of externalities and information leading to the danger of hold-up and free-riding, and it provides the foundations of institutional analysis of the relationship between law and development. At the level of the firm, there has been a parallel focus on the creation of long-term and relational contracts which has became the basis for re-examining capitalism as an institutional form rather than as a simple formula based on marginal principles or technological requirements.[41]

Institutions and development

Historically the State has been a key player in designing institutions to control and direct economic development. Laws are passed to create institutions that facilitate economic activity regarded as beneficial to the economic development of society.[42] Social institutions that are fashioned out of historical conditions to facilitate economic activities work to pass laws to ensure that further institutions are also market-enhancing. At the other end, there are human beings who attempt to manipulate the rules by influencing government, both officials and regulators, to gain concessions and work to impose unnecessary costs on competitors. While this is the negative side of institutions and not the purpose for which institutions are set up, the positive side is that new generations of individuals soon begin to enjoy the fruits of the activities of the institution and establish new practices till they become tradition and culture, as in the case where brokers' guilds of earlier centuries later became the stock exchanges. Along with partnership firms, companies, corporations, banks, mutual funds, pension funds, housing cooperatives, and so on, they comprise the main economic institutions in most countries today.

When custom becomes statute it is seen as an indication of the ability to control people through laws. Formal laws and a readiness to accept them are regarded

40 This was raised by the path-breaking *Rise of the Western World* by Douglas North and Robert Thomas (North and Thomas 1976) and became the centrepiece of North's *Institutions, Institutional Change and Economic Performance* (North 1990).

41 The literature on the firm that was the distinguishing focus of the work by Jensen and Meckling in the 1970s was defined further by Oliver Williamson (1982).

42 There is a long line of literature, from North and Thomas (1974) to Avner Greif (1992), focusing on the transformative role of new legal rules that protect Western societies from the excesses of the State and market failures in economic production.

as the characteristic of people in the developed world, but they are only poorly available in 'less developed' countries. The case of adherents of Islam, facing poverty and residing in low income countries, resisting any purchase of shares in companies that would deploy their capital either in usurious activities or for the production of prohibited activities such as liquor is taken to indicate a lower level of acceptance of economic laws (and a preference for religious laws). The emergence of economic laws as a set of conditions conducive to economic development has put moral and religious systems in disregard and they are awarded subordinate status.

The Darwinian proposition of the survival of the fittest has found a deep niche within the field of economics, where the survival of particular rules in some societies has been taken to indicate that they are superior to repealed/revoked laws and norms.[43] Consequently, economic rules are regarded as superior to those of moral or other authority. This ready acceptance of the biological principle in the formulation and adoption of laws is based on a confusion regarding the basis of morality, for it lies in the realm of sociology rather than biology (Hodgson 1993). There are differences in views in the schools of 'Institutional Economics' – the Old Institutional Economics (OIE) regards history as the sum total of social structures that provide hierarchy and thereby give form to society, and the New Institutional Economics (NIE) locates rights within individuals rather than organisations (such as firms and communities). The latter approach creates an exclusive focus on equality in relation to individuals, overlooking the examination of the legal concept of equity. The possibility of looking at equity was raised by the OIE as it focuses on class differences and group identities, but these concerns were replaced by marginal principles and a focus on market principles.[44]

The adoption of a principle of market logic has narrowed the biological analogy by removing the historical dimension from an evolutionary approach, replacing it by a linear thinking that regards new institutions as superior based on their ability to survive and continue, rather than as embedded in society and its hierarchies. While addressing inequality is a necessary requirement to redress any market failure, it is not able to deal with historical injustices, as these are on the whole meted out against groups and require legal redress, whether by the State or society. Equity will not result from ensuring that individuals get financial or other material compensation, for the nature of unfair treatment meted out in the past arose from forms of discrimination which related to identities that fell outside the market, such as those of the body, of the group or of occupation. The remedy for these can only emerge from looking at the social relations, the moral framework and the affective engagements that individuals partake in.

43 The current interest in evolutionary economics can be traced to the influential text by Nelson and Winters (1982).

44 Thorstein Veblen emphasised the importance of the class-based consumption in decisions regarding moral rules and social norms (Veblen 1994 [1944]). The central role of history in economic ideas is set out in Hodgson (2001).

The concept of reciprocity that can be found in Coase's suggestion of a 'readjustment of property rights' provides one way forward to improving these social relations between individuals. Only his rancher and corn grower would see the reciprocal wisdom of forming a firm to use combined assets of both in a way to add to the profits of both equitably, rather than going to court claiming damages on grounds of equality of right to property, even though the properties owned by each are not equal. Reciprocity also underlies all moral codes, and the presence of empathy or 'to feel for the other as oneself' is the basis for forms of mutuality. The possibility that individuals within communities, groups or institutions would highlight the need for reciprocity or morality to ensure either rights of the firm or for the public good of community, as they do to promote personal rights, can be invoked within a larger social framework (Ankarloo 2002b).

Vesting legal rights in an institution like a company or a corporation, and exercise of rights by members of boards of management holding wealth as trustees for shareholders, has not prevented members of management siphoning off profits due to the shareholders as their massive remunerations and retirement benefits (Heremans 1999). The law of equity, with ownership extending from the ostensible owner to beneficiary owners, governs trustees, yet the duty of trusteeship, prevalent till the nineteenth century in English law, has found itself overwritten by new legal rights that are now vested in the management of the company, thereby privileging greater accumulation for wealth rather than fair distribution of returns. Emphasising the dimension of morality in a firm, through the feature of embedding trust in the institution privileges the social dimension of work undertaken by of individuals/employees within their institution over the profit made by the organisation. This incorporation of historical social norms was however very rare in the social sciences.

At the same time, when Coase was engaging with real world trading matters, in the United Kingdom and the United States there was no study of law in development economics[45] in order to obtain an understanding of real world trading matters, only a retirement from the real world to the textbook world of microeconomics. Even in the developed countries, the work of Ronald Coase was sidelined into a sterile debate regarding efficiency within the 'law and economics' literature. The radical tendencies in development theory that were emerging out of Latin America regarding the failure of existing economic models to ensure the social transformation of developing countries and its replacement by an alternative economics were unable to gain centre stage (Sousa Santos 2003). Although Coase regarded property rights as a historically constructed set of rules that affected distribution in an economy, in the US the derivative work in the field of law and economics in mainstream economics departments continued to focus on economic forms in the market, and not on the law.

[45] The older school of law and development, which emerged after the Second World War, had fallen on its own sword by the 1970s, for it became part of the post-colonial imposition of legal systems on the developing world rather than a serious consideration of how existing systems of law in these countries could be brought into formal legal frameworks (Snyder 1980).

Market exchange, rule of law and economic development

Five decades ago development economics was a theory as well as a policy. It provided a number of economic models to bring about economic growth and thereby development of an economy. Developing economies found models that emphasised a staple-based approach (Snyder 1980) or even an export-based approach to development unable to provide stable economic growth. Industrialisation was regarded as the only path to ensure the development of newly independent nations.[46] While equitable treatment of marginalized groups and traditional sections was to be ensured through small-scale production units the accumulation of capital for investment to fuel and sustain a successful industrialisation policy was the single desired objective. The shortage of capital, on account of low domestic savings, was exacerbated by the difficulties of acquiring access to foreign capital that did not see the benefit of entering a traditional agrarian economy. Additionally, the experience of nations, particularly those in the Latin American region, was that the economic gains from trade were limited and faltering. While their constitutions and national documents lauded the importance of equality, the historical inequalities that had been meted out to them continued to thwart their attempts to join the developed world.

In recent decades, the possibility of putting in place as perfect a competitive and complete market economy as possible, by reducing the cost of information and contract enforcement, is the policy objective of development economics and institutions working in international development. The neoclassical model that provides the backbone of this economic model has pursued the maximization of efficiency by keeping out non-market features, such as emotions and beliefs, or by taking account of them as externalities within its rubric. In contrast to this rubric, there are common beliefs, historical traditions and even random events that reinforce hopes and fears in members of a society and its institutions, and these persist in determining actions of many human beings both outside and within the market, e.g., the opposition to trading on religious days that continues to be emphasized even today in many religions. On the one hand, they can support political reforms like democracy, protection of the environment, and the fundamental rights of individuals, including rights to life and livelihood, and help to view economic inequalities as an unnecessary detriment to economic growth and avoidable social cost. On the other hand, they can lead to restricted access to education, health, housing and markets, and give rise to social conflicts, adding to unnecessary social costs. The market is devoid of any historical dimension once it is removed from its social context and regarded as an institution that operates on an independent and autonomous principle of efficiency. Such a shallow institutionalisation of the market can only direct an economy to create a development path that is directed by efficiency considerations, even when these are actively opposed by historical events (such as colonialism). Models of economic development that do not contend with historical inequities are in danger of being

[46] Hoff and Stiglitz (2001) provide a useful review of how economic theory presented industrialisation as the way to ensure development.

upstaged by social movements demanding compensation, even legal rectification of past wrongs and injustices. The experience of developed countries indicates that historical adversities and inequities have been dealt with through adopting a range of political ideologies with associated legal systems (Buscaglia 2000) and all countries in the developing world share the strong desire to achieve the benefits of economic development. The common goal of economic development is, however, not realised through a single path or model, but by active state involvement in formulating and directing industry and society (Evans 1995). 'Transactions often reflect the larger forces that both support and obstruct the growth of legality, as well as the extraordinary fundamental transformations that are occurring in the Chinese economy and society' (Lubman 1999: xv).

Society strongly fashions the terms and pattern of economic development, and legal rules draw on social and legal norms in their endeavour to organise and regulate the processes of development. It is not uncommon for legal systems to work with customary services, as in the case of Malaysia, where early on there was an attempt to work with customary forms of Muslim *adat* to understand their legal basis (Hooker 1968). The power of economic development appears to emerge from harnessing social norms rather than as simple replacement by formal legal systems. It is in this context that the mainstream position, that the market remains untarnished and can be regarded as perfect and free of social costs, political pressures and processes, is problematic, even detrimental, for the process of development of economies and societies. It works against the possibility of seeking low-cost alternatives for current development goals, but more importantly builds historical inequities into the development model, thereby buying into instability, even violence, from the injured. It also denies the possibility of a more equitable and inclusive form of capitalist development where rules are devised from an expanded and richer rubric, where riches can be directed to remedy inequity and injustice.

Why rules and rubrics for riches?

The theories and policies of economic development that have been in evidence over the second half of the twentieth century do not seem to have taken on board the importance of the social, moral and affective. These themes were prominent in the work of Adam Smith and reiterated by Coase with a focus on reciprocity of actions to ensure a mutual satisfaction of needs through exchange and trade. The sharing of labour within households and communities was customary practice and reflected in customary law. It was not unknown to have reciprocity of labour exchange in the public sphere, and there were forms of division of labour prior to capitalism. For Smith the organisation across labour activities was a consequence of the market, but it required Coase to give a structure to labour organisation by showing the market to be an institution that contended with the firm. Smith saw labour as free from the shackles of the medieval apprentice system and the restrictions of the guild, while Coasean insights emerge from the recasting of the labour organisation as a firm, an institution that enhances the labour contribution through contracting within the firm.

Both Coase and Adam Smith regard self-interest as the primary driver for exchange and trade; there is little, or no, commentary on how self-interest operates within a social context. While economists focus on the criterion of efficiency and regard the self-interest as a narrow identity, there are social contexts where the creation of a moral norm, its compliance and enforcement, are located within an organisation or community. For instance, when a community makes a collective decision to punish the violator of a social norm by shaving his head, tying him to a donkey and walking it around the village or town, there is a willing barber offering to shave the offender, offers of rope and donkey, and volunteers to tie and walk the individual for no expense. That economists since the times of Adam Smith have chosen to only regard self-interest as 'the invisible hand' which ensures efficiency and least cost, and have not regarded respect for others or morality as possible solutions, is a reflection of the times those economists lived in and are living in. The ability of humankind to conceive of ideals that might be opposed to self-interest, and where notions of the universal good provide the basis for an alternate rubric, could change the relationship between riches and rules in the realm of economic development.

Investigating the role of rubrics in creating frameworks for understanding wealth creation and accumulation can be the starting point for exploring different rules that could provide different systems of valuation and significance, in relation to the processes and product of accumulating riches. The possibility of reordering rubrics to expose the rules of human interaction and gain a deeper understanding of the relationship between riches and rules has been a major reason for writing this book. If we are to go beyond the riches of the market to the wider remit of human development and well-being, it would be useful to begin by looking at rubrics closely, and particularly at those rubrics that dominate in the social sciences.

The rubric of efficiency that is central to economics is based on marginal principles. It is not directly linked to reducing inequality in distribution of wealth in society. Even a measure of income inequality such as the Gini coefficient does not provide directives for how economic policy could reduce inequality. A need-based equity coefficient would serve that purpose better, for example a state subsidy to satisfy the minimum economic needs of all citizens that would be an identifiable ratio of the GNP.[47] However inefficient or poor the provision of subsidy for making available 'minimum need goods' to citizens may be, it still holds the remedy to the inequality. At present the economic perspective is that any proposed rubric of 'equity' is oppositional to a dominant

[47] The Atkinson inequality measure does take into account movements in the bottom income deciles. The sensitivity towards lower income groups could provide the directive for awarding subsidies to ensure minimum economic needs, yet this initiative has not been taken. See Krugman (2007) for a discussion on the politics of inequality that militates against policy action in this sphere.

rubric of 'equality' and, further, that a rubric of equity does not fit into economic thinking and analysis.

Such objections do not take on board the possibility that rubrics themselves have a considerable effect on the rules they prescribe and on the pathways they identify and analyse for the accumulation and sharing of wealth. There is a need to look across existing rubrics which are guided by concerns that go beyond single disciplines, focusing on commodities and exchange. The implications of rules on social engagement need to take account of the needs and demands of communities and people rather than the short-term gain of a few individuals, however well placed and well endowed. The social sciences split human motivations and experiences, resulting in very partial understanding of identity. In economics there is a singular focus on personal motivations and preferences.[48] Yet social norms provide a menu of identities, and the advent of behavioural economics has provided one avenue into understanding why individual motivation cannot be separated into its constituent parts. It would be fruitful to go further down this avenue and ask what the other social sciences regard as aspects of identity. In law, the identity of a person is deduced from the beliefs expressed, and the court proceeds to ascertain whether the person's motives and related bodily actions should be deemed as lawful or otherwise.

Separating the individual from the social context, with identities such as the 'liberal' or 'poet', appears to have no place in the economic sphere and these are regarded as political matters or deemed to be in the cultural sphere. Yet these identities transform within these other spaces and resurface in the economic and legal spheres instigating unrest and heralding conflict. The violence of the *jihadi* or terrorist who undertakes political actions to compensate historical wrongs and contemporary injustice is one illustration of this phenomenon. If access to the law is to help everyone, it should treat and be seen by all as equal. If, however, the rule of law is equated with a bundle of private property rights then different groups would have different values for parts of the bundle and assign very different order to these parts.[49] Individuals do not operate in a vacuum but rather within the social contexts of larger human structures such as family, community and nation. Consequently, when neoclassical economic thinking regards the rules of capitalism as operating with a narrow rubric of self-interest to ensure the acquisition of riches, it is at best rather limiting and at worst inaccurate. Where the impact of development is felt within social spaces such as the household, the relations between men and women within the family and their contribution in the labour market cannot be fully comprehended by looking at individual preferences and productivity, but require an examination of social relations within both family and community, and it is to these matters that we next turn.

[48] Seabright (2005) points out that human beings take on a series of identities through their life course.

[49] Bardhan and Mookherjee (2007b) make the point that private property rights cannot be equated with the rule of law in a simple and easy manner.

2 All in the family

Gender and identity within the household

> What marriage may be in the case of two persons of cultivated faculties, identical in opinions and purposes, between whom there exists that best kind of equality, similarity of powers and capacities with reciprocal superiority in them – so that each can enjoy the luxury of looking up to the other, and can have alternately the pleasure of leading and of being led in the path of development – I will not attempt to describe. To those who can conceive it, there is no need; to those who cannot, it would appear the dream of an enthusiast. But I maintain, with the profoundest conviction, that this, and this only, is the ideal of marriage; and that all opinions, customs, and institutions which favour any other notion of it, or turn the conceptions and aspirations connected with it into any other direction, by whatever pretences they may be coloured, are relics of primitive barbarism. The moral regeneration of mankind will only really commence, when the most fundamental of the social relations is placed under the rule of equal justice, and when human beings learn to cultivate their strongest sympathy with an equal, in nights and in cultivation.
>
> (John Stuart Mill 1970 [1869]: Chapter 4, p. 95)

To be able to applaud marriage between like-minded individuals rather than regard it as a deluded dream requires the appreciation that both men and women can achieve the highest standards of excellence. The writings of John Stuart Mill on the position of women address those attitudes to and interactions between men and women that are the product of societal structures and social norms that construct and control gender relations and thereby determine and direct what are acceptable attributes and behaviour for men and women. The contours of gender are also significantly intertwined with patterns of ownership of human and natural resources (Boserup 1970). The presence of strong hierarchies in both the reproductive and productive spheres is a long-standing feature of human societies but takes on a particularly rigid spatial form in capitalist societies (Scott 1988).[1] Mill, in his treatise on women, addresses the need to do away with inequality in gender relations in both sexual

[1] Friedrich Engels provides a historical account of the family in *The Origin of the Family, Private Property and the State* (Engels 1986 [1884]).

and work worlds. These gender inequalities arise from interactions between cultural, social and economic aspects of family life that impinge on the household and community and construct both gendered obligation of duties and the rights to privileges. These gendered identities that permeate the local community are also reflected within the family and are visible both in key life events such as birth, marriage and death and in everyday activities of care, schooling and family chores (Tinker 1990).

Patriarchy, capitalism and the household

With the advent of the industrial revolution in England came a new form of labour organisation that resulted in a separation of workplace from the home which constricted the possibility of women with childbearing and caring responsibilities working in factories.[2] This shift in the opportunities for women was already preceded by changes to women's work in the agricultural world in the eighteenth century through legislation such as the Enclosure Acts in England that put an end to women's rights, such as gleaning (the picking of grain after the harvest had been removed from the field) and estover (the gathering of the hay after harvesting). While legislation in agriculture reduced areas of women's work, the factories of the new capitalist economy regarded women workers as a cheaper and more exploitable form of labour.[3]

Mill's treatise was a radical work as it confronted the established gender relations among the English upper classes. It addressed the tradition of political philosophy that perceived the world to be divided into two distinct arenas of the public and private that had emerged in the seventeenth century. This is a gendered distinction as it regarded the public sphere as male and the private sphere as female. This separation of the lives and locations of men and women has been termed 'the sexual contract' (Pateman 1988) where a gender hierarchy undervalues the contribution of women by pushing work out of the public sphere into the private sphere of the household.[4] The analysis of the changes in the nature and location of men and women's work in nineteenth-century capitalism is deeply rooted in the Aristotelian thinking of the first century BC which regarded women as emotional and men as thinking, for they were associated with nature and intellect respectively. It is noteworthy that the social norms of

[2] While Engels provided the original critique of the impact of capitalism and the growing importance of property rights on the position of women in society, there has been a longstanding feminist history on the relationship between capitalism and gender relations. See Joan Scott (1988).

[3] Jane Humphries was influential in bringing gender into the study of economic history. The consequences of new agricultural technologies on women's work in the eighteenth century is the subject of her 'Enclosures, Common Rights and Women: The Proletarianization of Families in Late Eighteenth and Early Nineteenth Century Britain' (Humphries 1990).

[4] Scott (1988) provides a historical account of the mechanisms by which this separation is engineered.

Athenian society are regarded as the epitome of equality and justice in the classical world and also as an exemplar for modern society in eighteenth-century English philosophical thought.

While the study of gender is situated in this intellectual tradition and is evident in numerous social science disciplines, it is not acknowledged within an economic analysis of processes of capitalism and its implications for international development.[5] These economic trajectories are regarded as positive phenomena that are invariant with regard to gender and drawing both men and women into the labour market in an identical fashion. The construction and consequences of gender relations are regarded as falling outside the remit of the market and economic exchange, and as being merely a matter of interest for the household. Despite this emphatic denial, the rules that control the actions of men and women within the household, in family and community contexts, are not in fact peripheral to everyday work and life.

Patriarchy, gender relations and household hierarchies

Patriarchy is a gender hierarchy that is based on a paternal rule, where men are the head of the family and that gives them the power to control women's behaviour and that of other lesser men within the family. The role of inheritance patterns has been central in upholding this system of gendered distribution of power.[6] The gender relations that are constituted within the local sphere under a system of patriarchy systematically impose gendered norms on every household by age and activity. The power of patriarchy to discriminate against women while separating work and life into male and female arenas has been scrutinised and critiqued by feminist social scientists in the second half of the twentieth century.

> Patriarchal civil society is divided into two spheres, but attention is directed to one sphere only. The story of the social contract is treated as an account of the creation of the public sphere of civil freedom. The other, the private sphere, is not seen as politically relevant. Marriage and the marriage contract are also deemed politically irrelevant.
>
> Pateman (1988: 5)

Western feminist analysis has focused on this separation of the public and the private sphere and called for a move away from a narrow regard which focuses

[5] The classic model of economic development through the industrial transformation of society does not distinguish between men's and women's work. See Lewis (1954). The macroeconomic analysis of development did not regard gender as a relevant category of analysis to the study of savings, investment and capital accumulation. See Nurkse (1953) for an account of how newly independent countries needed to focus on accumulation and industrialisation to ensure economic development.

[6] The impact of gendered systems of inheritance on the work and status of men and women is the subject of the now classic work of Ester Boserup, a Danish economist who was a longstanding researcher of agricultural economies. See Boserup (1970).

on women's contributions to the economic process, yet ignores the gender constraints imposed on these women within both the household and the labour market. This analysis has been strongly influenced by Marxist interpretations of capitalism, which depicted it as an exploitative and alienating system within which women were subordinated in the home and excluded from the world of work. The power of the family to control the work and lives of women and children by subordinating the status of women to that of a commodity to be owned by men has been a central critique.

> The family was a collective working group. The father was its head, but for survival the labor of wife and children was necessary. The introduction of individual wages and the end of the ownership of people, in serfdom, did not dissolve the economic and social control of men over women. The man remained the head of the family unit and he retained control over the ownership of property through primogeniture [or dependency of the family on him]. Both, his wife's capacity to labor, and her capacity to bear his children, were, still, part of his stock in the world. Moreover the notion that this was the order of the world was firmly embedded in political, religious and educational institutions.
>
> Rowbotham (1976)

It was the capitalist context within which patriarchy operated that became the focus of Western feminist analysis, and the exploitation and discrimination of women within factories in the manufacturing sector became the central research concern. The making of gender relations in industrial societies has consequently become a characteristic feature of feminist analysis within the social sciences in both North America and Western Europe. Elsewhere gender relations are examined in relation to agricultural livelihoods and informal and uncertain urban employment[7] located in the peripheries of capitalism rather than with direct reference to industrial employment in the factory sector. Though women's work is clearly affected by the pattern of international capitalist development, the study of economic development does not readily include any analysis of gender relations. This is a consequence of the established dictum that there exists two mutually exclusive spheres of the public and the private, and that economic development is situated firmly within the realm of the public while the family remains within the private sphere. Economic development models have consequently been 'gender blind' until the last quarter of the twentieth century.[8]

[7] Beneria and Roldan (1987) provides a detailed analysis of how subcontracting of women to do homework provided links between the informal and the formal manufacturing sectors.

[8] The work of Diane Elson has been groundbreaking in bringing out the extent to which there is a complete disregard for the consequences of gender relations on the nature of the labour market and the extent to which women can contribute to such a market. See Elson (1991).

The market has been regarded as an institution that is devoid of markers of family, driven only by self-interest and oblivious to altruism or other emotions, for it is concerned solely with economic efficiency and the ability and skills of individuals to achieve this goal. Gender discrimination is regarded as having no place in the labour market as the presence of both men and women is purely the consequence of their human capital and its associated skills (Becker 1981b). Economic thinking does not therefore turn voluntarily or even readily to the legal system to enquire about its thinking on gender justice within the market. The legal approach to remedies for gender discrimination and persistent inequalities has, in fact, emerged from the intellectual analysis within political science and sociology rather than economics. It is only when gender relations are aggravated by economic travesties that the need for remedy draws the attention of economists. So when the contradictions between the demands of capitalism and the prevalent gender relations throw up unexpected – even sometimes ridiculous – circumstances, commentary emerges. Furthermore, there has been little attention and even less consistency in the analysis of how gender relations and economic conditions of development are mutually constituted.[9] A telling instance of how development trajectories generate quirky if not knee-jerk responses from the household is evident from the case reported below.

econ vs social

> Recently, some primary and middle school teachers in Harbin [China] have eagerly and happily divorced [on paper] their husbands, even celebrating over dinner afterwards. The reason for this trend is that the education system disqualifies married female teachers from reimbursement for their heating bills.
>
> Shi Jikai (2005)

These economic actions undertaken by family members seem odd in the light of a dominant view that the family and household operate in the private sphere to support marriage, reproduction and child-rearing. Such contradictions emerge because of the separation of the economic and social, so that economics is considered to operate only within the market while it is the social and familial aspects alone that pervade the household. Such a distinction makes it difficult to understand how economic principles might have a role in the household, and equally how social, particularly gender, relations affect economic development.

Another situation where the oddity of separating the economic from the social in relation to household behaviour comes up in the case of the adoption of a new Islamic Family Law by Malaysia in 1984, hailed as a hallmark as it extended to women several grounds to begin divorce that worked to counterbalance a man's right to divorce his wife at will. It also made divorce and polygamy outside the court illegal. The law broke new ground as it entitled a

[9] The promotion of the Women in Development (WID) and Gender and Development (GAD) approaches in the international sphere are policy attempts to bring gender into the mainstream of development during the 1980s and 1990s within the UN framework.

woman to a share of the matrimonial assets even though she did not financially contribute to the acquisition, thereby recognising that her contributions as wife and mother were central to the acquisition of skills and abilities that were made possible by the institution of marriage (Anwar 2006). Other Muslim countries looked at Malaysia's law as a model for reforming marriage laws within a Muslim legal framework. This approval did not prevent criticism of amendments suggested to the Islamic Family Law Bill 2005, introduced in the Federal Territories of Malaysia, that used gender-neutral language and made divorce equally easy for both men and women. Objections were raised by feminist legal organisations, such as Sisters in Islam, that such amendments to the law subverted earlier advances in gender rights. The seemingly gender-neutral language used by the law which now put men on a par with women in relation to having access to *fasakh* rights (dissolution of marriage by order of the court) did not go far enough to remedy older forms of gender bias as Malaysian men who had not been permitted under the traditional religiously conferred right to polygamous marriage could, under this law, use the courts to get access to the earnings of their ex-wives.[10]

The law has the power both to recognise the role of women in the household, in the bearing of and caring for children, and to simultaneously reduce a woman's right to her own income and matrimonial assets; therefore it is a double-edged sword in relation to the economic rights that women have within the institution of marriage. However, it is still presumed that economic development occurs through the market, and since the family does not operate, directly, in the public sphere of the economy, it is not seen to share any characteristics with the marketplace. Neither is it regarded as being subject to market rules or contracts, and so it should not have any bearing on economic performance.

Gender relations in the world of work

The perspective that the household has no bearing on the market gave way in the 1970s to an understanding that men and women select a marriage partner based on a complementarity in their human capital. The work of Gary Becker provided the view that the decision of men and women to marry was based on a calculation of what would maximise their joint returns as a household.[11] Bringing economic logic into the household has led to the argument that the decision of a woman to withdraw from the labour market and become a homemaker after marriage reflects her lower earning capacity and better homemaking skills compared to her future husband. The predominantly male labour

[10] The Sisters in Islam website provides an excellent commentary on the impact of Islamic laws on gender relations in Malaysia. See http://www.sistersinislam.org.my

[11] The initial ideas were developed by Becker in his article 'A Theory of Marriage' (Becker 1973).

market is therefore regarded to be the result of a cooperative decision achieved by a sorting process which ensures that an 'economically rational' team of husband and wife maximise their joint preferences. The New Home Economics (NHE) adds the implications of positive transaction costs (*à la* Coase) to the older idea of comparative advantage (*à la* Smith) to try and explain that marriage reduces costs and the reassigning of duties between married men and women increases gains from specialisation.[12] This model of NHE appears to regard women and men as equal, in a manner that might appear to be very close to Mill's seeming dream of the enthusiast, and yet it is based on individual choice where women and men are treated identically by the market and where social structures do not enter in any shape or form.

The household as a Coasean firm

While it might appear novel to draw on the literature on the nature of the firm to explain the formation of households, there are interesting, even compelling, parallels of individual behaviour within both units. While the firm uses planning and coordination methods according to internal rules or memorandum of association and bye-laws of the firm or company, a family uses the hierarchy of patriarchy to exert gender power on its members to ensure that family members adhere to household rules and norms. The structure of these units seems to hold the key to success, with the size of the firm, expansion or contraction being regulated to meet the profit objective of the firm while the household structure is regulated by decisions on marriage and decisions regarding co-residence of extended family and kinship members in the household. In such a sense, it is not the individuals in the household who are akin to those in the market, but it is the organisation of the household that resembles a Coasean firm (Fennell 2003).

Using the tool of transaction costs facilitates the understanding of household interactions as a way of minimising costs of cohabitation, marriage and divorce and has become the starting point for a variety of technical models of the household.[13] These models drop the Beckerian assumption that the head behaves like a benevolent dictator, and the associated notion of altruism or 'other regard' as ensuring cooperation among household members, replacing it with the understanding that the household is a site where the threat of conflict is ever present. In place of the cooperative solution, the models identify mechanisms

[12] *A Treatise on the Family* was written by Becker in 1981 and took economic analysis, particularly the importance of bargaining and cooperation within the household, to maximise returns. His work was highly influential and gave rise to the New Household Economics.

[13] The work of Robert Pollak built on the explanatory power of transaction costs in explaining household decisions and patterns of work allocation. See Pollak (1985) for a useful commentary on the difficulties of analysing joint production, while the alternative of non-cooperation is introduced in Lundberg and Pollak (1993) through the model of separate spheres inhabited by a husband and a wife within a marriage.

within the household that are based on negotiation, even contracts, that operate within the context of well-established and policed hierarchies of gender. The 'bargaining' models shift the analysis from collective models to examining the negotiation and bargaining that individual household members undertake with regard to allocation of resources and the opportunities as the guiding logic for interaction in the family.[14] The context within which such bargaining takes place is provided by the relative 'fall-back position' of an individual and the 'social perception of the individual' by other members of the household. The fall-back position of an individual is related to the availability of an alternative to the allocation of resources, the opportunities and the work that has been assigned to the individual within the household. Where there is no alternative, or fall-back, the particular individual is unable to refuse even the most oppressive allocation of work. The 'social perception of the individual' is a combination of how other members view the economic and labour contributions of this member, 'the perceived contribution response' as well as the evaluation of others' well-being resulting from the individual's own ability to maintain their position in the household or 'the perceived interest response'.[15] It appears that both components of social perception tend to work against women within the household, as the social construction of gender within a society undervalues the economic and social contribution of women and also imbues women with a lower degree of awareness and articulation of their own self-worth. With the two features of 'fall-back' and 'social perception' that determine the manner in which bargains are devised and the interactions are riddled with the hierarchy of gender power, the contracts within the household carry a set of rules that have a greater cost than the contracts created within the hierarchy of firm.

The gender division of labour in the household is based on socially constructed gender relations rather than any hierarchy of organisation that emerges to combat the costs of the market. The inequity in the distribution of power and control within the household militates against the notion of equal 'bargaining' in the family.[16] So, notions of contracting within the household should not be regarded as simply in just another hierarchical unit but in a site of gender conflict and exploitation (Woolley 1985). This holds for all aspects of negotiation, choices and decisions made, within the household and the feminist analysis across the social sciences which maintain the separation of the public and private spheres[17] as well as new tendencies in economics which make out simplistic

[14] The work of Shelly Lundberg was influential in bringing a larger social context into the study of households and families.

[15] The importance of bargaining models was highlighted by feminist economists. See Laila Kabeer (1994) for an explanation of why gender hierarchies are so resistant to economic conditions. The particular role of unequal forms of inheritance, in particular in relation to land ownership, is the focus of the work of Bina Agarwal (see Agarwal 1992).

[16] The contribution of Amartya Sen to the study of gender inequalities in the family is well documented in the feminist literature. See Agarwal (1992) and Kabeer (1994).

[17] The collection of articles in Ferber and Nelson (1993) calls for caution in any continued opposition between the values that operate in the market and the household.

analogies between the market and the household, such as a ready association between the level of women's employment in the labour market and the relative importance or type of marriage contract.

> The relationship between employer and worker is contractual, and for many 'contractual' theorists the employment contract is the exemplary contract. Feminists have been greatly concerned about the marriage contract, but their writings and activities have been ignored for the most part, even by most socialist critics of contract theory and the employment contract, who might have been keenly interested in feminist arguments.
>
> (Pateman 1988: 5) [18]

There is also concern among feminist economists regarding the tendency to regard marriage and divorce within the household as events that are equivalent to acts of entry and exit in a market context respectively and treat men and women equally.[19] The reality is that the consequences of these acts do not have symmetrical consequences for the men and women taking part.[20] Despite the negotiation and calculation of costs, drawing on both individual 'fall-back' and 'individual perceptions' women experience greater economic and social losses with regard to resources and opportunities, both within the household and in employment and income-earning possibilities in the community and larger societal sphere as a consequence of divorce. There is also worry that there is a lack of recognition, in economic analysis, of the caring responsibilities that fall to women.[21] The undervaluation of all household work, and the predominant location of caring work within this sphere, result either in no, or a very inadequate, analysis of the importance of caring as a distinct sphere of gendered work. It continues to be regarded as an adjunct activity and is not yet considered a fully constitutive form of market labour. The prevailing framework of rules that separate out activities related to production and reproduction and assign different social norms to both, with self-interest operating in the former and altruism in the

[18] The importance awarded to separating public and private spheres in economics is accompanied by an insistence that if economics is brought into the household it would be fully applicable to key rites of passage such as marriage, reproduction and divorce. These tendencies are strongly opposed by feminist economists.

[19] The work of Frances Woolley was important as it recognises the value of taking economic analysis into the household. Yet it does so while being critical of the Beckerian view of 'altruism at home, and selfishness in the market' and at the same time emphasises how men and women have different gendered experiences of the same event. See Woolley (1993).

[20] See Paula England (1993) for an analysis of the consequences of regarding men and women as equal in the marketplace, while accepting the differences in logics of altruism and selfishness, in the household and market respectively.

[21] The continued disregard for caring work in the labour market and its relation to social expectations that women are primarily responsible for caring and the continued subordination of women in the household is the subject of Folbre's *The Invisible Heart* (Folbre 2001).

latter, occludes our understanding of negotiation and exchanges within the family.

Negotiation and contract in marriage

Household hierarchies result in conflicts and foment exploitation when there are unilateral actions in violation of the social norms, oral agreements and even negotiated roles, often on account of aggressive – even unprovoked – force by members located within the household hierarchy. Such actions might also be triggered by pressure from community-based social norms or large-scale economic or social shocks. While subordination arises through unequal power relations within a gendered set of rules that operate within a family and household, it is no easy matter to attribute subordination to a particular form of gender relations.[22]

There are no simple linear or direct relationships that identify the interactions between social norms that operate in society and forms of economic development: for instance, a contract cannot be regarded as a unique creation of the market within a capitalist system. Contracts are not entirely absent from the social spheres of society; they are not limited to a particular society, and also they are a feature that is central to the institution of marriage under Muslim law. The Muslim marriage contract makes provision for the promise to pay bride money (*mehr*) to the wife in the event of divorce. The contract also makes provision for the right of divorce to the wife under a prior agreement (*khula*) with the husband, to be made at the time of marriage. In addition, the contract requires the husband to provide maintenance to the wife, which is variously regarded as a debt owed to the wife (in the *Shafi'i* school) or as a gratuity given to her (under the *Hanafi* school).[23] The termination of a marriage is permitted under this marriage contract, subject to fulfilment of the conditions of the marriage contract.

The provision for full payment of *mehr* appears to be akin to the clause on 'liquidated damages' in standard commercial contracts for non-performance where the damage is 'computed in advance', i.e. liquidated, and specified in the agreed contract. However, there is no standard marriage contract and there are variations in the marriage contract which have emerged from cultural interpretations of the law in Muslim societies.[24] The variations in the marriage contract arising from interpretations by different Muslim schools of law

22 There is an uncomfortable ease with which Western social science has tended to regard feminist oppression as more readily present in non-Western societies. Okin (1989) provides a powerful argument for thinking carefully about gender analysis that cannot distinguish between freedom and cultural relativism. See also Seyla Benhabib (1992).

23 There are four schools of Islamic legal thought (*mahdab*) within Sunni Islam: *Hanafi*, *Maliki*, *Shafi'i* and *Hanbali*.

24 The ability of Islamic law to provide an element of autonomy from colonial rule in the case of Malaysia is the subject of an insightful article by Peletz (1993).

indicate that culture and social interpretation dominate contractual aspects. Family law has increasingly been treated as a private matter and the State has tended to restrict itself to matters that are deemed to be in the public sphere of the market. Yet there is a growing public demand for the State to deal with matters of property contestation in marriage, with disputes giving rise to an increasing number of amendments to the laws of marriage and divorce.

While the institution of marriage has remained within the private sphere, the spillover into the public sphere of the market of some of its aspects has become a matter for state intervention. With the growing importance of property in a capitalist world the State is forced to consider ownership in relation to both the rich and the poor sections of society. In particular, the foundational importance of the family led to rules relating to marriage to be among the earliest legislations undertaken by new nation-states. There are also national concerns about maintaining the family which are reflected in national legislation on divorce. State legislation has attempted to bring women into the modern world in relation to labour markets but has not wished to interfere in an undue fashion in family matters. The only significant exception is where gender legislation is central to a larger political or social project, such as modernising society or system transformation, as in the ushering in of socialism. For instance, the Marriage Law of 1950 in China was promulgated in the very first year of the existence of the People's Republic of China, to liberate women from the feudal shackles of the traditional family. Article 17 of the law of 1950 allows for divorce by mutual consent and dissolution of marriage in contested applications. However, there was considerable opposition to gender equality in marriage, most prominently displayed in relation to women's right to demand dissolution of marriage.

> The party state was a complex organisation in rural China. Village, town, district and court officials acted upon a variety of motives, not only in the interests of common gender or the perpetuation of patriarchy. Some village officials might try to prevent women from seeking divorce, from leaving the village, while others actually want them to leave to spare themselves the hassle; some supported the law just because it was promulgated by the same Party that gave them status. For their part, it appears that the court and district officials in rural areas were often more interested in enforcing the law than assisting men. It was this multi-layered and multi-motivational nature of the state that allowed room for women to divorce: if they were refused a hearing at the village or township, they could, and did go elsewhere.
>
> (Diamant 2000: 184)

There is no linear or straightforward relationship between patriarchy and economic development and countries that were deemed to be lagging behind in the industrial race cannot be presumed to have 'traditional' or 'under-developed' gender relations. Moving from a Western perspective, where gender relations are forged within industrial environments, to a broader and more nuanced Southern perspective permits a study of gender relations fashioned within the agriculture and service cultures which provide the largest contribution to the economy and society. Historical processes and national sites show that culture spills across nations and epochs, affecting gender relations in complex and important ways.[25] The historical processes that have constructed the national and local contexts within which gender relations are played out indicate the need for an understanding of gender that goes beyond the West, yet does not fall into the trap of regarding the non-Western world as a single entity.

While the act of marriage is regarded as a form of contract between parties in a number of modern societies, the huge inequality in the value accorded to men and women in these societies makes the marriage contract closer to that between a serf and owner rather than that of the employee and employer.[26] The notion of contract in marriage is not identical to that in the market as the husband has an unlimited claim on his wife and also children, who do not have recourse to any compensation or redress unless that has been formally negotiated prior to or at the time of marriage. The contracts between members of the household, along with contracts that create new households by the act of marriage, occur within a strongly gendered hierarchy of power. The adoption of laws relating to marriage and divorce reflected the slowness of recognising that there was an unequal treatment of men and women within the household, much less drawing on a gender-relations framework to understand how marriage and divorce affected the lives of men and women in a family environment.

In the case of Malaysia, where laws on marriage and divorce were addressed early on in the development process, there were concerns that the Law Reform (Marriage and Divorce) Act 1976 did not contribute to reconciliation; rather, it made both parties regard divorce as inevitable because of the absence of any clause regarding a reconciliation process (Hak 2005). The absence of a reconciliation clause prevented the possibility of negotiation and appears to treat marriage as a straightforward case of a contract, with divorce arising from a breach in such an arrangement. Yet it would appear that there is no easy way to analyse contracts in the household without taking into account the strategies

[25] The work of Chandra Talpade Mohanty has been influential in reconfiguring feminist research across North South locations. Her project since the mid-1990s, to create a new framework of feminist research that is based on cross-cultural understanding, has placed cultural practice at the appropriate context within which research paradigms and designs are pursued. See Alexander and Talpade Mohanty (1997) for an edited collection of views of the historical reasons for hierarchies and differences in feminist analysis, and Talpade Mohanty (2003b) for a personal and pedagogical reflection on the purpose and practice of feminist analysis and struggle.

[26] The legal similarity of husband and wife to that of master and servant was brought out by the work of Susan Moller Okin. See her *Women in Western Political Thought* (Okin 1979) for a review of classical authors on the role of women, and her *Justice, Gender and Family* (Okin 1989) for an analysis on contemporary thinking on gender and justice.

and reasoning used by household members in negotiating the exchange in relation to their location within the household hierarchy.

Contracts, markets and gender relations

Gendered relations in the household impose unwritten rules on its members. The possibility of members breaking away from the household hierarchy of power can be achieved through economic empowerment, i.e. the ability to contract economic rights and duties, or through a more ready and valued recognition of their contribution to meeting household obligations of care. The nature of the family, located as it is in the private sphere and dealing with matters of affection and care, has not been examined at any length within mainstream economics. The computation of the costs of care, child-rearing and emotional support is a latecomer to the study of the labour market and even to the understanding of the economics of the household.[27] The recalibration of values within the household, through more equitable gender relations, requires a fundamental re-weighting of activities termed as caregiving within the household. If it is done, then the ability of individuals to bargain in the household will be akin to altering the terms of the Coasean contract. If there is a shift, from focusing on income-earning activities undertaken in the labour market to the much larger number of unpaid hours expended on care and affection within the family, then such a revaluation might be feasible. Where the full cost of child-rearing is brought into the calculations of contribution by individual family members, there would be a fundamental renegotiation of the importance of non-market, affective activities within the household.[28]

If a household's total income remains the same but the woman's income increases, the woman begins to exercise greater say in household matters. The case of the Grameen Bank in Bangladesh shows that women who join community microcredit groups begin to exercise greater say in their households. It is the opportunity to work and organise, which creates options outside the household, that increases the bargaining position of women and entitles them to rights in society that were previously the sole right of the rich and powerful, and often only male members in the community and household. The ability to change gender relations within the household through expanding external relations permits women to challenge the power hierarchy and improve upon their negotiations and contracts in the household. The possibility of using contracting as a form of power within the household and community could permit more equal gender relations, but this equality is still one that does not do away with gender differences; rather, it results in a more equitable treatment of men and women in the community.

[27] Folbre makes this the central point of her book *The Invisible Heart*, and focuses on the implications of the longstanding neglect of care in economics on how gender relations are viewed within the discipline (Folbre 2001).

[28] The gendered manner in which childcare is accounted for in the household is the subject of England and Folbre (1999).

> [T]he family as a jurally defined, corporate kin group is distinguished from a household as a collection of kin and sometimes non-kin who share a common residence. The corporate nature of the family derives from the jural rights to property, usually land, which its members hold in common. (Yanagisako 1979: 153)

The State has tended not to change marriage laws that might undermine the family, and the Indian and Malaysian legal systems have been slow to change the laws in the direction of gender equality or even make modifications of family law to ensure gender equity in relation to community interpretations. The reluctance of these governments to meddle with family law is largely because the family is seen as the bedrock of private life and the stability of societal rules and behaviour. In particular, there is concern that changes in family law would be seen as undermining the power hierarchies within the household, which are critical for investment in human capital and social capital, and might therefore undermine accumulation processes within the household that are critical prerequisites for market expansion and wealth accumulation.

Investment in marriage and children

The notion of marriage as a site for investment has been focused on by the new household economics (NHE) but this is not something new; rather, it is inherent in the dynamics of the household. The strong sense of investment is closely related to asset accumulation and inter-generational inheritance within the household. In the case of marriage, there is a transfer of wealth. In some traditions and culture this is by the bride's family to that of the bridegroom (dowry) and in others with a reverse payment, from the groom to the bride's family in the form of bride price.[29] The difference between the neoclassical notion of investment and that which emerges from an anthropological study of marriage is that in the former the investment is marriage-specific and relates to a single marriage partner, while in the latter it is family-specific and extends to all the relations that the incoming partner has with all members of the marital family. Where the marital relationship is embarked upon solely on the basis of the knowledge of cultural norms, it may not be conducive to partner-specific investment.

In a majority of cultures, it is the wife who enters a new household and is investing large amounts of time and effort getting to know the hierarchy and arrangement of individuals within the family. She also attempts to gain information regarding the specific characteristics of her husband through such a process. Her ability to observe and learn about the particular demands of her husband would take many years and require her to traverse the hierarchy from

[29] See Goody (1962) for an early commentary on the role of property rights in gender relations

young bride to mother and senior matriarch (Kandiyoti 1998). The making and remaking of relations by the young wife through her life cycle in her marital home makes for a very long horizon of investment. In her life trajectory, children are regarded as an investment that will help her achieve a respected woman status. This private benefit to women of having children in a traditional agricultural household is distinct from the investment that children provide to parents as a form of pensions. The contribution that children make in a woman's life in her marital home might therefore be greater than the economic contribution that they make to the household. This conception differs markedly from the neoclassical understanding that children are a public good that benefit all in the household but where the private costs are borne disproportionately by the mother/women in the household.

In traditional agricultural households, women do not have the option of choosing between being a homemaker and an employee in the labour market. In such conditions the marital home does approximate to a large organisation, but as a situation similar to that of an apprentice or servant in a guild rather than that of an employee in a firm. The patriarchal property relations that operate in traditional agricultural communities do not allow individuals to exit from a household, the absence of a fall-back position making it impossible for women to negotiate or resist subjugation in everyday life. The impossibility of exit in a traditional agricultural household and the strong patriarchal hierarchy within such organisations give rise to social relations that are closer to those in a guild or closed group rather than a market. In such a situation, both marriage and divorce are not a matter of individual choice but a mediated action by the household and community. The institutional basis of the NHE does not deal adequately with the corporate entity of the agricultural household, which follows cultural norms and not market principles.

The social and cultural context of agricultural households has a bearing on the implications of marital breakdown and the likelihood of divorce. As women in their lifetime, in their marital home, have to establish and repeatedly renew relations with their husband's kin, the cost of exit would be the total investment in maintaining this large network of relations. The wife who leaves the husband's home has not only to face a cost that far exceeds the loss of investment that is husband-specific, but also a withdrawal of the support and status that has been gained over the years of marriage. In the neoclassical understanding of divorce, adopted within the law and economics framework, divorce is regarded as a consequence of rising costs of negotiation in the marriage, or a rearrangement in the household and work distribution between husband and wife that is increasingly regarded as unfair (see Nock and Brinig 2002). The notion of fairness in a marriage, and the intent to prevent free-riding, lie behind recent calls for additional sanctions against lack of due care in marriage, through the introduction of the covenant form of marriage (Rowthorn 2002). The thinking is that divorce is chosen too readily by selfish partners who do not want to make asset-specific investment in a marriage, and so there should be further social sanctions against divorce, to be instituted by the State.

Equally, in societies where the cultural norms of a traditional agricultural world still reign, the act of divorce amounts to dishonouring the marital family. The consequence of a divorce is that it renders the woman an outcast from the home that she has invested in, widely and repeatedly. Where the cause of marital breakdown is an erring or selfish husband, the calling for a further strengthening of social norms supporting the institution of marriage will not help, and reparation can come only from a focus on reprimanding the erring individual. Cultural norms govern individual action or personal choice or preference in the matter of divorce, and these are rooted in the investment in household relationships. Consequently a cultural reprimand or cultural compensation is needed, and it has to be case specific and cannot be written into the state law. In such cases equitable justice through family courts seems to be the only solution.

Hierarchies, divorce and domestic violence

Where the inequities in the division of labour within the household are viewed as unacceptable, there emerges a threat to the household union which might result in separation or divorce. Such a change in the status of the individuals might have a negative impact on the household honour and therefore be regarded as an inferior, even unacceptable, situation by powerful members of the household. The patriarchal head would therefore seek to prevent separation or divorce. Divorce or separation not only affects the status of the household but also alters the legal and traditional rights of the individuals concerned. Divorce also destabilises the household, while marriage (not divorce) contributes to stability of the State, significantly even if remotely. The feminist reasoning that contracting within the household has a different social basis, not found in the economic basis of the firm, has been sidelined by recent arguments in law and economics, which do not make much of the difference between the socially binding union of marriage and the voluntary federation of economic contracting parties as a firm; their focus is more on legal enforcement of promised duties and obligations in the family and in the firm. One area of particularly heated debate has to do with the duties and obligations under laws relating to marriage and divorce, because laws are drafted by reference to a black-and-white definition of legal concepts that are mutually exclusive, whereas concepts of duties and obligations in family relations are inclusive of one another. The Chinese experience in codifying their laws in the area of family concepts, given below, is of interest, in the danger from divorce to patriarchy which it highlights and the importance of duties, imposed on the married by patriarchs, to cater to the stability (political sensitivities) of the State.

> [T]he history of divorce law and policy under Communist rule in China shows that, in the absence of clearly specified and detailed grounds for divorce, the courts tend to do their best to keep the couple together rather than to end a marriage … in contrast to the situation regarding marriage,

> in which state law in a sense is prepared to acknowledge 'private' or de facto arrangements. The Chinese Communist authorities have always retained an exclusive right to grant divorce, and buttressed this position by maintaining a strict rule against bigamy. The unwillingness to afford any kind of official recognition to 'de facto divorce' is indicative of the political sensitivities surrounding the dissolution of marriage in the Chinese social context.
>
> (Palmer (1995: 122)

With the adoption (in China) of a new constitution in 1978 there was the introduction of a new Marriage Law in 1980. Article 25 of the 1980 Marriage Law recognised the freedom to divorce. That did not make '*de jure* divorce' easy, but only a possibility. The Inheritance Law of 1985, the Protection of Women's Rights and Interests Law of 1992, the Marriage Law of 2001 and Article 3 of the revised Marriage Law all prohibit domestic violence. Under amendments to the Revised Law of the People's Republic of China on 'Protection of Women's Rights and Interests', passed in 2005, a prohibition is placed in Article 40 of the Revised Law of 2005, in relation to the illegality of sexual harassment.

If a couple choose to divorce then, generally, family law imposes a payment to be made by the husband to the wife, to compensate for her loss in her share in the joint income. The compensation may well be the last step in the dismantling of the household. The move to separation or divorce is a decision that is made by the concerned parties and can be regarded as a form of negotiation where the parties are still evaluating the costs of returning to the market.[30] A recent case in the evolving Chinese legal system is of interest.

> On March 2 in the Luqiao District of Taizhou city, Zhejiang province, citizen Chen took his wife to court, seeking a divorce from the wife, and also petitioning the court to compel the return of a 19,000 yuan betrothal gift and payment of 10,000 yuan in compensation for emotional distress. That day, the Luqiao District People's Court formally accepted this case. According to plaintiff Chen's indictment, at the beginning of the first month of the lunar year, Chen's wife, without having secured her husband's agreement, went to the hospital to have a fetus artificially removed. Chen believes that because he is legally married to his wife, both parties should jointly enjoy the right of procreation. The wife's conduct, [in] unilaterally expropriating for herself that procreative right, calls for a grant of compensation for emotional distress, in accordance with the law. Wu Weiqing, a lawyer for Zhejiang's Haihao law firm, believes both husband and wife enjoy an equal claim to the right of procreation, and although at present the law has not made a definite ruling, a wife's secretive extraction

[30] A useful collection of articles on the use of law and economic thinking to analyse marriage and divorce can be found in the edited volume by Rowthorn and Dnes (2002).

> of a fetus can constitute encroachment upon the husband's procreative right. However, speaking from legal theory, as the conduct of Chen's wife has already encroached upon Chen's right of procreation, Chen is entitled to advance against his wife a claim for emotional damages.
>
> ('Today Morning Express', taken from the *Yanzhao City News*, 7 March 2007)

The law and economics literature regards the ability of individuals to take the first step to file for divorce as a reaction to, and amelioration of, the increasing transaction costs arising within the marriage, on a 'no-fault' basis. The focus of a 'no-fault' divorce is on ensuring a fair rearrangement of property rights rather that on staking a claim for injury to the person and the associated evaluation. This perspective has come to be regarded as reducing the sanctity of marriage, or at least reducing the incentive to stay in the marriage, as such a ruling works to reduce the amount of care and negotiation within the marriage (see Rowthorn (2002a). In a similar state of affairs, in relation to the idea of the 'contract', the courts of law dealing with torts read into contracts a 'duty to care' and 'strict liability' for failing in duty for any reason, in many cases of commission of tort or civil wrong. The onus to care was put on the economically stronger party and strict liability on the party engaging in dangerous activities resulting in injury to others for any reason. Analogously, 'duty to care' can get linked to the inequity in income between the spouses and imposed on the economically stronger partner. With regard to strict liability, it needs to be assessed in a context where both infidelity and domestic violence within a marriage, for any reason, are viewed as serious marital wrong or tort. Legal perceptions of marital wrongs have not been as consistent as the perceptions have been of material wrongs, over the last three centuries, since the former is thought to be more private than the latter.

Domestic violence has not, so far, been viewed as arising from negligence inviting strict liability for compensation in torts.[31] Where domestic violence is stated to be an affront to a person, the established legal procedure in Western courts has been to seek a solution through further undergirding of the rights of the individual. Domestic violence has increasingly come to be regarded as a human rights issue and one that should be viewed as a universal concern that goes across all societies (Thomas and Beasley (1993).

> Domestic violence violates the principles that lie at the heart of this moral vision: the inherent dignity and worth of all members of the human family, the inalienable right from fear and want and the equal rights of men and women.
>
> (Thomas and Beasley 1993: 37)

[31] (CEDAW) The UN Convention on the Elimination of All Forms of Discrimination Against Women came into operation on 3 September 1981 as part of an international initiative to recognise domestic violence as an affront to human rights.

Any assertion of rights at the individual level without taking into account the relational aspects tends to break off relations and will be counter-productive. To bring domestic violence into the analysis, society needs to provide additional relational worlds, such as those of employment, outreach and education, that encourage an individual to reconfigure her fall-back position and force other members to change their perception of the individual. In Malaysia, though figures for female education and health had gone up in 2005, according to the Human Development Report, this did not trigger an increase in employment. Cultural norms had prevented women from entering the labour market, and this is not an exception as it had also been the case in Japan in earlier decades. The Malaysian organisation Sisters in Islam is arguing for a law against domestic violence, in recognition of violence against women as an area where both public and *Shari'a* law need to work to ensure that communities change their interpretation of the law, alongside changes in the national legislation on domestic violence.

The Domestic Violence Act (DVA) in Malaysia is a significant achievement as it is one of the few pieces of legislation where a process of consultation and negotiation has involved both the State and victims of violence and their support groups. The campaign for a DVA began in 1985 and the negotiation for the legislation, which began in 1989, took five long years, not least because all issues over conflict of jurisdiction had to be meticulously considered by all those involved. The difficulty of addressing these abuses within the household arises from the prominence of the economic model which prevents a more familial and affective model of the household from taking centre stage.

> Among non-market transactions, those occurring between kinship groups or families dominate [attention]. The family is a group of individuals related by blood, marriage or adoption but its significance as a social institution comes from the activities it accommodates. The institution takes the form of rights and obligations associated with and defining the role of the family members, thus forming a comprehensive transaction, or contract, or set of interrelated contracts (husband–wife, parent–child, wife–mother-in-law, etc.). Terms such as contract or transaction usually connote voluntary association. This seems natural in the case of marriage, where entry into the roles is voluntary on the part of the spouses or the families of origin.
>
> (Ben-Porath (1980: 3)

> In the Malay village, gender differentiation was commonly expressed not in terms of biological makeup but in terms of morality. A basic concept of man's role was guardianship – of his sister's, mother's and daughter's virtue. By extension, all village men were responsible for the moral status of all village women.
>
> (Ong 1990: 261)

On the other hand, maintaining the virtue and honour of women helps maintain hierarchy in families, while drawing on notions of shame and guilt provides the instruments of patriarchal control in the family. The influence of patriarchal hierarchy on household decisions regarding women's presence in the public and private sphere has created fundamental contradictions between women's contributions to income from working in the marketplace and their contributions to care and family through working at home.[32] The economic logic pushes for looking at women as economic agents and their contribution to be measured by the value of the work that they undertake in the market. There is, however, no easy way of evaluating the responsibility that women shoulder in relation to childbearing, child rearing and childcare for the benefit of the family and society. In fact, the activities of caring that women engage in are swept into the grey zone between the public and private spheres and are hugely undervalued in both spheres. It is only when women are given opportunities for employment that they seem to be able to reform their men's attitudes towards valuing women and working towards women's empowerment.

Gender relations, legal rules and cultural norms

The possibility of a broader and more inclusive analytical framework (for the household), which introduced a gender sensitive and culturally embedded set of tools, arose with the concerted work of feminist social scientists.[33] In particular, feminist frameworks around patriarchal models of the household move far away from market logic to social construction of identities. The overemphasis on the market in the West has led to inattention to the cultural and social context within which economic aspects of household negotiations take place. The cultural norms of society interact with household hierarchies in particularly intricate ways to produce local patterns that closely affect negotiation within the household regarding gendered work and social valuation.[34] The 'implicit contracts' that emerge through contested negotiations in the households, in different nations, are criss-crossed by ideological, historical and religious considerations and overlapped by economic as well as cultural considerations.

> The assumption, of women as an already constituted and coherent group with identical interests and desires, regardless of class, ethnic or racial location, [which] implies a notion of gender or sexual difference, even patriarchy, can be applied universally and cross-culturally.
>
> (Talpade Mohanty 1988: 64)

[32] The work of feminist thinkers in the social sciences was important in bringing in the complex set of social relations that affect the lives of men and women differently. See Hart (1992) on Malaysia and Folbre and Abel (1989) on the United States.

[33] Our knowledge of the impact that national and international frameworks make on the construction of gender relations in household, community and economy is the result of pioneering work by heterodox social scientists. See Michael *et al.* (1989); Beneria and Feldman (1992); Kabeer (1994).

[34] See Collier and Yanagisako (1987) for a classic work on how gender plays a powerful role in everyday life. Jacka 1997 provides a powerful sketch of how gender relations play out within the context of large-scale migration during the reform process in China.

The demand for gender equality has encountered legal conservatism in Malaysia, essentially cultural in nature. The difficulty in demanding gender equality is that it is based on Western notions of equality that emerge from the particular forms of social differentiation and hierarchy prevalent in those societies. The opposition to gender equality emanates from a distrust of concepts from the West which are seen as post-colonial impositions rather than as genuine matters for concern in the non-Western world. The slow acknowledgement of Southern feminisms within Southern societies has also resulted in a reluctant recognition of inequalities generated by hierarchies of gender in these societies. The obfuscation of gender inequity due to the resistance to the cultural dominance of Western models of the family, household and gender politics has resulted in contradictions between the global demand for gender equality and the manner in which national governments are putting forward gender laws to facilitate economic development.

The demand in the UN, since the Declaration of Economic and Social Rights in 1945, has been for recognition of women and children as distinct individuals, who must be respected as full humans beings in their own right. Claims for human rights have been opposed as a product of Western cultural imperialism by scholars outside the global North.[35] The furore surrounding these issues has shifted the focus from gender and other inequalities that are meted out under patriarchal regimes to decrying any move to a single historical trajectory of Western-style liberal democracy. This shift has been a detriment to understanding how patriarchal national governments can affect the relationship between household hierarchy and individual human welfare. However, there are exceptions where governments do attempt to bring in equity, as illustrated by the following example.

Seven women in Haining city of Zhejiang province, China sued the City Planning Bureau, the Urban Residents' Committee, and the Neighbourhood Committee Office for not being treated equal to men in applying for land for construction. Haining City Court and Jiaxing Intermediate People's Court confirmed that the City Planning Bureau's decision to reject the application for an administrative license by returning the application materials represented a violation of the law (Meng Wancheng *et al.* 2007).

'[C]ross cultural feminist work must be attentive to the micropolitics of context, subjectivity and struggle, as well as the macropolitics of global economic and political systems and processes' (Talpade Mohanty 2003b: 501).

The marital promises, and resulting rights and duties, are not dissimilar to those of commercial contracts, but everything in marriage is not voluntary. Marriage implies force of tradition and culture. In commerce and marriage, rights and duties are context-specific instruments. If the instruments are sought to be applied out of context, because of ignorance of the context, misunderstanding between the parties will result, and it may not be right to trace

35 Okin (1989) provides a valuable analysis of the difficulties that universal categories face in the context of cultural understandings regarding gender rights.

them to tradition and culture instead of to the inability to counter their force coming through interested others. But misunderstandings do cause suffering where the contexts have been forgotten by everyone and yet there is much generalised clamour regarding the need to uphold tradition and culture. People's need to use force on others can be conveniently attached to available handles in tradition and culture, and the handles remain alive thereby. Contracts that are implicit in contexts as different as the 'casting couch' and the making of suicide terrorists by promises of payment to their families indicate how mixing up contexts makes cultural norms, including gendered norms and even law, ambiguous.

Gender relations, judicial ruling and property rights

The State has traditionally intervened in decisions of marriage and divorce to reduce the inequity brought about by the changed status of individuals. Such interventions cannot be successful if they focus on the individual or the market value of properties; they must look to the community and nature of hierarchy and investment in human relations therein which do not lend themselves to market valuation easily. However, the State is not a neutral arbiter as it is a fundamentally patriarchal institution that has the ability to promulgate on, and to regulate, human behaviour, and by doing so control and reorder gender relations (Connell 1987). How the State will first reorder its own attitude to gender is the more important question.

The most important of the state interventions is the right of the State to arbitrate on matters relating to property, particularly in relation to the right of inheritance. In the case of intestacy the State plays an important role with regard to the rights and duties between husband and wife, and between father and children. The rights and liabilities in the matrimonial contract are laid down by law, and typically are a mixture, with a part based on modern law, a part on customary law and a part negotiated by the parties concerned. If the State is to enact a law to reduce the inequality and oppression of patriarchal property rights it would do well to look at the manner in which a market-based valuation of household activity undervalues and underprivileges the contributions made within the organisation of the traditional household. The ability of the patriarchal head of the household to regard his wife and children as his servants, and in extreme cases as property itself, prevents such a reframing of the valuation of activities of the household, without the introduction of opportunities outside the household (Sen 1999). Fairness in a divorce settlement requires an evaluation of the contribution made by both parties to the marital family and evaluation cannot be according to neoclassical principles, which restrict the frame of evaluation to the nuclear family. Where the marital home is leased or owned, the State must, foremost, protect the right of the divorced wife to her house, in which she was living during her marriage, irrespective of who is the owner of the house. Where the woman is accorded the same rights as her husband to the marital home, she has the same liability to eviction as did the husband.

Determination of properties, with unspecified shares of individuals in rights in joint ownership of them, arises in cases of succession and marital breakdown. That requires, first, determination, by law, of what are the joint properties with unspecified shares, since thereafter (in properties with shares specified by law as in most intestate succession cases, or in some marital agreements specifying shares) the filing of suits in courts is the way to resolve differing views on interpretation of law. There may be demands for amendment of law which communities may consider unfair. But where law is silent on measured division or on non-capitalised labour of parties hiding in tangible assets (as in most marital breakdown cases) law requires courts to make equitable division after equitable determination of divisible properties with unspecified shares. In marital laws covering divorce, there are divergences in law, as well as approach to equity, across cultures.

Medieval English law saw the couple as one person, but common law viewed them as separate owners of separate properties. In England the courts of equity introduced a doctrine of equitable separate estate for a married woman, out of property given to her by words, express or implied, for her sole and separate use, which thereby went out of the control of the husband. In the UK, the Royal Commission on Marriage and Divorce (1951–5) said that the current accepted views in the UK of the wife's status required her possessing a separate property, and not property jointly with her husband. It was also the natural and normal desire in people to acquire property of their own. It rejected the preference that exists in many European countries for viewing property of husband and wife acquired after marriage as common property. It said they always have the choice to opt for joint ownership when acquiring any property and that would override the presumption in law when purchase is in the name of either of them only.

Laws in India, covering the majority, similarly recognise the right of the wife over the property which she brings with her into the marriage from her parents, with variations under regional personal laws. On death of the spouse the property rights of the widow (or widower) may not be subject to testament of the deceased spouse, unless right to transfer a share of property by testament overrides customary or scriptural laws on intestate succession. Intestate succession usually provides for common or joint ownership by specified descendents, their spouses and the widow of the deceased, with specified shares.

Muslim personal law, in India, lays down the woman's share in the property of the parents at roughly half the amount granted to male descendants. Muslim law prohibits more than a third of property of a male passing by will, the rest being reserved for specified heirs, with specified shares, as per social law. The Muslim Women's (Protection of Rights of Divorce) Act 1986 provides that a divorced woman is entitled to 'a reasonable and fair provision of maintenance'. That clearly requires equitable determination by judge or court of one kind or another. Muslim law creates *Waqfs* as welfare institutions for the destitute and mandates that Muslims finance them through obligatory donations termed *Zakt*.

> While Shari'a contributes to some commonalities in gender and family relations in Muslim societies there are marked variations in the uses and interpretations of Shari'a that evince a lack of consensus among Muslims and should deter overgeneralizations about Islam. Many factors contribute to these variations, including different schools of Islamic jurisprudence and the histories and politics of religious institutions, conversions, reforms and education. However the most important variable is the State.
>
> (Hajjar 2006: 5)

Women without any property are in no position to create an understanding of their rights in others, nor to generate fear in those who are to maintain them for failing to do so. It was this powerlessness of women that was the focus of the Indian Criminal Procedure Code of 1898 that granted maintenance to all neglected wives. The area of property of spouses has been the major realm of state intervention, with an increasing number of amendments to the laws of marriage and divorce in the area of division of property. The growing importance of property in a capitalist world where asset accumulation is a central focus is reflected in the concerns of the State, in relation to both the rich and poor sections of society. This is occurring both in societies that draw on the notion of marriage as a contract and in those that regard marriage as a sacrament. The institution of marriage has remained within the private sphere, but with the spillover of property rights into the public sphere has become a matter for state intervention.

The right to property for women has raised a debate in India about changing inheritance rules for women, to ensure that women are able to have an equal share under Hindu law so that they do not continue to be regarded as property but become co-sharers in property.[36] There are other areas that remain unresolved in the law, such as the manner in which marriage as such gives no right to share in the property acquired after marriage by the couple (though the instrument of prenuptial contracts has emerged to deal with this lacuna). If husband and wife are viewed as operating as co-sharers in an equitable firm, then there is an unspoken agreement to share happiness and sorrow equally, which creates the presumption that all savings used to acquire property after marriage should be treated as a half share for each partner. The context of marriage proposed by Mill would be approximated to in such a case, but for it to be sustainable would require any alteration of rights to be brought about by bargaining and promotion of understanding rather than threat and violence.

Conclusion

The inequality and inequity in duties and obligations between men and women are deviations from moral and legal codes which create disorder and suffering,

36 See Agarwal (1992) for the case for changing inheritance laws in India to ensure a new gendered distribution of assets.

mostly to women. The legally inferior status of women in productive, reproductive and caring spheres is deeply ingrained in cultural norms which resist legal reform. The investment which women make in others with whom they relate by marriage, and through having children, may give them emotional satisfaction but little economic security or empowerment over their own lives. This leads to their work in the household being undervalued and their due share in the household being expropriated by others, while being within a growing 'triple burden' of work (production, reproduction and caring). The way gender relations operate in the household is also reflected in the manner in which gender equality is built into laws and customs in society. The reluctance of the legal system to go beyond simple formulations of gender equality, to unpicking the finer texture of community and cultural understandings of gender equity, results in continued erosion of women's power and entitlements in family and society.

Duties and obligations are concepts relevant to moral relations in society as well as to adaptation into enforceable laws of the State. Duties and obligations have been erased from family law, particularly in relation to marriage and divorce. The focus of contractual matters has been useful in bringing to the fore the control exerted by the household hierarchy. However, on account of the almost exclusive focus on marriage and divorce, the everyday relational aspects of gendered lives have continued to be overlooked. In the extreme, reforms of existing laws of marriage and divorce have made for increasingly inimical approaches to women's rights and their economic and social independence. The current renditions of relationally sensitive laws emerge out of cultural contexts, which privilege social norms over legal rules.

That gender relations go far beyond the contract of marriage, and are much more far-reaching than marital events, requires they be studied on a broader canvas. This is provided within the context of the community, for it is at this level that the moral and ethical worlds operate. The local sphere which is dominated by groups of households, and where lives are lived and inequalities are experienced, is that important interface between the individual household and the state system.

3 Group rights, distributional conflicts and the making of unequal identities

> Use fairness in governing the state.
> Use surprise tactics in war.
> Be unconcerned and you will have the world.
> How do I know it is like this?
> Because:
> The more regulations there are,
> The poorer people become.
> The more people own lethal weapons,
> The more darkened are the country and clans.
> The more clever the people are,
> The more extraordinary actions they take.
> The more picky the laws are,
> The more thieves and gangsters there are.
>
> Therefore the sages say:
> I do not force my way and the people transform themselves.
> I enjoy my serenity and the people correct themselves.
> I do not interfere and the people enrich themselves.
>
> I have no desires
>
> And the people find their original mind.
>
> (Lao Tse 2007)

Human beings, both as individuals and as members of families and households, see the world around them both as a source of opportunity and a site of threats. As the venerable Lao Tse, Chinese philosopher extraordinaire, advises in the above extract, the ability to bring about the best rather than the basest in humans requires that the State desist from being an intrusive or increasing influence, for that does not bring out the creative or entrepreneurial aspects in people's lives. The State provides the framework within which they can devise their strategies to survive and aspire to grow rich. Imposing more and harsher laws is detrimental to harnessing the energies and spirits of individuals in order to create new levels of wealth generation and accumulation. It thwarts their natural abilities and generates animosities so that mistrust and deceit mar their abilities and their instincts are limited to eking out a livelihood.

On the other hand a complete absence of laws of the State also hinders human endeavour. Humans do not find it easy to ensure that their economic activity will result in a better future for them.[1] Despite an individual's hardest and even best efforts she might not be able to make significant improvements in her earning capacity or be able to accumulate assets through the accrual of wealth. Often the obstacles that prevent individual advancement are created by human groups themselves. Social markers are often regarded as one such obstacle to economic development, for they are seen to control and constrain individual behaviour through the formation of dominant groups.

The disapproval of large groups in the economic sphere arises from their tendency to exert inimical control on the competitive market.[2] The presence of groups in economic activity has been regarded, at best, as regrettable and at worst as reprehensible. The existence of a single monopolist or an organised cartel, as a large group, in a market, is always the object of condemnation and they are sought to be replaced by a number of smaller firms. The negative power of the large group over smaller groups is thereby removed. It is regarded as far better to have a large number of small firms whereby the power of the large groups is replaced by the competitiveness of the small groups and individuals. This simple notion of competition, where small firms use price as a signal for efficient production, has occupied centre stage in economics since the late nineteenth century. There is, however, the possibility that power might still lurk within a competitive framework, as economic outcomes are not necessarily willingly accepted by the competing parties, but emerge out of contested exchange (Bowles and Gintis 1993).

Groups are akin to the conscious lumps in the pail of milk that caught the economist D.H. Robertson's attention in the 1930s. Groups do emerge in the economic arena and the usual economic explanation is that groups form when individuals join together in the pursuit of a common objective or good which is not attainable through individual action. Mainstream economics also recognises collective action as acceptable behaviour where the market is unable to provide a commodity, since the cost of production to be met by the private producer far exceeds the price that society is willing to pay. That is, there is a case of market failure, and the excess cost, termed a *negative externality*,

1 The difficulty in overcoming natural and human constraints has been the subject of much classical literature. In Chinese landscape painting the power and dominance of nature has been the central theme from the ninth century under the Sung dynasty. See Clarke (2000) for a modern analysis of the ecological implications of Taoism and the regard for nature as a supreme force.

2 The inefficiency imposed on the economy by imposition of economic instruments such as taxes has been calculated in terms of the loss of consumer welfare, and termed a deadweight loss. The use of Harberger triangles to measure the costs became commonplace in the 1960s. See Hines (1999) for an explanation and evaluation of this measure.

militates against the possibility of private production of such a commodity. An established form of collective action in an industrial world is the trade union which wrestles to obtain 'worker rights' and a fair share of income for the members of the union as they are not automatically proffered by the market (Offe and Wisenthal 1980).

Collective action is not regarded as the *best* solution in economic thinking and the preferred route to efficient solutions is that of writing enforceable contracts. The Coasean solution of contracts within a firm has generated the thinking that just as economies choose their preferred contracts, so polities will select their preferred institutions. The notion that individuals will choose those institutions that are best suited for economic development has been cast into a Political Coase theorem (Acemoglu 2003). If the Political Coase theorem could operate, i.e. individuals could calculate the cost of alternative political institutions, then it would be possible for individuals to contract for political solutions, in a manner similar to that which is already possible in the economic sphere.[3]

The idea that groups may not merely be a secondary solution to overcome externalities (where there is private cost far exceeding the public payment), but can play a primary role in the lives of human beings, had not been considered within modern economics till the closing decade of the twentieth century. The possibility that groups might contribute positively to the identity of individuals, and that individuals might voluntarily, even actively, seek group identity, was largely absent in the economic literature. New thinking by Akerlof and Kranton provided a welcome change, highlighting the importance of identity in understanding individual behaviour in economics. They point out that identity can be based on individuals' perception of themselves, or on others' perception of them, or on a third party's ability to influence their identity and on the individual's desire to achieve/acquire certain characteristics. Such identities are not external to economic activity; rather, they fundamentally influence the individual's economic behaviour (Akerlof and Kranton 2000). For example, the extent to which an individual finds a match, between her own beliefs and preferences with a firm's style of management and strategic approach to its business, is emerging as a key factor in the individual's decision on choice of employer. The deciding factor for an individual, in choosing between working for a company or as an external and independent player in the market, is not based on any difference in the costs of operating within both structures but on the ability to share a common identity (Akerlof and Kranton 2005). The centrality of individual rationality, as opposed to group motivation, is now beginning to get dislodged, and there are increasing indications that the key to individual behaviour lies in the interaction between the group and the individual.

3 This raises a problem in the political sphere, for it is the State that enforces contracts; so contracts written by the State with the rest of society will be non-enforceable and create a commitment problem. As economics makes a foray into the sphere of politics it draws on game theoretic propositions to analyse the conflicts that operate within institutions and nations. See Powell (2006) for an example of a political scientist using the commitment problem to explain national collapse into war.

The manner in which individuals respond to organisational structure is a latecomer to social science, for the importance of the family group in the formation of individual identity was widely accepted within the field of development psychology by the mid-twentieth century.[4] The ability of the family and other social grouping, such as class and race, to influence individual identity is closely related to the communal sense of trust that creates a sense of membership within the group and does not necessarily disappear in the thoughts and actions of an individual, who has separated from the family group. The lasting legacy of group identity on the motivation and behaviour of individuals within the study of human psychology has not found easy acceptance in economic analysis. The adverse impact of this failing is to be found in the difficulty that economists have when encountering individual identity that is inexorably intertwined with social characteristics and markers.[5]

> social order is impossible if the individual is governed by unfettered self-interest, for such a system must eventually lead to a Hobbesian war of all against all ... while the self-identity approach may not be compatible with the cynical image of human action that has come to occupy the social sciences ... it [identity] has no difficulty in accounting for the dead seriousness that is sometimes expressed in status systems and or the violent turns that they [systems] sometimes take ... What is at stake in these struggles (among other things) is the individual's sense of the [his] value and importance of [his] life itself.
>
> (Hatch 1989: 351)

The acknowledgement that social groups have an impact on understanding individual decision-making, within the very heart of the capitalist system, permits us to study social norms, such as morality and reciprocity, that have hitherto been restricted to specific subfields, such as the literature on common property resources. This redrawing of the economic terrain, to include social norms, brings up the possibility that the affective and communal dimensions of social life might be reflected in, rather than retracted from, the market. That possibility requires a re-examination of group identity and common property, in relation to the economic activities of individuals.

Groups in the arena of common pool resources

Common pool resources (CPRs) are a particularly interesting subfield, as they are non-rival but excludable goods, i.e. these resources are accessible to only

[4] The work of Sigmund Freud was a formative influence on this field of research and was elaborated on in the work of Erik Erikson. See Erikson (1950).

[5] The importance of social and multiple identities has become a centrepiece in social psychology but has found stony ground in economics until the recent literature on the multidimensionality of poverty. See Hogg and Vaughan (2002) for an exposition of the multiplicity of social identities as constitutive of each individual.

those individuals who are deemed to be members of a particular group. In this sense, CPRs are different from open access resources that can be used by all who might pass by or come upon a 'public resource'. CPRs can be created within a community by all in the community, for use of all without rivalry, but those outside the community are excluded. CPRs can also be created by an external authority or by an internal norm. The greater the interest in any collective good of the community as a norm in any single member, the more likely he will work towards creating CPR even if he has to pay all the cost himself (Olson 1965: 34). There is also the interesting possibility that collective action by a group can create a 'club good' that might generate a 'public bad', i.e. as a benefit for a 'club' as a group, but inimical to the well-being of the whole society, such as the right to bear firearms as a member of the National Rifle Association (Olson 1982). The group mechanisms that encourage self-governance that contribute to maintaining common pool resources without government or other external form of regulation have become an important focus in the study of CPRs (Ostrom 1990). The exploration of societal control and protection of CPR is at odds with the traditional understanding that the State has priority with regard to ownership and regulation of such resources.

The State and group rights to the forests

The importance of common property, as a form of use and control of forests, gave way to increasing colonial demands for state and private ownership, during the nineteenth century in the forests of South Asia and East Africa (Sivaramakrishnan 1995). The market opportunities for private financial gains, by dealing in the considerable commercial value of particular species of timber, provided an attractive opportunity for introducing state monopoly into this domain, notwithstanding the much higher costs that were to be borne by others, such as the loss of livelihood for forest-dweller groups, forest tribes and other indigenous groups living in the forests. The trend of converting forest property into state property required private individuals to obtain contracts from the State for the removal and use of wood and other forest produce. The trend continued into the post-colonial period, with increasing pressure for the market to be regarded as the appropriate mechanism for the distribution of natural resources. There was little pause for thought, or consideration for the historical trail of denial of community rights in and usage by the public of the forests as livelihood and social structure (Guha 1989; People's Union for Democratic Rights 1982).

The blind disregard for traditional, communal and indigenous rights to the forest, and to natural resources within it, displayed by the state juggernaut of forest law, met with confrontation from the community and groups in civil society, and they have used both violent and non-violent forms of protest and resistance in voicing their demands for recognition of the time-honoured and traditional rights to traverse and draw on the forest and its products. The clash over the ownership of the forest and its primacy as a form of life and livelihood has been wrought with distributional conflict and the contestation of rights.[6] At the heart of this conflict is the manner in which state power uses politics, rhetoric and knowledge to give the highest priority to current economic value and market opportunity over cultural, traditional and indigenous forms of society. The full range of stakeholders associated with a CPR is not adequately identified, which leads to a poor computation and underestimation of relative costs and benefits of the different systems of resource management (Adams *et al.* 2002). In the case of forests, there is a need to undertake a full study of the history of ownership and stakeholder usage for 'there is a dialectical relationship between discourses of rules and discourses of protest, and we can advance the study of this relationship by treating resistance as a diagnostic of power' (Sivaramakrishnan 1995: 3).

The power of the State, particularly colonial, legislation to seize land and to deny, even write off, existing land rights has denied indigenous people of their traditional lands, as in the case of the Orang Asli, the original peoples of Malaysia who were excluded from any legal deed to their traditional lands. The British colonial administration took the formal position that they were supportive of the laws promulgated by the princely Malay states and such laws decreed that land was the property of the kings. After independence this omission was carried over into the national policies of Malaysian government. The National Land Code to provide a uniform system of land ownership that was introduced in 1965 continued to draw on the Australian Torrens system of land registration that had initially been brought in by the British colonial administration during the 1930s (Means 1985).[7] As independent Malaysia was a federation consisting of thirteen princely states, the federation required the promulgation of laws that operate across all states. The National Land Code proceeded to vest land rights of individuals only upon registration in the Land Registry; however, this was contradictory to the procedures used by the twelve tribes of Orang Asli as they passed their rights from generation to generation through customary law (Cheah 2004).

The path of forest development drawn up by the national administration did not take account of the traditional livelihoods or customary practices of indigenous peoples. The official policy regarded these communities as falling outside the formal market system and their peoples were deemed to be primitive and not comprehending of the processes of modernisation (Hooker 1965). It was only in 1996 that the long-standing denial of the rights of the Orang Asli became a matter of public attention, when the federal government used the

[6] The tendency to overlook the rights inherent in the way of life of groups that have traditionally resided and drawn on the forest persists across modern states. The conflicts between tribals/indigenous forest people and the modern State pepper the history of the twentieth century, such as the case of the Chiapas in Mexico and the Orang Asli in Malaysia.

[7] The Torrens system of land ownership is based on a Hanseatic system of land registration that was initially introduced into Australia by the British colonial administration.

Land Code to compulsorily requisition the land of the Orang Asli Temuan tribe, to facilitate a road link between the new Kuala Lumpur International Airport and Kuala Lumpur city. The tribe members were given fourteen days to vacate their homes and given monetary compensation for the loss of their homes and crops but not for the loss of their ancestral land. The Temuans refused to relocate or accept the compensation offered by the State and the police had to forcibly evict them from their lands.

The Temuans took their complaint to the High Court of Malaysia and sought the restitution of their right to ancestral land. This case, known as the *Sangong-Tasi* case, brought the matter of indigenous land rights and its abrogation by the federal legal system into the limelight. The treatment of the indigenous people as mere tenants on state land since the early twentieth century was regarded as unacceptable by the court. In its 2002 decision the court recognised that the rights of the Orang Asli were different from the private land rights determined within market contexts. The Orang Asli did not obtain only livelihoods, i.e. economic products, from the land, but their very way of life was directed by the spirits of their ancestral land. It therefore decreed that the 'native title' of the Orang Asli could not be treated as though land was a mere commodity and on a par with private land holdings; rather, it should be regarded as a way of life that was based on a system of beliefs linked to the land (Cheah 2004).

The recognition of traditional rights held by indigenous groups within forests has emerged out of hard-fought battles. The wresting of rights for indigenous groups from governments is laudable, but it remains difficult to ensure that recognition is translated into more inclusive land-use patterns. In India, the 1990s saw a new form of resource management termed Joint Forestry Management (JFM) that was introduced to ensure that all the relevant stakeholders were brought in, and to permit a more inclusive use of the forest. The JFM was hailed as a new managerial form of organised resource use and generated a wave of social forestry programmes in Indian districts. Despite the creation of a new framework and the considerable fanfare with which the programme was brought in, it failed abysmally as there was little attempt to restructure the highly top-down management structure of the bureaucratic administrative and forest services. The so-called managed forestry approach was riddled with official interference and evidence of the abuse of official power. The JFM programme was unable to vest any power in the local communities, whether by intent or poor design, and hence the district initiatives became short-termist, driven by commercial interest, and were unable to prevent premature exploitation of the trees (Sundar and Jeffery 1999).

The difficulties faced by the State in recognising and designing common property resources are widespread and cross over different development paradigms. At independence in 1949, all land, including forest land, in China was declared to be state property. The Chinese approach to forest management during the first half of the 1950s was modelled closely on Stalin's understanding of controlling and exploiting nature (Bao 2006). In the period from 1956 onwards, forest land was awarded to private households but this policy was revoked during the years of the cultural revolution from 1966 to 1976 (Long and Zhou 2001). It was only after the start of the economic reforms of the 1980s that there was a reconsideration of the rights to the forests with regard to usage and management of resources.

On 20 September 1984, the National People's Congress Standing Committee adopted the Forest Law of the People's Republic of China, This law was formulated to protect, nurture and rationally utilise the forest resources so as to speed up the greening of the country's territory. The law was designed to bring into prominence the roles that the forest could play with regard to storing water, saving soil, adjusting the climate, improving the environment, and supplying forest products (Xi 1999). The remit of the law was largely to change incentives with regard to the conduct of forest and forest-tree cultivating, planting, logging and utilisation, and to regulate the operation and management of forests, trees and woodlands.[8] The strongly developmental spin placed on the use and conservation of forest lands has implications for the rights and lives of indigenous people who have long-established customary laws with regard to the forest lands in far-flung areas of the country. The Minority Regions Autonomy Law (1984) was promulgated to provide an increased degree of administrative freedom in devising and directing regional development strategies. The intention of the central authorities was to reduce the relative backwardness of these regions through these legal changes by introducing market-oriented approaches as suggested in the Forest Law of 1984. The sale of user rights and the growth of tourism have emerged as large revenue earners for the provincial governments but they have also come into conflict with the traditional ways of the indigenous groups such as the Dai and Junuo in the province of Yunnan. The market-based approaches to user rights have devalued traditional ways of knowledge transfer regarding flora and fauna (Liu 2007). In its place there has developed a very avaricious approach to extracting value from logging and forest clearance leading to cases against private individuals and groups, as in the case of Nincheng county, which borders Liaoning, Hebei provinces and Neimenggu Autonomous Region. Here, violations of forest use were found in five state forests in 1998 which were investigated by the county prosecution team and resulted in punishment being meted out to 125 individuals (Xi 1999).

The politics of common property is contest-ridden. Existing laws are rarely invoked, for affected parties prefer to turn to customary laws to deal with disputes in the forests. The violation of common property in the forest sector arises from the disregard of the modern State for the groups that live by sets of rules that precede capitalism. The indigenous/tribal/traditional peoples are

[8] The Forest Law amended on 29 April 1998 to introduce the transferability of use rights in a range of forest types: timber forests, economic forests, fuelwood forests, that these could last up to seventy years and be renewable.

regarded as lesser and the appropriation of their resources as legitimate for the furtherance of economic growth and capitalist accumulation.

Expanding the collective arena

The possibility that common property provides more than a joint right to ownership and an economic way of life has not been fully considered even in the more heterodox approaches to resource management. The power that is manifest in resources goes beyond their market value, taking on a set of ascribed meanings and communal values that mask the purely economic contribution that they make to the lives of individuals within the community. The economic revenue stream, in effect, depends on the cooperation of the community and their ability to utilise mechanisms that allow 'collective spreading of risk' to overcome their individual vulnerability to shocks. The success of common property resources lies in the ability to draw on 'collaboration as a way forward' (Vira *et al.* 1998) with the concomitant creation of a common identity through this process. The collaborative process is not one based on equality of status or even income, but on the shared urgency of risk in the continued existence. It is the need to use a valued resource that brings individuals together to reduce risk by using collective mechanisms to mitigate costs. The collaboration continues in the presence of social and economic hierarchies within the group. At the same time, the existence of the collective and shared risk-avoidance groups does affect the identity of individuals and the value they attach to group benefits.

> if a government or some collectivity wants to encourage cooperative behaviour, it must create a focal identity among its citizens. Various repressed groups that fail to rise up collectively against their oppressors probably do so for reasons of an absence of focal identity among themselves. Prevention of a focal identity is a useful instrument for a tyrant or a powerful government to employ in trying to prevent some group or nation from acting cooperatively within itself. The aim must be to destroy the group's ability to form a focal identity. Through a deliberate policy of splintering them into various overlapping and conflicting identities it can keep the group under control and keep at bay the possibility of group rebellion.
>
> (Basu 2006: 31)

The move from earlier colonial, and then Marxist, notions of ownership of forests, lands and natural resources has been towards models that draw more on market framing of resource ownership and use. In the attempts to maintain common property resources, there has been a conceptual shift towards stakeholder management models that facilitate collaboration across groups in maintaining the resources in the forest sector. The movement away from legal diktat has gained momentum in recent decades and comes about as a severe reaction to state monopoly and imposition on natural resources.

Legal power, group rights and claiming resources

In many societies there is a history of communities confronting the power of the State to wrest away group rights. In pre-modern times, in Western Europe, there appear to have been three types of collective action: *pro-active*, *reactive* and *competitive*. They were put to use respectively for demanding new rights, for protecting existing rights from being usurped by the State, and for ensuring a fair distribution of rights by competition (Tilly 1977). These confrontations emerged because of moves by the State to control the power of the community. In the twentieth century, particular forms of collective action emerged to respond to the social dilemmas that are imposed on communities by the State as well as other social forces (Basu and Kohli 2000). One particularly contentious area of confrontation is protecting long-standing community forms of natural resource ownership which increasingly appear attractive to the State and corporate world as they look further and deeper for new sources of wealth. Conflict also arises with regard to the management of these lucrative assets and the growing inequities within members of the group.

In the non-Western world there has been a preponderance of social dilemmas thrown up by the colonial administrative process. The colonial mechanism was bent on rationalising categories of social activity, on classifying the actors and in imposing iron rules of behaviour in the colony. The process emerged from combining Western notions of justice with the newly drawn classifications of the local people and their practices through lenses and discourses that were familiar to the colonial administrators (Said 1978; Mamdani 1996). The newly independent nations of the twentieth century have been confronted by the challenge of economic development, in the face of many historical injustices. Historical claims have been met by recommendations that the market-based model of growth be used to ensure that trickle-down benefits reach these groups. This market-based analysis is unable to value traditional ways of life, and yet the management approaches of multiple stakeholders do not provide a full sense of the relationship between the law, group rights and claims for ownership.

In India today, the administrative and judicial bureaucracy continues to follow the colonial system. The central administration imparts justice under all enactments and at all levels including rural areas. The subordinate courts specialise in small-value civil and petty criminal cases which are also handled in judicial or administrative magistrates' courts. The traditional groups of five elders who may be from the village or religious/caste councils continue to settle local disputes, based on their understanding of local traditions and personal laws. These councils do not consider themselves as being under the new state laws any more than they did in colonial times. In 1960, the village *panchayat* (council) was entrusted with judicial powers, as a measure of decentralisation of judicial power to grass-root level.

In Malaysia, the nation inherited a legal system constructed by the British for colonial administration and the nation placed the colonial civil law above the customary and religious *Shari'a* laws. The colonial policy of bringing in and working with foreign populations resulted in the Chinese hegemony on the financial sector, with Indians working in the plantations, while the indigenous Malay refused to move out of traditional small-scale agriculture (Hill and Kwen Fee 1995). The ethnic differentiation of Malaysian people into Malays, Chinese and Indian that was emphasised by the British Malayan administration has remained in place in the independent nation of Malaysia and has become the most common category of social distinction. This feature of ethnicity has become part of national policy since the formulation of the New Economic Policy (NEP) brought in by the Malaysian government after the ethnic riots of 1969 and designed to ensure coexistence between the indigenous Malays (*bumiputera*), and the Chinese- and Tamil-speaking populations in the country. The preferential rights awarded to the Malay population under the NEP gave greater access and ownership of land to Malays in the countryside, while bringing in statutes to ensure that there was Malay representation on the board of every business. The statutes, under the NEP, gave *bumiputeras* a greater basket of rights to help advance their economic position in Malaysian society; it was based on arguments of equity across races, since Chinese- and Tamil-speaking groups were in a better economic position. Critics have opposed this notion of social justice, pointing out that it is against the notion of equality of opportunity, and that Chinese and Indians do not have access to redistributive mechanisms to improve their economic and social well-being (Gomez 2004).

In recent times, there have been debates on whether the NEP should be brought to an end, after operating for nearly forty years. It is now emerging that there has been differential benefit from the NEP among groups of Malays, with poverty pockets emerging among Malays as well as other ethnic groups (Brown, Ali and Muda 2004). Another area of contestation among Malays themselves has been the legal reform process, going on from the 1990s, that has shifted the 'conceptual balance of the law' from Western notions of equality and democracy, to providing a greater role for religious *Shari'a* law. This move away from secular conceptions of the law and welcoming religious principles is regarded by some as remedying the original imbalance in the legal system coming down from colonial times (Hamayotsu 2003). The notion of equity that is present in religious and traditional law might not sit easily with the advancement of the Western concept of individual legal equality, but it does provide the well-understood community sense of 'fairness in inequality', and such communal and group senses of equity and fairness are being emphasised in multi-ethnic Malaysia.

The importance of historical legacies is evident across the developing world. The Chinese legal system underwent reform at the end of the nineteenth century, during the last decades of the Qing dynasty, and later under the leadership of Sun Yat Sen, in an attempt to modernise it in the early decades of last century. This Chinese legal reform project of the early twentieth century was stopped short by the establishment of the People's Republic of China. The Chinese constitution, established in 1954, articulated the right to equality, yet the legal rules of the 1950s were largely written in relation to the class struggle, and therefore the remedying of group-based inequalities, that had brought the Chinese Communist Party to power and resulted in the setting up of the PRC (Potter 1994).

The property laws that were introduced in the 1950s were also strongly influenced by the Soviet legal system. The laws brought in by the new communist government were closely aligned to the needs of material development and the law of productive forces as set out in the Stalinist model of development (Bao 2006). The fundamentals of the socialism-oriented new laws were to bring in a form of equality that eradicated class distinctions, with an underlying notion of equality of rights rather than opportunity. The limited role of the resulting civil law was a reflection of socialist thinking, that the law being a part of a superstructure would atrophy with it, with the removal of economic inequalities from the society. The people's State (and not a body of laws) was seen as the central pivot for the maintenance of law and order in a socialist society; it would prevent the re-emergence of class distinctions, through a revisionist impulse, among bourgeois elements in society.

The re-engagement with legal reform, in China, began in 1980 when the Third Plenary Session of the Eleventh Congress dissolved the pre-existing laws and embarked on a new system of laws (Otto *et al.* 2000). The process of reform was directed by the need for economic transition from the existing socialist models of development to a new market system for economic advancement, but one which retained the structures of socialism under the control of the Communist Party. The Economic Contract Law of 1981 permitted individuals to contract such that economic transactions could be regarded independently of the class or social status of the contracting parties. The Chinese constitution was overhauled in 1982 to ensure that legal principles and rules were brought closer to the objectives of economic reform to transform China into a high-growth, market-oriented economy.

The renewed Chinese interest in legal reform regards law as an auxiliary to the State as well as its need to maintain political control (Potter 1999). The thinking that law should support and work as a subordinate feature of the political process has been increasingly questioned by Chinese jurists, and there is a consistent effort to separate law from concerns of class and state power and bolster it so that jurisprudence is made distinct from economic concerns of the State. Such a shift promotes close links between market activities and economic valuation as well as permitting careful consideration of legal terms and concepts imported into Chinese law (Keith and Lin 2001). The drafting of economic laws in the 1990s has been based on legal understanding among China's legal establishment that the law is the political instrument to change national institutions and bring them into line with the demands of the new model of economic development (Seidman and Seidman 1996).

At the same time, reducing the extent of state control over laws could topple the system of political control and bring in divisive and destabilising forces through the increasing presence of external bodies, or even international interference. The need to maintain a common understanding of Chinese socialism is central to preventing the unravelling of the social contract that is emerging between the Chinese State and its citizens (Tang and Parish 2000). The notion of the Chinese citizen or *Zhongguoren* as a symbolic political identity has provided a single marker that has, to date, unified the country against external forces. The cementing force of identity has weakened with the considerable economic and social changes brought about by a quarter century of reforms that have ensured two decades of economic growth. In particular, the rapid increase in growth has resulted in a rising volatility in private incomes, the 'little emperor' syndrome displayed in one-child families, and the reduced social support from the State for the elderly, and has pushed individuals to develop local networks, such as exercise groups, and seek spiritual sustenance from religious organisations (Peerenboom 2002).

The state view of how law affects group identity and the inequalities that they have undergone is markedly instrumental in its orientation. The use of social markers such as ethnicity and class has been consciously drawn on by independent nation states, whereas colonial administration had been highlighting visible social markers, such as race and caste, in a subject population.

'The world around both developing and the former socialist countries looks at law as an instrument for radical social change' (Seidman and Seidman 1996: 44). That instrument was used in earlier centuries by colonial powers to follow a divide-and-rule policy, and it is used today by governments to control the population, sometimes to prevent rebellion and at other times to ignite civil, often violent, disorder (Tambiah 1989). The presence of group identities does not always trigger disruptive tendencies in the political and economic spheres, and powerful emotions such as nationalism are able to keep in check group identities, so that they lose their aggressive and exclusionary tendencies in the presence of stronger and unifying national passion (Hobsbawm 1990). The different impacts that group identity has, on the political stability and historical trajectory of a country make it a key concern in social science, but more importantly group identity is also an intrinsic part of human life (Stewart 2001). The ability of group identity to provide a socially acceptable basis for pursuing an equitable political solution has worked effectively in Asian societies over the second half of the twentieth century. The ready justice of social equity provided the foundations of legal structures, in the early decades of post-independence planning. In contradistinction, the Western notion of individual equality remained either a distant dream or even a disreputable hangover from a colonial past, in the heady first decades of nationalist planning.

The laws of social justice were devised to remove social obstacles that hindered the economic progress of the individual.[9] The pursuit of possible liberties by the individual were subordinate to confronting the denial of certain rights to an individual on account of social attributes associated with membership of a

[9] Deshpande (2005) compares the impact on laws of social justice to overcome markers of race and caste.

disadvantaged or subordinated group. The strongly enunciated need, in national constitutions and other legal documents, regarding the matter of negative liberties far outweighed the valuation of positive liberties.[10] The granting of negative liberties provides a focus on historical social injustices as were meted out on groups. The primary emphasis on negative rather than positive liberties could be regarded as the first phase of economic development. Conversely, it also raises the interesting matter of whether the pursuit of positive liberties should be as much a matter that falls within the jurisdiction of the law as has been the case of ensuring negative liberties to marginalised and peripheral groups with regard to natural resource use and management, as well as the broader terrain of ensuring economic development.

The power of social justice that emerges from a common notion of equity is able to drive economic development even in the face of economic and social inequality among individuals in a community. Equity treats individuals with regard to where they are located so as to ensure that each is treated 'fairly', which permits social and economic inequalities to be addressed where they are the most acute and disturbing. The call for equality, with the associated positive liberties to action, opportunity and resources, is based on the notion that the starting point for all individuals is identical, which is far from the truth in all, but particularly in developing, societies.

Group inequality and social consciousness

Social relations are not based on equality but on hierarchy, in the household, in the community and even in the workplace. These hierarchical relations can take on either a corporatist or a clientelistic form.[11] Hierarchy pervades both economic and social life and contributes to maintenance of social relations, by ensuring the observance of social norms and passing strictures and censures for associated violations. These hierarchical relations between groups within a society are not always harmonious, and are often sources of anger that can whip up revolutionary fervour among disadvantaged or discriminated groups. The hierarchy itself might be the symbol of oppression, but equally the contradictions emerging from the differences created by hierarchy have themselves become points of conflagration setting alight passions and leading to bloodshed. Inequality across groups has often been cited as a cause of conflict and violence (Tambiah 1997). In particular, the large variations in resources, power and control that are controlled by various groups are regarded as a cause of aggression, invasion and war.

[10] Isaiah Berlin (2002 [1958]) introduced the concept of two types of liberties, negative and positive, where the former were freedoms from restrictions such as fear and hunger, and the latter freedoms to act, such as speech and action.

[11] The importance of patron–client relations and their generalised presence of these networks in the economy and society is comprehensively examined by Einsenstadt and Roninger (1984).

Hierarchies driven by national elites are used by states to maintain control of the social and economic activities of individuals.[12] Modern states and individuals, who are aspirants to the political power of the State, have used ethnic and religious identities for political purposes. The State and powerful groups of individuals have worked, and are reworking, historical memories of groups to mobilise support for the leaders of the group (Hobsbawm 1990). Historically, political identities of individuals in groups and nations have been used by rulers and governments, as well as rebel or revolutionary leaders, to drum up support for their political ends.[13] Manifest inequalities in political and social spheres that accompany hierarchies in societies provide both obstacles and challenges, motivating aspiring political leaders to reach higher rungs of the political hierarchy. In a democracy, there is equal freedom to all to take part in political processes and others do not have the power to impose an identity on anyone. Nor do they have the right to impose markers on the aspirant.[14]

It is, of course, not just states and political aspirants who make use of hierarchies and inequalities in existing groups. In fact, groups do form around a desire for a particular economic, political or social advantage, and they make use of mechanisms of lobbying through existing sources of institutional power. They even work towards the formation of new institutions, to gain social status and increase their political power (Olson 1993). The success of a group is measured by the extent and magnitude of the gains that it is able to wrest away from the State in furtherance of its particular objective.

Group identity, social norms and social capital

The provision of individual rights is regarded as a legal way of reducing inequality. The notion of 'affirmative action' used in state policy is a way to redress group inequality and bring deprived and excluded groups into the mainstream of society by allowing them to play a full economic and political role in society. In such a policy action, the group identity is maintained, but is no longer a basis for voicing discrimination or oppression; it is more an expectation of reparation of historical wrong by authorities in the society. Rights granted to individuals ensure that they are able to undertake actions, whether in economic,

[12] The study of the role of the elite attracted economists, sociologists and political scientists in the first half of the twentieth century. See the work of Vilfredo Pareto (1968 [1901]) for an economist's perspective on why the role of meritocratic elites was commendable for organising and controlling the economy and society; also the work of G. Mosca (1939 [1896]) and C. Wright Mills (1956).

[13] The use of ethnicity by the State and revolutionaries has become a subject of increasing interest since the 1960s, when the poor ability of national development planning to alleviate poverty and discrimination of deprived and discriminated minorities started to emerge in statistical and social science analysis. See Bates (1986) for a review on Africa, and Tambiah (1997: introduction) for a general overview.

[14] In a similar way, the economic right to acquire a place in the economic hierarchy, or the power of wealth, is available more readily in a market economy than in a planned administered economy.

political, social or religious spheres of life, without their legal rights being thwarted by others. An individual's rights, in practice, are dependent on recognition and accommodation of those rights by others as no different from their own. So, equal rights which are present in all reduces to fair competition among them.

When that expectation fails, the deprived and excluded expect their rights to be upgraded into a privilege that will place them in an activity, position or condition wherein they would not otherwise get selected, in fair competition. Fundamental rights of individuals are the rights to personal life and liberty, religious belief, choice of profession, trade, occupation, business, assembly, association, movement and residence, speech and expression. These rights of an individual can provide a basis to combat restrictive practices in society based on race or religion, provided others see the restrictions as illegal violation of the rights and eschew practices emanating from historical discrimination and restrictions imposed on deprived and excluded groups.

Restrictions imposed by the institution of the family on contracting with individuals outside the familial sphere make the point that local reciprocity in such contracting could work against the functioning of generalised forms of reciprocity.[15] In contrast, restrictions imposed by the government on bureaucrats speaking critically of their employer, i.e. the government, or those imposed by the school management on the wearing of a religious headdress or veil, fall into a different class, as they work towards fostering generalised reciprocity within an institution.

> Amoral individualism ... exists where there is neither familial nor generalized trust, where narrow self-interest literally permeates all social and economic activity, and where members are isolated – either by circumstance or discrimination – from all cohesive social networks.
>
> (Woolcock 1998: 172)

The law favours such generalised restrictions directly or indirectly by tacit delegation of implied legislative powers to heads of civil service and principals of schools, as these hierarchical forms of control discipline their population. Where a law is introduced to end discrimination, there is the expectation that individuals in the society will follow the law because of a change in behaviour. The law works because new social norms have deemed discrimination as unacceptable, and therefore the multiplier effect of sanctions against violators would work to affect individual behaviour.

Social networks are regarded as beneficial, for they provide a gauge for measuring individual behaviour, and that helps in regulation and direction of behaviour. These networks are seen to operate at both micro and macro levels, and they can ensure that individuals follow socially acceptable patterns of behaviour and that individuals imbibe social consciousness and reap the emotional

[15] The importance of generalised social norms is the foundation of the work of Mark Granovetter (see Granovetter 1974).

benefits resulting from socially integrating knowledge and learning. The importance of social capital, a term used to describe such knowledge and learning, is to be found in the tradition of the common law that emerges from social norms within communities, based on patterns and habits of social networking.[16]

In England, the link between equity and justice can be traced to the chancery courts that were charged with enforcing equity. The common law in its entirety was reduced to an institutionalised shadow in the equitable Court of Chancery. The ecclesiastical and chancery courts enforced Christian obligations which said that property is a shared concept and that a legal owner can be obliged to an equitable owner. This notion of 'trust' was woven into a patchwork of common law norms. The Chancellor meted out justice based on written pleadings and the application of the Roman laws. The chancery court granted specific performance of contracts and allowed borrowers under mortgage to recover their property even after the lapse of time limits for redemption under an equitable right of redemption. It also granted injunctions to prevent infliction of unjustifiable harm and allowed discovery as a means of investigation of fact.

The common law in England operated such that juries hearing cases could only work with ideas prevalent in society and not on the basis of any written law. The common law courts could not be given any instructions on normative aspects of acts of will, and they tended to be better at identifying trespass in torts within feudal society. Under common law, the land belonged to the Crown, and only its enjoyment and succession as an estate of the Crown was accorded to others (Glenn 2004: 235–6). In all this, equity acted on human conscience and 'followed the law' but did not replicate any of the remedies of common law. Relations between common law courts and chancery court were stormy, and compromise of sorts was reached in the seventeenth century. Thereafter common law dominated human thought, overriding the influence of the concept of equity, and after the reform of common law in the nineteenth century, the courts of common law and equity as well as ecclesiastical courts were combined and the higher courts named as courts of justice and equity (Glenn 2004: 255–6).

The common law co-opted local diversity in norms, leaving juries to their own devices. The common law tradition emerged in response to the historical difficulties encountered by the Norman conquerors over their English subjects in the fourteenth century. The tradition of overlaying a legal system upon existing practices is not unique to England. The importance of customary laws, and the power of social norms that lie within, has long been valued in other societies.[17] The power of custom to invoke moral and equitable social norms has informed the Shasta country ranchers (Ellickson 1986). There appears to be a range of historical institutions that cognise moral values and draw on social norms to

[16] Social networking does not always lead to emotional integration, as for example where the norms are 'an eye for an eye' and 'finders keepers'.

[17] The tendency to regard social norms as inadequate or in need of being shored up by formal rules is oblivious to the possibility that rules could result in the destruction of existing social norms. See Pildes (1996) for a commentary on how laws might destroy social norms.

ensure economic development; in fact, the 'legal traditions of the world' (Glenn 2004) show that there is no single path to legal development.

The notions of equity and equality originate in tradition and modernity, respectively, and are based on very different considerations. Equity emerged as a powerful mechanism for social change and economic development in the eighteenth and nineteenth centuries, with a strong association to fairness. The focus of this tradition has been on the ideal of fairness. Equality, on the other hand, while having intellectual routes to European enlightenment, acquired a particular stridency in the twentieth century, particularly in advancing individual rights, autonomy and enterprise.

The language of equity is most evident in the emerging South American legal literature, where there is a demand to redress historical injustices imposed on indigenous people, some commentaries tracing the discrimination and exploitation back to the colonisation by the Spanish and Portuguese in the fifteenth century. There has been a particular emphasis on the forcible appropriation of land by the colonial administrators which tore asunder community life by forcibly acquiring traditional lands (Faundez 2000). A different form of resistance to forcible state exclusion and expropriation can be seen in the form of 'passive resistance' developed by Mohandas Karamchand Gandhi, in response to his experience of racial discrimination by the British in South Africa and later in India. This form of opposition posed a serious challenge to the sharp intellect of the British judges in British India. They found it very hard to reconcile the duties imposed on Indians by the British Indian colonial laws with the principles of the right to natural identity available to British subjects by virtue of being born and living in the land of their birth. The ideal of absolute rights to act according to one's will and over one's possessions that came with modernity and industrialisation bequeathed absolute rights, independent of one's birth, race or wealth. This sense of equality (of freeborn Englishmen) was a specificity emerging from historical events in that society.[18]

The importance of history in determining the particular form of equality and reciprocity that operates in a society was a matter of concern for eighteenth-century intellectuals such as John Stuart Mill and de Tocqueville (Pildes 1996). The forms of equality and equity that emerge in a society are embedded in the very interstices of the State. The sense of equality that lies within the rule of 'equality before law' has acquired the status of a universal ideal. This sense of idealised equality has been the major determinant in the development of the legal system in the twentieth century, where the Weberian view that legal-rational thought would prevail has found much favour.[19] Yet the ideal does not take root in an identical fashion nor does it follow a single path (*à la* Barrington Moore) in all developing countries; rather, the introduction of the 'rule of law' is understood within the context of political authority and rule. The

[18] It was based on the understanding that these personal attributes were not significant to the future exercise of one's free will.

[19] I am grateful to the late Sir Robbie Jennings for sharing his knowledge of the early experience in the arena of law and development as set out in the French legal literature.

intellectual power of the 'rule of law' as a universal principle applicable to all is often contradicted by the parochial demands of dominant groups. In the presence of opposing tendencies the primary consideration in creating a set of rules is to ensure the economic advancement of the nation. To ensure this outcome, rules are sometimes made to constrain the ability of those who affect the economic decision-making process of other individuals in society.[20] Rules are made to reduce friction between individuals and to promote economic transactions. A constitution could be regarded as a collection of reasons and associated rules that have been selected by the public through its elected representatives to advance social and human development. Constitutions do have qualifications to be prescribed by law, to ensure that reasonable restrictions can be imposed on individuals who can obstruct human advancement.[21] Where law-making disregards historical injustices it imposes future costs for economic development. Additionally, the costs of non-enforcement of just laws creates new bases for experiencing inequalities which further aggravate already affected groups.

The view that the constitution, and the legal principles that it enshrines, should result in minimal interdependence costs (e.g. the cost of group dithering and delay) for individuals informs law-and-economics schools in the United States (Buchanan and Tullock 1962). The law-and-economics literature in the United States in the 1970s drew on a market-oriented perspective. Regulation was brought in as a method to overcome market distortions by contracting transactions and thereby changing the incentives for exchange and production.

Regulation is not a recent innovation, but is to be found in the first law-and-economics movement that was underway in the United States in the 1890s (Hovenkamp 1990). The existence of legal aberrations that have resulted in market imperfections has been dealt with by bringing in a regulatory regime that rewrites the incentives through changing the contractual environment, where rule-making and law enforcement operate to enhance the logic of the market. The sunk cost of these laws results in new incentives and sanctions for the operation of firms at a lower running cost. While regulation reduces market imperfections the regulator does increase the power of the market through his actions. The opposite reason of reducing the power of the market has also been highlighted as a reason to bring in regulators as in the case of ensuring public goods such as water supply (Prosser 1997). Regulation is consequently not a simple instrument for dealing with externalities but a powerful tool for bringing in the social dimensions of economic exchange and production.

Laws, regulation and historical situatedness

In the nineteenth and twentieth centuries, in most developing countries the enforcement of enacted laws in the local sphere was the task of the magistrates

20 The analogy of Ulysses and the Sirens, where the latter called sailors to their death and therefore needed to be controlled, is often cited in this context.

21 International agreements too resort to such devices, to accommodate the pressures from the dominant groups.

and local juries. The role of political institutions, such as the judiciary and the police, functioning under the control of judicial magistrates, to advance the rule of law was not without a cost. The presence of these new political institutions did not necessarily mean that they had the capacity for effective enforcement of all laws. The inequalities that emerge through the inability of political institutions to carry out all that is laid down in the law can become the basis for overthrowing a political system. Any change in the law enforcement system does not automatically imply an improvement in the enforcement of laws to achieve all that is laid down in the laws. The game of passing the buck between the police, piling up undecided prosecutions in courts, and the judiciary, complaining of an inadequate number of judges to provide justice in time, continues, with the changes in the system making no difference to the game.

The Political Coase theorem (of least-cost political institutions) is not an adequate solution for dealing with political bids. While law enforcement is regarded as a public service which is universally accessible to all citizens the ability to make political bids subvert such provision. Those who are able to make high bids for such services can convert the public provision of services into a new market for enforcement services. In situations where there is an acute shortage of public goods and services even the most professional of police, magisterial and judicial administration cannot prevent the public services from being bid away by powerful groups. The widening of inequalities, between groups in the local sphere and groups in the central sphere, complements the unequal legal assertion of individual rights, enabling accumulation of wealth in a few hands in the metropolises. These practices are not unique to a particular country nor are they uniquely linked to a particular stage of economic development.

The emergence of terms such as the 'Asian rule of law' arises when economic performance and the role of the market dominate over any analysis of the legal system in place in an economy. The tendency to see economic regionalism or cultural facets, in legal traditions is propelled by a failure to distinguish, equality before law, from the application of the legal principle of equity. The concept of equity is currently viewed as a legal principle of the second order, employed to make pragmatic correction to adjust for inequalities, but is also wrongly viewed as having subjective elements, overriding an ideal of 'legal equality' which is, in fact, a subjective element, incapable of objective determination.

> The natural rights theorist ... claims to discover an intrinsic order in social relations, an order it is his purpose to make explicit and to develop. For him the universals that describe this order – rights, rules and institutional categories – have an existence and a worth quite independent of the particular interests that may take advantage of them. Thus the natural rights thinker treats the system of private law concepts of contract and property and the doctrine of separation of powers in public law, as if they had an autonomous logic that survived in all their transmutations.
>
> (Unger 1975: 72)

A variation that has longer standing is the evolutionary view of common law that highlights dominant human tendencies within the local sphere. The incorporation of the habituated forms of interaction, prevalent in the society, in the development of the common law, based on a principle of equal rights to all, did draw a response from lawmakers. That response, however, lay in the making of statutory laws and not in the disposal of cases by which common law developed. It is focused on statutory laws on individual rights emerging as an efficiency-enhancing set of rules. The provision of rights to individuals, through legal rules that define rights *ex ante* and incentives to govern behaviour *ex post*, provides the context for economic activity.[22] This perspective of equality in economic activity regards non-excludability of others and rivalry in matters of public goods as a part of the 'law of equality' itself. The non-excludability of legal rules lies in the fact that once laws are formulated they apply to all individuals, at no additional cost. Once a given rule is in the public domain it becomes public information and it is impossible to charge a fee for its use; it is costless to resell. No one, equally, can be excluded as a potential rival. Legal equality does not prevent economic inequality nor stop motivations arising from perceived inequalities.

The 'public choice' dimension of the law arises from the American school of public choice that has focused on the inimical nature of the State and the self-seeking attitude of its agents. The judiciary ensures that rules are enforced in society. The Posnerian view is that judges are insulated from interest groups on account of their high salaries and public position and consequently are able to take an objective stance with regard to legal rulings (Posner 1993). This raises questions regarding the neutrality of the judiciary, and concerns expressed on the consequences of judicial intervention and action on grounds of public good or public interest. The emerging scepticism regarding the neutrality of the judiciary has drawn on historical evidence on the class-driven nature of judicial decision-making, and the more current concerns arising from the 'public choice' literature about self-seeking individuals solely interested in making private gain from public office.[23] The emphasis on how individuals are affected by social norms and the role of the judiciary in changing such behaviour leaves out the dimension of social groups and older concerns about class and equity.

Social groups, inequality and political lobbying

The major paradigms of economic development are located at the level of the individual. The evaluation of national growth is undertaken through an examination of distribution of income across individuals, i.e. measures of income inequality, but has not taken regard of other social inequalities. Other inequalities

22 Economic Analysis of the Law brings in the economic concepts and tools of cost and competitions to analyse the observance and non-observance of the law. See Cooter and Ulen (1988).

23 The Dickensian claim that 'the one great principle of the English law is to make business for itself' does not seem to be too far off the mark, even in the twentieth or twenty-first century.

that exist, such as those across ethnic and racial groups, have come to the foreground as a cause of internal conflict in societies. The interpretation of these wars is that ethnicity is a force for confrontation and war (see Heyer *et al.* 2002, 2003). The emergence of such a perspective on group conflicts has given rise to a new research paradigm that looks at the 'existence of severe inequalities between culturally defined groups' (Stewart 2000: 3) which are termed as *horizontal inequalities* (HIs) to differentiate them from individual income inequalities measures, which are termed *vertical inequalities* (VIs). HIs are a major cause of animosity in a society, yet there has been little study of how to reduce HIs; and VIs just measure the distribution of economic wealth. Even less attention has been paid to comparisons between types of inequalities. There are two other types of inequalities that were identified with regard to common property resources, those of within-group and between-group differences and they are referred to as heterogeneity (Olson 1965). While the concept of inequalities and heterogeneity of attributes in individuals located within a group and across groups has emerged as a key aspect of the management of resources, it has been unable to gain ground in the broader economic literature on economic development. The focus on group-related inequalities remains peripheral to the study of economic development (Stewart 1990).

An HI is multidimensional and can be identified across economic, political and social dimensions. This alternative way of conceiving of inequality provides not just another perspective, but also a richer set of attributes to understand discrimination and deprivation. The manner in which inter-group and within-group inequalities interact is not immediately obvious. Stewart points out that where a high level of vertical inequality is present a large HI might reduce the potential for conflict, as the heterogeneity within the cultural group would work against a consensus on political action (Stewart 1990: 11).

The concept of HI has provided an additional intellectual tool for understanding the relationship between ethnicity, culture and conflict.[24] It has also opened up the contours of economic development by bringing to the fore the hierarchies and structures that configure the canvas on which development takes place. By distinguishing between vertical and horizontal forms of inequality it forces us to consider the different axes of engagement that development both encounters and brings about.

The long-standing absence of inter- and intra-group analysis within economic development and its relationship to political power and social justice can be ended by bringing the vertical and horizontal axes into the frame of analysis. The significance of and difference between inter-group inequalities (IGIs) and within-group inequalities (WGIs) provides a way forward for understanding the impact of inequalities and looking for new ways to rectify these injustices. For instance, the typical economic remedy for inequality (taken to mean VIs) has

24 Both the UNDP and the ODI research frameworks on conflict and development draw heavily on the concept of HIs to explain group conflicts in multi-ethnic societies in Africa and Asia.

been to provide income or other forms of financial compensation. If there is to be a reduction of IGIs it would require measures of inter-group inequality that affects the ability of individuals within these groups to exit the group. Such remedies cannot emerge from a market-based approach as the nature of IGIs is not based on material inequalities alone but also on perceptions of these inequalities (Stewart 1990).

An individual's perception of her inequality in relation to that of others is based on a subjective sense of grievance. It raises the possibility that where IGIs are cognised by individuals in a group accepting this inequality on the understanding that WGI can be reduced through work and effort, IGIs too will diminish as other groups increase their acceptability of their working group. Such a group configuration creates a tacit agreement between group members to play by the rules of the society. In the case where IGIs are large there may be a high level of resentment but, as seen in the HI analysis, it might not lead to recrimination and retribution, where high WGIs work against the ability to rally the group around a single strategy. The remedy for IGIs in the presence of WGIs appears not through market solutions that focus on the individual, but by bringing in the avenue of community-based solutions that provide increased acceptability, rights and privileges to the discriminated group as a whole.

Bringing together the concepts of IGIs and WGIs provides a novel opportunity to understand how inequalities are perceived and responded to both by the State and the politically powerful and by the individuals who are members of lowly groups and associations in a country. The ability to identify the different impact that market-based and claim-based (community-based) approaches have on less well-off groups and individuals has become a matter of considerable academic and policy interest (Mitlin and Satterthwaite 2002). National governments have tended to prefer market-based approaches to rectify distributional conflicts in the economic arena. The option of using community-based solutions is rarely used as it requires a longer time horizon within which communities need to be engaged and their views taken on board. Where national legal actors have engaged with groups discriminated against in society they do provide valuable insights into the manner in which linkages can emerge between national entities and sub-national level identities, in society. Figure 3.1 provides a schematic representation of the interactions between the State and its people in the process of dispensation of justice. The schema highlights the linkages between the State as the maker of legal rules and how it uses economic values, such as market as well as societal claims made by groups, in ensuring that justice is meted out and inequality reduced.

The schema highlights two methods of obtaining rights that have engaged national governments: self-determination, which is imposed by communities confronting the State, and welfare, which has been promoted by mainstream macroeconomic models. Figure 3.1 delineates the hierarchical aspects of the relationship between the legal authority and the community. The enforcement of legal rules by the State on the community concerned with obtaining justice is indicated by a vertical bold arrow line connecting *legal rules* to *community*.

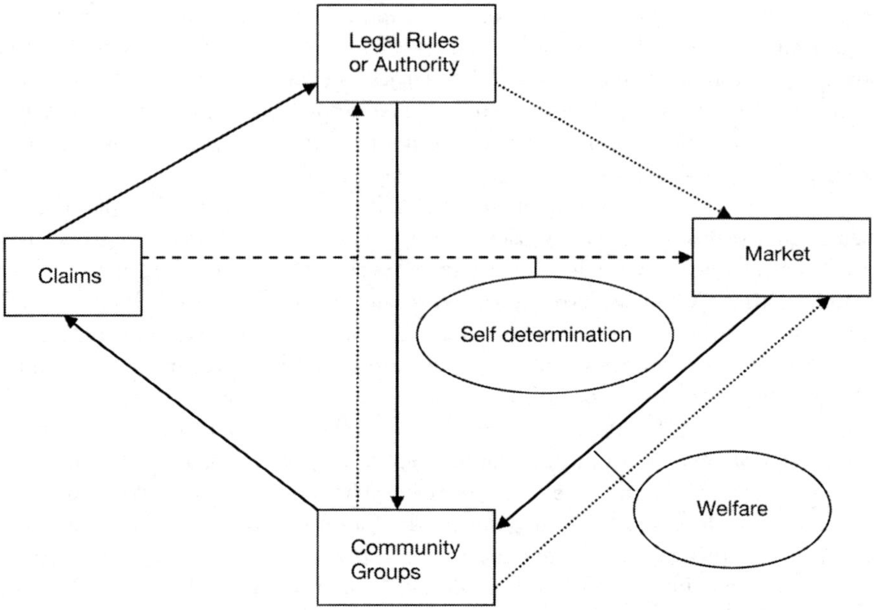

Figure 3.1 Current interactions between the law and community groups.

The claims made by the community are for equity between and within the groups to right historical wrongs of discrimination and exploitation of the group[25] as well as for equality of the individual, to rectify the inequalities at birth and those meted out through life.[26] So, a bold arrow connects *community* to *claims* as a way to approach the State as *lawmaker*.

The presumption is that the lawmakers are sensitive to the community's aspirations of equality before law and equity in opportunities to achieve a basic level of economic well-being, such as the satisfaction of the minimum needs of human beings. So, a bold arrow connects *claims* to *legal rules*.

While communities can interact directly with the State as lawmaker, the light dotted arrow connecting *community* to *legal rules* indicates an alternative route taken by communities to approach the courts. Individuals can also be enabled by the State to access markets directly. The community appears to mediate its demands through the market (economic) and claims (political) approaches. The light dotted arrow connecting the *lawmakers*, or legal rules, to the *market* identifies the situation where regulation or rectification of the market is

[25] The World Development Report 2006 (World Bank 2006) brings the notion of equity back into the development policy literature by focusing on the importance of legal rules and reforms in setting right historical forms of mass exclusion and deprivation.

[26] The World Development Report 2007 (World Bank 2007) emphasises how inequalities through life can adversely affect an individual's opportunities of work and wealth creation.

undertaken to overcome unacceptable practices such as anti-competitive behaviour in the market.

As already stated, the bold arrow connecting *claims* to *legal rules* represents the normal route for grievances that are brought to court through processes akin to class action to rectify past inequalities such as ethnic discrimination. The interaction may also arise to reverse the impact of recent actions of the State or private parties – such as the building of dams or felling of forests – since such development processes adversely affect the lives of communities. These claims which demand the attention of the government have the capability of amending the rules to ensure that a measure of equity is brought in. The inequity gives rise to claims by way of petitions to the court by the aggrieved groups or to 'public interest litigation' on behalf of the poor groups. The more demonstrative forms, such as agitations and social movements to remedy the differential opportunities across social groups, do not have a direct route to the courts. It remains at the discretion of the court whether or not to intervene on the community claims, and the linkage is consequently represented by a dotted arrow.

The authority for law enforcement is a matter of how the law is interpreted. If agitations and other forms of militant action by groups are deemed to fall in the political arena, then social unrest generated and giving shape to a set of claims may or may not be taken to court. In cases where these voiced claims are converted into formal claims that are heard by the lawmakers and rule-enforcers, the two sides of the diamond (claims and markets) work in tandem. Contrarily, despite the social agitation for land by marginalised groups such as the Chiapas in Mexico or the Maoist groups in India, such groups have been denied legal voices as they are deemed to be outside the legitimate political spectrum and regarded as guerrilla or terrorist organisations.

The market also affects the community directly in relation to prices which can bar effective entry, and the bold arrow linking *market* to *community* represents this significant connection that exists between the two. Laws that affect market conditions, such as breaking up monopoly, have a ripple effect on the community as the reduction of market power permits more individuals to gain access to commodities. In the case where the law upholds the right of an individual it is a signal to others to accept the ruling, which therefore has a multiplier effect in society. The dotted arrow linking *legal rules* to *market* represents the assertion by the State of the right of the individual to trade in the market. Legal rules become more strongly oriented towards the market in advanced stages of economic development. In situations where markets are well developed, the dotted line might be replaced by a solid line.

The thin arrow line connecting *community groups* to *market* represents access of the individuals to the market through supportive state measures such as the provision of welfare, particularly income-support schemes.

Claims that are enunciated but not taken to court become a basis for direct forms of action, and social movements do affect the nature of the market, as in the extreme cases of forcible land appropriation by slum dwellers or agricultural labour. So, the broken arrow connecting *claims* to *market* indicates that such influences over the market do not occur easily; this is a path of self-determination for a group, for it to claim to become sufficiently strong to influence the market. Initiatives taken by governments, for empowerment of poor groups, identify policies on 'welfare schemes' and for 'self-determination' in individuals and groups (Mitlin and Satterwaite 2002).

The policies, unlike flows, are indicated by ellipses. A welfare policy is a form of equitable compensation. Welfare policies can be combined with participatory policy by granting greater access to the beneficiaries in some economic activity by the State. In the 'participatory policy' a market-type approach gets combined with a welfare policy and involves a move towards self-determination. The greater the participation, the greater is the motivation to create an asset rather than to remain a simple transfer of income. Increasing the participatory element emphasises the move towards self-determination or the move towards market and away from pure welfare. The *self-determination* ellipse represents policies that direct the flow from claims groups towards the market. The *welfare* ellipse represents pure income transfer, which may have an adverse impact on the growth of the market by cutting into savings for investment.

Participatory policies that promote self-determination prevent dependency on state welfare and improve the chance of success of the pro-poor policies. The market can also be manipulated to provide equitable relief to disadvantaged communities, as in the case of price subsidies and fair price shops. This tendency is shown by the dotted arrow connecting the market to communities. There is always the possibility of the claiming individuals switching between claims and market-based approaches, depending on their economic strengths and weaknesses.

The presence of active groups in the community expands the basis for bestowing ownership rights. Their equitable claims are best asserted through addressing and highlighting the horizontal inequality between groups, which is manifestly visible. The contribution of the judiciary at the national level, in promoting self-determination, has helped to focus attention on the benefits arising from the claims-based group approach. Claims from groups are a potential springboard for advancing community-level enunciation of equity concerns, through creating a discourse on equitable rights. If more equitable rights get written into laws then many group claims for acquisition of assets could be successful. If these were individual claims they would take the market approach. While rights are negotiated in the political arena the development of the public domain in sub-national spaces promotes equity in laws at local level. The understanding that inter-group inequality is the result of absence of equity in law and policy helps claims to be asserted logically and argued on principles of equity. For example, opportunities for housing; utilities such as sanitation, water and electricity; and services such as education and health care, are denied to many groups on the grounds of insufficiency of state funds. The budget is akin to a financial law but is misrepresented as insufficiency of funds only to some groups. The inequity in the budget and its enforcement by the financial administration is not regarded as a matter for examination by the judiciary.[27]

The market implies purchasing power. The exclusion of groups from the market and their simultaneous denial of group rights stir up strong emotions that can create acute desperation and even acts of violence. Their agitations have invited threats of contempt of court for demanding equity. These agitations do not take place at the national level but tend to be fought at the local level. Their struggles are therefore the subject of sub-national discourses on equity. This raises difficult issues as there are different understandings of the concept of equity, at the national, sub-national and community levels.

All higher courts are courts of equity and justice. They are not simple interpreters of law, but also dispensers of the justice of equity. Equitable justice becomes complicated when there are contradictory equitable claims, or an equitable arrangement is contested by groups, at various levels. Equality can only be achieved for the satisfaction of minimum human needs. The satisfaction of higher levels of created demands has to be left to individual efforts. Inequity in allocation is patently unjust when budgeted funds supplement individual efforts on development beyond minimum needs of some groups without having met minimum needs of all.

The Indian constitution was drafted in the context of large-scale economic reforms to achieve a strong and modern economy. The utmost care was taken in the drafting to avoid judicial interference with economic reforms. The right to property was subject to laws to ensure economic reform, and the constitution visualised that such laws would affect property rights. The court struck down law after law on land reform, passed by the legislatures, for violating the right to property. In the case of a law with differential rates of compensation for taking over of private property by the State, where rates tapered down as the value of the property went up, the court responded that this was discriminatory and a violation of equality before law. The Supreme Court struck down the laws, saying that if the market value was not to be paid as compensation it would be a violation of the fundamental right to property. The Indian Parliament responded by passing a law to amend the constitution to exclude laws promoting economic reform from judicial review. The Supreme Court struck the amendment down, saying that lawful compensation cannot be illusory as it would result in a deprivation of property. The constitution was then further amended so that the term an 'amount' replaced the term 'compensation' for taking over land under the land reform acts. The court then decided to interpret 'amount' to mean 'fair amount' putting the lawmakers in a quandary. A further amendment of the constitution sought to remove right to property from the category of 'Fundamental Rights' in the constitution, and it

[27] The National Audit Offices in most central and sub-national governments do examine the expenditure patterns but do not raise questions about the allocation of funds in the budget itself.

was made an ordinary right as per law. Presently the constitution says no person is to be deprived of his property save by the authority of law (Sathe 2003: 46–9).

This series of cases in the Indian courts, where the abridgement of property rights to improve equity was resisted by the highest Indian court, underlines the reality that the landlord's right to property had more sanctity than the right of the tiller. It was only after the green revolution in agriculture became widespread in India and the powerful landlords became rural capitalists that the State changed its views on private property in land holdings (Sathe 2003). These forms of persistent inequity in treatment by the courts have cast doubt on the ability of the law to transform social relations and ensure economic development.

Asserting group identities and affirming resource rights

In India where there has been a caste system in operation for much of its history and where at least 52 per cent of the population belong to Other Backward Classes (OBCs) today there has been central legislation that provides for 27 per cent reservation for OBCs in educational institutions which was challenged before a constitutional bench of the highest court. The 93rd Amendment to the Constitution passed by a central legislation in 2005 created an exception to the principle of 'equality before law' that had till then governed admissions to educational institutions. The constitutional bench had asked why identification of all OBCs was a prior condition to the reservation of 27 per cent of seats for OBCs, since it was public knowledge that the percentage of OBCs in the population was certainly larger than the stated 27 per cent. Also, as identification of all OBCs could take years to be completed there was a query regarding whether, as a pro-tem measure, reservation for OBCs should not be made pending full identification. The bench also observed that in the case of 20 per cent of the population in the US who were of black and Hispanic origin and where 80 per cent are whites, only a minority suffered from discrimination and resultant backwardness. This contrasted with the situation in India, as previous legislation had restricted coverage to the categories of scheduled castes and tribes which make up only some 20 to 30 per cent of the population.

In many Indian states there are already official quotas for employment in the public sector and in quotas for admissions in educational institutions for the Backward Classes in operation. The lists of Backward Classes were constructed by the Backward Classes Commission in these states and the quota was implemented on this basis, even prior to the 93rd Amendment. It raised the question of why, if legislation for a quota for the poor could precede their identification and enumeration in the population, this was not possible in the case of legislation, for creating reservations for OBCs. The court agreed: why not?

The provision for affirmative action in the Indian constitution has had mixed results. At the national and regional levels the social mobility achieved, epitomised by the rise of political parties of rural lower caste (*dalit*) such as the

Bahujan Samaj Party,[28] has been applauded. The picture is different at the sub-regional and local levels, where it is the strongly repressive effects of caste discrimination that are more evident in the rural areas. It is only in urban India that there are any signs of social mobility (see Béteille 1991). In the post-tsunami reconstruction in the state of Tamil Nadu, the sharply exclusionary nature of the caste claims made itself heard when members of high-caste groups protested against the architectural plans to provide similar housing for high- and low-caste members of the community. Their objection was that if the *dalit* acquired houses comparable to those of the higher castes this would upset the local caste hierarchy and asset-holding pattern.

Malaysian economic policy has been based on ethnic lines for more than three decades since the launching of the New Economic Policy (NEP). The NEP came close on the heels of ethnic riots in Malaysia in 1969 and was consciously constructed as a vehicle for the social and economic transformation of Malaysia. The threat of civil unrest arising from the high level of inter-group inequality between the Malay and non-Malay races was recognised as a trigger for future outbursts of ethnic violence by both the ruling party (UMNO) and the minority political parties. There was a strong desire in all political parties to ameliorate the potential for further ethnic violence, with the senior members of the Malaysian Chinese Party and Malaysian Indian Party actively participating in drawing up the NEP document. The success of the NEP, during the last quarter of the last century, in ensuring the economic advancement of the *bumiputera* population, is regarded as a success by all communities.[29]

The policy has operated in Malaysia from 1970 giving significant advantages to the indigenous Malays, or the *bumiputera* population. On the other hand this has restricted the relative group rights of the two minority races, namely the Chinese and the Indian groups. The close attention paid to reducing inequity between groups over the last twenty-five years has been accepted by Malaysians as its focus has been on developing a citizenry marked by ethnic distinction while relegating equality of individual rights to a lower level of importance. Having classes of ethnic citizens and creating horizontal legal inequality between groups by design did improve equity between ethnic groups. There has been some suggestion that the Malaysian state will be reworking the NEP guidelines and will reintroduce a new form of ethnic policy for future decades, and this has raised concerns among the citizens of minority ethnicities that an excessive emphasis on equity would work to further reduce their ethnically based individual rights and thereby hinder their future social advancement.

A noteworthy feature of the Malaysian model of development is that the NEP was never given the legal status of a constitutional law but was located within the policy space, and ordinary laws and rules were framed accordingly. Nonetheless, the policy operated through the 'group claims' channel and

[28] Brass (1995) provides a useful narrative on the rise of rural farmer-based parties in the 1980s.

[29] I am grateful to Seri Ramon Navaratnam for sharing his knowledge and experience of the NEP.

attained the status of a quasi-rule which changed the modes of engagement between the national State and the communities, as set out in Figure 3.1. It is also significant that the proposals to bring in a new and modified NEP into the Malaysian policy space, in the current national plan, underline the need to ensure that the gains in group equity translate into individual advancement through market-based competition. The use of policy space, rather than law and justice, to advance group equity through greater flows between claims and market-based solutions would strengthen the sub-national ability of self-determination to find participatory 'demand-led' solutions, as reflected in Figure 3.1.

In the United States the problem of racial heterogeneity in urban planning hails back to the black ghettos in the 1960s. Heterogeneous groups differ in their preference structure, making it harder for economic planners to ensure adequate provision of services (Baqir *et al.* 2004). In the case of provision of schooling it is the case that school districts with racially heterogeneous communities face a greater challenge in increasing attendance rates (Hoxby 2003). The persistence of group identity can also oppose nation-making and therefore the erasure of such identity becomes a high priority for a new state,

The Chinese socialist revolution under Chairman Mao that led to the creation of the People's Republic of China in 1949 is one such case. The socialist policies of the PRC were geared to ensure the socialist transformation of the economy, with policies of collectivisation followed by the Great Leap Forward. This was followed by a decade-long 'cultural revolution' designed to erase class consciousness in the Chinese psyche and create manifest equality seldom seen before in history. The laws brought in during the 1950s were devised with the intention of remedying earlier class differences. Everywhere class dominated and often defined all other forms of inequality. This enabled the State to draw upon individual talent that had been freed of historical inequalities of status as the new mark of class.

In the era of economic reforms since the 1980s, ushered in under Deng Xiaoping, there was a shift from ensuring equity to a more market-oriented equality. The urge was to ensure economic competition through harnessing state assets while also encouraging individual enterprise and a move to private ownership of corporate and personal assets. The PRC therefore adopted a new set of norms and rules. The common ownership of all property in China managed through the state leaders gave way to joint ownership and to opening up state-owned enterprises and service provision to the domestic and later international markets.

The transition to the market economy has not been trouble-free, as distributional problems have emerged under the new norms that require a review of group equity and individual rights. The growing divide between the rich and the poor, the urban and the rural, has brought status back into the social sphere in China. The freedoms in the commercial and productive spaces created by the economic reforms have provided new avenues for the huge pool of human capital that has emerged over the last three decades. The State needs economic and human development to ensure that its polity functions effectively, just as the multinational company needs political and legal stability to ensure economic enrichment.

The following news items illustrate the impact of these transitions that are working towards the decentralisation of legislative rights but are still subject to national laws.

Wang Shurong, a peasant engaged in agricultural cultivation, recently discovered inconsistencies between the 25th provision of the Land Management Regulation of Hebei Province (entitled 'Authorisation Required for Agricultural Cultivation of Land') and the 57th article of the Land Management Law [National]. The former stated that authorisation was required for use of land in fishery and husbandry, and the latter did not. Wang Shurong subsequently wrote a letter to the Standing Committee of the National People's Congress recommending that the local regulation of Hebei be amended. On 27 May, the 10th Standing Committee of Hebei Province People's Congress passed a proposal, 'Revision to the Land Management Regulation of Hebei Province', which abolished the 25th provision of the Land Management Regulation.[30]

Liu Yong, a research associate at the Development Research Center of the State Council, revealed that during the 'Eleventh Five-year Plan' period China will begin planning trial administrative district reforms. The plan for reform includes establishing a dual structure (province–county) regional government system, as well as eliminating the administrative layer in cities and towns. With the exception of the national capital, provincial capitals and a number of major cities, in principle, administrative duties in all cities will be turned over to the county governments.[31]

The responsible person of the Municipal People's Congress Legal Affairs Committee stated that henceforth the legislative program will be strictly controlled and legislative resources will be used prudently. The measure is meant to address three large problems with Chongqing's local legislation: inconsistent rules, unclear content, and difficulty in implementation and conflicts with higher-level legislation.[32]

As there are multiple legislative bodies in China, conflicts of law occur frequently and the current constitution has established the principle of constitutional review and a 'legislation recording and reviewing system'. The legislation recording and reviewing system is related to constitutional review, but there is also a crucial difference: this system does not include a review of problems concerning conflicts between China's constitution and central laws promulgated by the National People's Congress. The impact of the legal reform has been much debated in China, and Professor Cai Dingjian, director of the Research

30 Zheng Ran, 'Letter from Peasant Leads to Change in Local Rule and Regulation', *China Legal News*, 6 June 2007, available at www.chinalegalnews.com.cn

31 Xu Lifan, 'China Plans to Construct Dual Province–County Government System', *China Times*, 1 September 2005, available at www.chinatimes.cc

32 Li Guo, 'Chongqing Gives Notice that it will Control Local Legislation and Prudently Use Legislative Resources', *Procuratorial Daily*, 10 October 2005, available at www.jcrb.com, taken from *Workers' Daily*.

Centre on Constitutional Law at the China University of Political Science and Law, believes that China's 'legislation recording and reviewing system' focuses primarily on whether local regulations conflict with the constitution, the central laws and administrative rules and regulations. China's constitution stipulates that only local regulations must be submitted to the National People's Congress for recording but the 'Legislation Law' has subsequently expanded the submission of legislation for recording to include administrative rules and regulations. Moreover, it is stipulated that local regulations must be reported to the State Council for recording. There are many rights that cannot be enforced because there are no relevant organisations to implement them, or because there are no procedures to be followed. However, the most worrying aspect is when the institutions have been established but they do not do anything, and the laws exist only on paper.[33]

Although the Chinese constitution contains guidelines on the respective powers of the central and local governments, they are not easily enforceable. There is also a lack of corresponding concrete laws and regulations to carry out these guidelines and a very inadequate set of supervisory mechanisms to guarantee that these guidelines are followed. While current constitution does provide for central and local governments to function on the principle that power is officially shared between them, it does not clearly differentiate between central and local powers. The constitution enumerates the powers and responsibilities of the State Council, but fails to specify which powers and responsibilities are reserved only for the State Council and which are concurrent with those of the local governments.

It has been suggested by Chinese jurists that when the constitution is amended in the future a special chapter be devoted to establishing the principles of central and local relations. This will permit a full outline of the scope of central power and its relation to the autonomy of the local governments. It will also identify the residual powers of the central government for laying down new acts for local governments. The above goals could be achieved through a judicial review of central and local relations. One suggestion is that the Administrative Tribunal of the Supreme People's Court should handle disputes over ordinary powers and over division of interests between the central and local authorities.[34]

> The rapidity with which the law is changing in China with a relative lack of understanding of its implications for locally held views on social justice has led to a knowing disregard for the law by groups of citizens. Quite a few villages in Zhejiang have largely resorted to 'settling in private' after a

33 Wang Yijun, 'The Most Frightening is When Established Institutions Do Nothing and Laws Exist Only on Paper', *China Youth Daily*, 22 December 2005, available at www.cyol.net/

34 Xiong Wenzhao, 'Differentiate between Central and Local Authorities through Laws', *China News*, 10 December 2005, available at www.chinanews.com.cn (taken from *Outlook Weekly*)

criminal offense has occurred. This method of resolving cases in private mostly pertains to cases of rape, hooliganism, bigamy, and intentional injury. In some counties and towns, more than 50 percent of the cases are privately settled. The reasons for this are as follows:

1 Those involved in serious criminal cases often view the offenses as ordinary civil disputes – rendering big issues small or minor, and rendering minor issues insignificant.
2 Many victims who have been unlawfully violated believe that 'public prosecution' will bring them no personal benefit; instead they seize the opportunity to fish for money, consequently seeking out the perpetrator on their own accord and settling the matter in private. The suspects, afraid of legal punishment, pay up to make the issue disappear.
3 Many parties do not wish to hurt friendships or create enemies, and mediators use all kinds of excuses to suppress the cases. Since the role of mediator is usually played by a village cadre or a powerful member of a clan, this increases the lineage's ability to constrain a victim, so that even if the punishment by mediator is unfair, victim will not seek legal protection.
4 Cadres at some levels worry that if there be too many reported cases, it will affect their end-of-year comprehensive management examination and appraisal ratings, therefore their approach to criminal offenses is 'do not turn over disputes to higher authorities, but resolve them internally'. Some village cadres try to extricate the criminals from the responsibility of their offences.

(Yu Xiaozhou, 'How "Settling in Private" became Standard Practice for Criminal Cases in Villages', *Zhejiang Legal Daily*, 6 January 2006, available at zjfzb.zjol.com.cn).

What the changing legal terrain for social justice indicates is that greater judicial presence is a welcome feature, but it needs to be applied cautiously. Laws that attempt to rectify historical wrongs encounter the deep fissures caused by severe inequalities across groups. The adverse impacts of inequity arising from social exclusion based on race, ethnicity and caste need to be explored, in relation to both inter and intra-group inequality.

It would seem that the extreme use of race in the apartheid policy in South Africa till the end of the 1980s accentuated a particular form of inequity, and it was therefore regarded at national and local levels as a priority area for the eradication of that inequity in identity, which was an immoral inequality. The removal of other historical inequalities through use of affirmative action seems to have succeeded in Namibia and South Africa. A large part of the success in South Africa was founded on the creation of government institutions such as the National Truth and Reconciliation Commission under Rev. Desmond Tutu which helped to heal the wounds and cleanse the guilty (Faundez 2000).

Judicial activism for equitable development

The current focus on more equitable development is noteworthy and indicates that the redressing of group inequalities would be a central pillar for advancing on the sustainable development path. To ensure that the judiciary is regarded as an independent body and driven by an abiding interest in the public good rather than private gain, the actions of the judicial arm must be viewed as non-partisan.[35] There are always fears that this sense of objectivity and impartiality in the judiciary may be seriously compromised when there are competing claims on judges by their own group and by other groups in society. Contrarily, the convictions held by the judiciary and their considered deliberations on both the letter and the spirit of the law have also radicalised legal systems in some parts of the world. A verdict of 'judicial activism' has been served on the pro-active role adopted by such judicial establishments. The ability of activist judges to considerably advance the rights of individuals and/or groups in society have come to be regarded as a valuable resource in ensuring social transformations. The rise of pro-active judicial processes such as the use of public interest litigations in India have drawn considerable attention to the progressive power that could potentially vest in the judiciary (Iyer 1991).

The radicalisation of the judiciary increases the focus on a claims-based approach to obtaining group rights in contrast to the individual-focused market-based approach that had been advocated in the earlier legal literature (Ogus 1994). The reason for associating the market with the latter approach lies in availability of law enforcement to the highest bidders for it. The cost of accessing the judicial market, for any individual, is reduced when there is an accompanying group claim for redressing historical inequities. The expansion of the Habermasian public sphere through the success of community-led group demands, has attracted both activist judges and lawyers to the field of public rights. This concern goes far beyond the traditional interpretation by Coase of 'law', as a set of efficiency-enhancing rules (Prosser 1997). These changes in the orientation of the judiciary have shifted the balance between market- and claims-based approaches towards addressing concerns regarding different dimensions of inequality.

The community- or group-based claims secures the ability to compete in the market by way of prior equitable empowerment. The State needs to assert equitable justice for de facto protection of the *de jure* individual rights. That would make for more effective and sustainable eco-political equity as a solution to the problem of inroads of inequitable market equality into moral equality. Ensuring a more equitable and inclusive development of economic well-being

[35] The non-partisan nature of the court has been questioned in recent analysis,

> When the Court takes sides in the culture wars, it tends to be with the knights rather than the villeins – and more specifically the Templars, reflecting the views and values of the lawyer class from which the Court's members are drawn.
>
> (Romer v. Evans: 652).

(not just statistical national product) can result only from a more holistic moral understanding of unequal human identities. Local meanings of individual rights and right to equity arise from the contestations in the life of individuals and groups.

The push towards the legal provision of rights to individuals at the bottom of the social pyramid flies in the face of the restrictions on them already imposed by the market. The first priority must be social equity to maintain the social fabric. This is not a unique feature that is relevant only for the late developers in the world economy. There was a restriction on individual rights in many states of the US, not only by the states, but also by the federal US government, to counter economic depression in the 1930s. The Supreme Court expressed its view[36] that in mortgage moratorium cases, the right of the State to enact laws to delay or postpone payments to the mortgagee was in the public interest. The court upheld the right of the government to rewrite the rights of the mortgagee in the mortgaged property because there was an economic crisis. The court noted that the right of the citizens to contract had at all times an implied limitation that such rights could be restricted by governmental power in order to protect health, welfare and safety of citizens. That a contract contrary to public policy is not enforceable is expanded by the governments in the case of an emergency. In times of war such power of the government gets used extensively. Even in peace times the legislature imposes restrictions, as purely an act of will, on right to contract, in the interest of public health or morals. Private riparian interests become subservient to a public right when a dam is constructed by the force of will of the majority. The power to contract carries with it an infirmity of restriction by the State. Recognition of public needs, relation of individual right to public security, are ongoing processes, as are development and growth.

Firm control, capitalist advancement and inequitable development

The use of group claims to advance economic enterprise and thereby to drive the capitalist system provides a new dimension to bringing about economic development. The impact of societal structures or organised forms of power on generating and harnessing wealth accumulation permits the analysis of the practice of discrimination in the modern economic corporation. Discrimination within an industry or across industries can no longer be regarded as a suspect claim in modern economies in the face of evidence that groups too practise discrimination, and racial, religious and gender discrimination has been reported in a range of workplaces – public and private offices, schools, healthcare institutions. The use of social markers brings in a subjective discriminator into decision-making, where age, gender or race might be drawn on to screen labour market entrants. What subjective features do is to complicate economic decisions. The linking of subjective considerations with financial profits is clearly

36 Home building and Loan Association v. Blaisdell, Supreme Court of the United States 1934, 290 US 398, quoted in Williams (1956: 266–73).

reflected in the central levers of capitalism as a system where the subjective interests of individual capitalists do not overwhelm the economic benefits of the system but are identical with them.[37]

The firm gains economic power as it accumulates and concentrates capital. Additional power is obtained from the particular location of the firm within the global supply chain, or what could be termed the consequences of 'where in the system the firm decides to invest'. The firm also has power within the organisation and can demand the obedience of its employees as part of their contractual obligation within the system. So the firm as a 'self-regulated system of contested sovereignty' is a key institution that wields power and authority in both internal operations and the external industrial environment (Dietrich 2002). The size and concentration of capital in current operations is a source of power in itself.

An additional source of capitalist power emerges from directing capital to new areas, thereby fashioning and fulfilling new and unmet social needs in society. The latter can be termed the 'directive power' of capitalists, while the former is the 'accumulative power' of growing capital assets. The authority to chart new waters in the global system is regarded as worrisome, while the accumulation of wealth is deemed as laudable. The orderly and predictable process of accumulation through the market and the use of competitive forces is the acceptable face of capitalism, while the use of power to steer into new waters is regarded as a cause for the downfall of capitalism. The importance of 'access to capital' as a power, on the one hand, and the detraction of the 'dark side of ownership' that seeks to reduce investment in areas that will meet social needs, on the other hand, has come in for particular criticism (Rajan and Zingales 2004). The negative impact of the dominant capitalist derailing capital on account of individualistic entry into new areas results in calls for removing capitalists from the driving seat in society.

The 'directive power' of the firm or company does possess a negative aspect that permits it to commit misdemeanours arising from its dominant social position, but it also has a positive one to fulfil social needs. Where the flexing of the authoritative arm of firms results in activity that appears unwarranted by the social needs, it is often deemed as immoral by the larger society. The imposition by firms generates retaliation both from individuals and organisations who sue the firm where the laws of society allow such recourse. The law is regarded as an appropriate mechanism to control errant behaviour of firms,

37 It was Paul Sweezy who provided a commentary on the coalescing of the subjective interest of the capitalist in reflecting his status as a wealthy individual with the objective need of capital to find the highest returns. See Sweezy (1971 [1941]) for an analysis of how the subjective and objective elements of capitalism work together to ensure the advancement of the system. Half a century after the original analysis of the tendencies of capitalist development, there is evidence that capitalism has diversified into a varied set of conditions in response to different social and cultural subjectivities of nations. See Hall and Soskice (2001) for a presentation on the varieties of capitalism that have come to exist in Western Europe and North America.

because management of firms, like individuals, is regarded as self-seeking, and needing external control and containment. In this context, the law is regarded as a framework within which individuals are required to behave in a socially acceptable manner. The framing of the law is seen to be responsive to the ethical, moral, cultural and customary practices prevalent in society. In fact, the legitimacy of laws is effectively derived from outside the words of the statute, and is to be found in the shared values of all individuals in the society.

When firms are both viewed, and view themselves, as akin to private individuals they see the law as only an unwelcome constraint. As the law is regarded as a restriction on firm behaviour, it creates a perception that the bypassing or circumnavigating of the law is the best possible route for that individual or firm.[38] Firms consequently clamour for deregulation of legal constraint. This is driven by the desire to rid themselves of any fetters to accumulate capital and make profits by following their desires. Their belief that regulation will cramp the ability of companies is based on a 'red traffic light' understanding of the law, which posits useful regulation to be a constraining force. The possibility that regulation can be a force that fosters wealth creation by extending the terrain of production and provision of additional resource, i.e. a 'green light' does not dawn on them (Fennell 2007a).

Corporations wrestle with the State over what they consider unfair controls and restrictions. Yet the 'red traffic light' mentality of no restrictions on their acquisitions does not prevent the corporate sector from demanding reduction in state control while lobbying for further rights from the State; thereby bringing out the green light role of the State to give away their power over acquisitions. The dual nature of the relationship between the private firm and the state legal system is reflected in the defensive and offensive manoeuvres and manipulations of the State. The demand for reducing regulatory controls is a form of defence against state power, and the right to claim and enforce patents makes use of state power offensively.

The potential power that firms possess of operating in tandem with one another, at the level of the industry as a whole, has almost disappeared from economic analysis, together with the possibility that such operations might increase the opportunities for economic advancement of the industry. The room for business manoeuvres in economic analysis seems limited to actions of firms operating within the marketplace by using price mechanism and non-priced (non-transferable) instruments affecting economic behaviour. This space will explode if the covert ways in which industry gets the State to make laws and rules are brought into economic analysis. But what will be significant in the explosion will be the expansion to its real size of the power of the firms and industry and limited individuals constituting it vis-à-vis the power of the State composed of all individuals therein. In other words, it will be a paradox of the

[38] There is also resistance from within the institution of the firm itself; from employees who become whistle-blowers and occasionally succeed in obtaining remedy against undue influence and pressure from the company.

power of the part being bigger than that of the whole in its influence. It will show that the national institution of law with all its hierarchy of power yields to the influence of sub-national institutions whose power manifests.

In the United Kingdom, regulations set out by the Financial Services Agency have not prevented mortgage lenders from dipping into the sub-prime market with its greater exposure to risk. Nor have regulations prevented companies from underhand practices in auditing, such as that which led to the Enron scandal in the United States. In fact, the ability of large corporations to mismanage funds surfaced in the Enron disaster; and that led to the more stringent requirements set out in the Sarbanne–Oxley Act. Corporate power was exercised to make illegal payments to political parties, on a quid pro quo basis, over considerable periods of time in the US, and it constituted a misuse of trust.

Figure 3.1 sets out the social schema that shows the ability of the legal system to ameliorate the social conditions of the marginalised, which again depends on its ability to identify forms of group inequality. Where equality is restricted to the individuals, the law is limited to granting only access to economic opportunity through granting market access. The sole champion of the poor, the marginalised and excluded groups is the judicial activism that has increasingly been seen as the saving grace of what is otherwise a moribund legal system. The current rubric which regards claims as simply a form of contract between parties desiring an exchange of goods and resources cannot comprehend that those located further down the social hierarchy could be other than inchoate. The legal system has become subordinate to the market and can only see the social unrest as a source of opposition to the wealth accumulated by corporate institutions, and therefore the State itself. The ability to contend with the disquiet of the marginalised and the dissenting voices from below and afar requires a broader and more dynamic view of the law, as a force that can itself direct the rubric of development, by moving the spotlight from the court to the community. It is only by understanding that the *Sangong Tasi* has legitimacy, as does the *Narmada Bachao Andolan*,[39] not because their demand is more legitimate than that of the corporate entity or State but because their knowledge and way of life is what makes for the survival of natural resources that are so central to furthering the power of the firm and further wealth accumulation. It is only by making a reading of the law from where groups are located that the legal system can provide the wider rubric where both the market and claims are instruments that can work towards national development.

[39] See Sathe (2003) on the dynamics and demands of the Narmada Bachao Andolan.

4 National and sub-national institutions

> It is power and power (*danda*) alone which, only when exercised by the king with impartiality and in proportion to guilt either over his son or his enemy, maintains both this world and the next.
>
> The king who administers justice in accordance with sacred law (*Dharma*), evidence (*vyavahára*), history (*samsthá*) and edicts of kings (*Nyáya*) which is the fourth will be able to conquer the whole world bounded by the four quarters (*Chaturantám mahím*).
>
> Whenever there is disagreement between history and sacred law or between evidence and sacred law, then the matter shall be settled in accordance with sacred law.
>
> But whenever sacred law (*sástra*) is in conflict with rational law (*Dharmanyáya* = kings' law), then reason shall be held authoritative; for there the original text (on which the sacred law has been based) is not available.
>
> (Kautilya 1915: Book III, Chapter 1)

Kautilya, the prime minister of Chandragupta Maurya, speaks of the role of the king, the head of the State, in this extract from the *Arthashastra* written in the fourth century BC, and of how his dispensation of justice affects the functioning of society. He recognises the power of the king in the administering of justice and calls for an adherence to the edicts of rationality in this act.

The importance of kingly law has given way in modern societies to state power that is closely aligned, if not actively aiding and abetting, the proponents and processes of capital accumulation. The State has the primary power to control and directs the activities of its people and has the right to signify importance and assign wealth to places within its realm through how it shapes both the contours and fabrics of society and its economy and polity. The intentions of the State are, however, still the subject of public scepticism in the modern era. In particular, there is an increasing sense that the State has its own and often opaque agendas that are in effect, if not intentionally, oppositional to the public interest.[1]

[1] The notion of the State being opaque to the general public brings in a new dimension of state activity, which intends to hide (increasing the information asymmetry) but not necessarily to steal (corruption-based activity). Arpaporn Sumrit, my doctoral student, who has been researching rice liberalisation in Vietnam, has labelled this feature of the State as 'murky', a comment I have found very helpful in thinking through state agendas and governmentality.

Capitalists and state-led development

The worries about the opacity of state intention and purpose have generated public and group demands for the right to separate the purposes and outcomes of their strategies from those of the State. This tendency is recognised within the social science paradigm in the rising tide of claims for legal rights to fend off the clutches of state power. Notions of the rule of the 'economic (licence) raj' first found an audience in the 1970s, in the context of developing economies (Krueger 1974; Lal 2000 [1983][2]). It was subsequently reworked into the image of the grabbing hand two decades later in the context of transition economies, by drawing on these earlier concerns and anxieties within the social sciences.[3]

This scramble by groups to wrest away rights and to break asunder from the shackles of the State are found in a number of conceptual castings. The Hobbesian dilemma is one such enduring formulation which, however, sees the State as a necessary evil to curb the excesses and self-destructive nature of individuals. The laws that developed around property in the nineteenth century were directed towards privileging the emerging capitalist class but were couched in language such that the general public would accept and respect the law, as a legitimate social institution (Cole 1999). The dominance of the classes of the merchant, the manufacturer and the financier, over the public, was achieved by protracted struggles with the Crown in the nature of collective action.

On the other hand, there is the invocation of the nineteenth-century Darwinian model of 'natural selection' which favours the survival of the fittest and states that it is only those strategies that are 'fit for purpose' that will continue to thrive within a given state structure. The successful attempt of dominant classes to create laws that protected their activities from monarchical demands for payment, both financial and personal, as a symbol of their allegiance, represents a necessary condition for modern economic development (North 1990). The creation of rules by legal institutions, such as the English Parliament, was the most distinctive feature of the seventeenth and eighteenth centuries. The overturning of the divine right of kings and the enforcement of royal laws by a judicial chief appointed by the Crown, who exercised his rule of law as an enforcement of law, before which all were equal, played a major part in the development of legal institutions.

The subjective view of the jury or the judge is never totally absent, with Thomas More reminding us that the arm of the law is related to the intellectual reach and the understanding of the judge. The very concept of equity in English law emerged out of a consideration of fairness in the decision of Lord Chamberlain on behalf of the king. Here justice was done on the basis of the subjective view of the Lord Chamberlain, leading to the adage that 'equity is measured by the length of the Chamberlain's foot'.

[2] The original 1983 pamphlet was republished as Lal (2000).
[3] The grabbing hand was popularised by the work of Shleifer and Vishny (2002).

In contrast to claims of individuals, the power of collective action is far greater, for it can bring a sizeable number of individuals together as a section of society of State, to protest against or confront the power of State. A shift in perception of political power, which is brought about by the State bestowing or safeguarding the rights of a group, affects not only the group but redistributes the ease with which groups throughout society can access political power (Knight 1991). The reconfiguration of access to power affects how other groups regard their own prospects as well as those of other groups, and this can generate a competitive battle between groups. Of course, it is also possible that groups compete against one another in order to maintain their existing status and wealth (Fennell 2003). Such forms of competition are not those of the marketplace but are those of communal clashes and civil action. Collective action can change the rules in the very arena of contestation, i.e. the rules of political behaviour, which are not available to the individual or firm in relation to the rules of the market.

New political ideologies make an impact on the State and on the representation of the people in the legislature.[4] The legislature is also responsive to social disruptions. For instance, the political role of labour power arose from the congregation of labour to counter the hierarchical supervision in the factory (Berg 1982). The demands of organised labour for an improvement in conditions of work and pay were at the heart of the conflict of interest between labour and capital. It was only in the socialist and communist legal systems that there was guaranteed employment.

While capitalism as a system is regarded as beneficial, for it increases the size of output and reduces the cost of goods, the process of creative destruction unleashed by capitalists does have losers. The trade unions are opposed to these changes and want to maintain status quo (Thompson 1966). The bureaucracy too wishes to control the process of change, and this tendency has been put down to the desire of the bureaucrats to enrich themselves by supporting the wealthier sections of society and pauperising the poor and voiceless groups in the State. Legal institutions are set out to provide justice to its people in the face of these powerful political forces by bringing in a sense of equality under law and instilling a concern for the equitable redistribution of political and economic access in society.

The core of the model of social justice to ensure fair treatment of groups, in terms of equitable access, is at the heart of the political and social reform movements that emerged both within industrial economies, such as the United Kingdom, and in relation to agrarian and often colonial economies, such as South Africa. Shifting the balance of power between groups so as to ensure better access for those at the margins of society has been an uphill task.

Ensuring the fair treatment of groups becomes particularly difficult where there are systems of government that follow federal principles. This is because

[4] (Cole 1999). 'An Unqualified Human Good: E. P. Thompson and the Rule of Law' at http://www.indylaw.indiana.edu/instructors/cole/cole.htm

the existence of a federal structure creates multiple sites of state power that are linked to the centre but with the autonomy to make administrative and financial decisions regarding the path of development. A federal legal system that needs to take into account group aspirations at both the national and the sub-national level is open to manipulation by the powerful situated within different sub-national jurisdictions, with the possibility of conflict between sub-national entities and the national State. Federalism as a system of national administration and political decision-making has been adopted by large nations, particularly those beset by deep-seated differences of ethnicity, language and cultures. In the context of developing countries, federalism has also come to be regarded as a more effective way of ensuring that development efforts do remain the prerogative of a central administration (Kee 2004). The difficulties which a federal structure, providing authority to sub-national territories to take political, financial and administrative decisions, imposes on national sovereignty and development planning have made the legal and administrative framework of federalism hard to implement and sustain (Tanzi 1995).

The debate whether the centralised or the decentralised state structures of fiscal, administrative and managerial functions are better placed to deliver the goods and services that bring about human development has been the rage in international development institutions through the 1990s.[5]

The move away from a historically informed social science and its replacement by more discrete and technical, and consequently narrower and shallower, corpuses of knowledge, has had the effect of erasing the overarching links between political power and state structures in defining and administering the law. The manner in which decentralisation and federalism have come to be regarded as two blades of the same scissors that will cut out excessive state interference is the result of a dangerous type of intellectual short-circuiting. This seeming simplicity of transferring power to sub-national levels without understanding its relations to historical experiences within each nation also obscures the many distinct schools of thought that exist within the social sciences regarding the manner in which different nations entered the global trade arena and appeared in world markets. For instance, the European tradition has been strongly influenced by an evolutionary approach, while neo-classical analysis, favoured in the United States, has the clear hallmark of the Chicago school of economics which has taken a static, even ahistorical approach to the law.

Second, the history of countries must be regarded as the central context for adopting particular state structures of administrative and fiscal arrangements. In the case of Malaysia, the administration and political control has traditionally been strongly influenced by the rulers of the thirteen constituent kingdoms. This administrative structure was supported by the British colonial administration in the late nineteenth century, which recognised the rights of the sultans

[5] The reverberations of the French Revolution in England compelled politicians to enlist the support of workers to pre-empt the possibility of a revolution on British soil.

to rule their kingdoms in a federated manner while classifying the areas of Malaya, Penang and Singapore together, as unfederated states to be known collectively as the Straits Settlements.[6] The Malaysian constitution, under the British, was built on a federal structure, with the thirteen states and their rulers having a strong say in the manner in which national law is made and implemented. This Malaysian form of federalism was distinctive in that it was based on a rotating headship of the federation from among the thirteen rulers (sultans). The ceremonial head of state continued to be head of the federation after independence and wields considerable powers, including a veto against the prime minister of the country (Hooker 1968).

The importance of historical developments in creating a nation and launching it on a development trajectory is also evident in the case of China. The country had a unitary system of administration and financial management between 1949 and the 1970s. Through the 1980s, there were economic reforms that reorganised production but did little to shift the levers of power. It was in the 1990s that there was evidence of a shift in the location of power, and the reforms of 1994 changed the tax-sharing arrangements so that provinces were required to become revenue-generating units and to no longer be mere units of revenue expenditure. This shift had resulted in a move to a system of fiscal federalism that has been further supported by administrative and managerial devolution. The growing move towards a federal structure is evident across sectors with the *bao-gan* (household) becoming the key institution in rural policy (Oi 1999) and the district at the administrative level responsible for rural industrial production and service provision. Despite the considerable spate of administrative reform, the Chinese constitution does not yet provide a wholly clear exposition on the distribution of power between centre and provinces, or on the nature and procedures that constitute legitimate centre–State relations (He 2008).

The growing attention accorded to the importance of federalism in the administrative process is accompanied by greater attention to the legal implications of such forms of devolution of financial and administrative functions.[7] The ability of decentralised administration to transfer considerable powers to local structures of the State does not arise solely from its proximity and therefore knowledge of local production processes but is dependent on local political economies as well (Bardhan and Mookherjee 2007b). The importance of political and social structures in determining the consequences of policies of decentralisation that operate through existing forms of centre–State relations has emerged as a new area of concerns in the first decade of the twenty-first century.[8]

[6] See Chapter 3 for a commentary on the view that decentralisation of power transfers authority and therefore representation at the local level. Of particular relevance is the notion that decentralisation and greater power of sub-national territories are concomitant processes.

[7] See Harper (1999) for a historical treatment of the transfer of power from colonial to federal structures.

[8] See Nirvikar Singh (2007) on the importance of federalism and decentralisation.

Using a legal lens to examine the nature of centre–State relations and associated implications of decentralisation reveals yet another important dimension of federalism, that of its superior ability to give due attention to social justice and equity (Bird and Ebel 2006). This dimension of social justice might occur even if the economic efficiency of decentralisation does not emerge as an immediate result of such reform. In national contexts, the decisions of the central government might appear to citizens in the local sphere to be made at a considerable physical and political distance and, also as difficult to decipher, the more proximate the site of state power, the more visible the practices of enforcement adopted by the local judiciary.

The importance of federalism as both a mechanism for resource mobilisation and allocation across the states, provinces or other types of sub-national units within the nation, and a schema to contain and even defuse ethnic conflicts was understood in social science in the early decades of development studies, but has now disappeared from the framing of economic analysis and policy.[9] This has been accompanied by rising murmurs which have grown over the decades, and there is now a loud clamour for at least a nuancing of the law to take into account local interpretations, if not a revoking of national legislation that denies sub-national and local understandings and meanings. On the other hand, there is a rising international demand for a global system of legal principles. The rising benefit of a uniform world undergirds current neoliberal interpretations of the development processes where globalisation-brought-about free trade is hailed as the new engine of growth.[10]

State jurisdictions and societal interpretations of the law

People within a local sphere understand the law from the way it is enforced, particularly the role of judges in such enforcement. Perceptions of any divergence between the letter of the law and the practice of the law are based on how justice is witnessed in everyday life (F. Benda-Beckmann 2002; K. Benda-Beckmann 2006). Where local communities perceive a displacement of the intention of the legislature by the judiciary, disillusionment sets in regarding the ability of the national legal framework to address and advance the social purpose of the legislation. The gaps and schisms between the stated purpose of law and public readings and understanding of the law have led to the scuppering of cases, and a growing concern about the inability of the legal system to comprehend the lives of ordinary people who reside in marginal worlds yet are regarded as jurisdictionally falling within the nation (Strathern 2005). Public disaffection with national laws is therefore compounded by a growing inability in the local public

9 Placing decentralisation in the limelight has revealed unexpected flaws, such as a wide variety in the capacity of the local state to deliver services, See Bird and Rodriguez (1999) for a commentary on the uneven performance of the decentralisation process in the Philippines with regard to achieving poverty alleviation.

10 See Enloe (1977) for a lucid analysis of the economic and political arguments for federal structures in development.

sphere to make sense of legal rulings in the manner and language set out by the courts.

The existence of different legal traditions is acknowledged by legal scholars, and yet there exists thinking that the convergence in legal systems between the 'West and the Rest' is a laudable process and could be achieved in the twenty-first century.[11] The simplification of a legal tradition to market-friendly rules or the demand for a ubiquitous but meaningless need for the 'rule of law' has reduced the role of law to a mere precondition for economic development. In the process, the importance of policymaking and power in making laws and thereby fashioning both social and economic relations has come to be ignored by comparative political studies of legal systems in developing countries (Tanner 1999).

The disregard of legal structures is part of a larger inclination to take the administrative governmental processes, both the legislative and executive aspects, as a mere backdrop to the development process. The importance of local and sub-national institutions and norms in absorbing, and adapting to, the new laws introduced into a society has disappeared from view, as legal and administrative matters are increasingly regarded as outdated props of an older system or, worse still, as an obstruction to market-based development. This is shortsighted and even dangerous for societies which operate through social norms, and the interaction of these norms with laws is critical in understanding how they are received and responded to within social contexts. It might be the case that collective action is more unlikely where executive and judicial powers act to check and balance one another.

Fashioning State–society relations and federal structures

The collective and the individual interact to ensure the maintenance of laws in a society (Potter 2001). That modernity brings about a set of interactions around the wresting of political and property rights from the State, followed by a second round of battle around social and economic rights, is how development has been experienced in the twentieth century (Hirschman 1991). The right of the individual and groups to control the might of the state power remains a key feature of progression in modern societies. They redress imbalances in power distribution that have arisen by way of collective actions in the past, many of which have been forgotten.

The particular arena of State–society that evolves within a nation emerges from its own history and within the context of national and local social structures that direct individual and group behaviour. There are strong political and

[11] While globalisation results in markets becoming more interlinked, this does not imply that all economies that are drawn together are regarded as equals. There is a strong tradition of regarding non-Western legal systems as a setback for international trade and negotiations. See Duncan Kennedy (2006) for a review of how waves of globalisation have impacted on legal institutions and legal thinking.

economic hierarchies within the State which test the ability of individuals and groups in society to contend with them. Social structures in turn are aligned to these hierarchies. Society is the term used to designate those parts of the hierarchical structures that do not legally constitute the power and hierarchy of the State.[12] While the State is the dominant structure in developing countries, society has the ability to refashion the levers of power as well as change the balance of power between the State and groups, and among groups.

The ability of individuals and groups to access prosperity depends on acquisition of rights and participation in the policies and functions of the State for creation and sharing of wealth in the future. There are strong political and economic hierarchies within the State that direct, control and contain the accrual of wealth which would be diametrically opposed to any major reformulation of the sites of power and decision-making. The centrality of politics and economic power in maintaining the stranglehold of the State is an abiding feature in organising society.[13] Political and economic power flows through political and economic hierarchies that exist in society, and in the developing countries it is the hierarchies of the State that command the organisation of society. State hierarchies perform the difficult, even politically perilous task of linking the actions of groups and individuals in society to those hierarchies that dominate a society.

The most dangerous state actions relate to the redistribution of national resources in a new nation. The inability of many developing countries to radically transform the ownership of resources, assets and income have been a long-standing indication of their failure both inside their nations and in the international arena. Yet there are a varied number of reasons for the hapless performance of the state apparatus to effect such changes, even when the legal provision is drafted and ratified in their national constitutions. Where groups within society that have chosen not to participate in state processes make demands or obstruct reform in the ownership structure of national resources and assets, the State faces a huge dilemma.[14]

12 The considerable influence and impact of a legal system on the social and economic actions of a citizenry and the existence of different legal systems across societies has been the central subject of legal history in the second half of the twentieth century. See Berman (1983) for a study of Western legal systems and Goldman (2008) on how globalisation has affected these legal traditions. This has not prevented popular commentators and even academic discussions in mainstream economics from making quick and easy comments on the urgent need to put in place a single set of legal rules. See Shleifer and Vishny (2002) on the need for Western economic laws in post-Soviet society.

13 The study of State–society interactions within economic development as a separate area of study has evolved from a long-standing interest within political science. See Evans *et al*. (1985) for a powerful analysis of the critical role of the State in patterns of development. These themes have been taken forward into a State-in-society approach that was put forth by Migdal *et al*. (1994).

14 Mushtaq Khan has provided a compelling analysis of why political structures and power-sharing among political groups is such a central feature of development. See Khan (1996) and more recently Khan (2003).

Past collective actions as well as the seeds of future ones inhere in socio-political hierarchies; even their description is not without subjective motivation. Groups in society are driven by the desire both to continue to dominate the political and economic landscape, and to deny other potential competitors for power, the ability to take over the reins of government.

> The historical process of nation building provides us with many examples of the interplay between the economic and political interests of dominant groups, with [their] imagined group identities, generating new social norms that are given the social status of 'tradition'.
>
> (Anderson 1991: 42)

The process of economic development that is brought about in a newly independent state creates a series of inequities and generates a process of economic differentiation by the selection of a particular pathway of development. Historical analysis shows that the rights awarded in national legal frameworks, such as the constitution, derive from a range of considerations, from the furtherance of the principles of equality with focus on individual freedom, to aiding and abetting the advancement of dominant classes (Rosenberg and Birdzell 1986; North 1990).

The legal process of creation of rules and individual and group identities works to buttress the sense of emergent homogeneity across social groups. It works to unify a nation and brings about consensus formation; the hallmark of successful national struggles to establish independent nations (Hobsbawm 1987). The emergent individual and group identities within the new nation and the directives of the State jointly work to set out the type of rights that are incorporated into the legal framework of a country and that sets off the legally constituted institutions of the nation. The national identity is not a permanent rallying point, neither is it a durable form of social cohesion, for it can become a symbol of repression and give rise to group reprisals.

The State and its agents undertaking economic development increasingly face the wrath of groups that no longer regard the national growth as being equally distributed, and regard themselves as being bypassed or even denied the fruits of development.[15] The continued attempts of individuals and communities to wrest rights from the State and participate in governance by the State meet with a holding action by the State aimed at containing disparate and often destabilising demands from groups in society. This two-way process of interaction between the lesser power of many aspiring groups or society of individuals vis-à-vis the greater power of State has been termed by Joel Migdal 'strategies of survival' (see Migdal 2001: 252). The control of resources and the associated nexus of power, in groups and the State, are at the heart of this battle where

[15] Where the State is forced to make peace with dominant societal groups it is referred to as 'political settlements' by Khan (1996). He makes the case that if such payments are not paid out, political collapse of the government will be the consequence.

State and society emerge as competing orders (Lambach 2004). State and society interact to legitimise, in their own way, forms of human interaction between them. The historical context within which current political events unfold through the lifetime of individuals, in various presentations noticed by them, provides the backdrop and the context for types of interaction between State and society. The future is fashioned by actors noticing certain aspects of events, and these are selected by them out of their memories and expectations, and not by the mere occurrences in recorded history.

Where the State is mired in a feudal and traditional past there is the emergence of a neopaternalistic form of interaction.[16] Pre-existing social formations are replaced by the State for meritocratic principles to advance economic development. The legal–rational framework that emerges encourages a cohesive process of modern state formation. If the process of change results in a splintering of groups with no cohesive source of central power, there emerges a fragmented multi-class state (Kohli 2004).

> Collective action becomes contentious when it is used by people who lack regular access to institutions, who act in the name of new or unaccepted claims, and who behave in ways that fundamentally challenge others or authorities.
> (Tarrow 1998: 3)

The demands for property rights and access to new channels of resource flows by groups that have hitherto been denied access to official avenues of mobilisation and accumulation of wealth can be a potentially disruptive source of lobbying. The manner in which state power acts in legitimising the interaction between State and society is crucial.[17] The view that what the State needed to ensure was the construction of a unified set of legal postulates for development floundered when early attempts at importing legal rules from one society into another had deleterious effects on the development process (Chua 2003). The importance of working within a well-developed body of the law does not need to preclude a healthy respect for the plurality of legal traditions (Glenn 2004).[18] The legal importation of rules from Western societies and polities, in the belief that these were rational and therefore conducive to economic development, has been regarded as consequential of Weberian thinking.[19] The tendency to regard 'rule of law' as a single and universal principle with inadequate recognition of

[16] See Chapter 3 for illustrations of protest and social movements by forest dwellers and other marginal groups.

[17] Khan points to the persistence of patrimonial structures that operate through patron–client relations in states that remain caught up in feudal structures. See Khan (2003).

[18] The nature of political modernities is presented in Migdal (2001) as a combination of state and non-state actors. Principles for legitimate interaction can emerge from within the State, from outside or from a combination of the two.

[19] The foundational position of Roman law in Western legal thinking provides both a well-established entry into the subject and a clear basis for understanding the implications of different systems, such as that between the Roman and common law traditions.

historical or cultural differences between societies, that must be established in both transition and poor economies to facilitate the initiation and/or maintenance of the development process, does not take into account these historical differences that have given rise to very distinctive social and political structures.[20]

> Contentious forms of collective action are different from market relations, lobbying or representative politics, because they bring ordinary people into confrontation with opposition, elites or authorities. Collective actions have power because they challenge power holders, produce solidarities, and have meanings in particular population groups, situations and national cultures. (Tarrow 1998: 4)

The ability of social movements to doggedly confront and sometimes to even radically transform power relations is representative of this historical process. The creation of a federal state structure is one form of dealing with existing group differences and conflicts based on differing historical trajectories and geographical repositories which can work towards remedying both historical and geographical inequities. The tiered system of federalism where sub-national territories have the right to decide the economic and social policies for their constituents permits the existence of identities within the national State that do not have to contend with the other sub-national entities at the national level. This is an interesting policy of containment that can successfully diffuse the large-scale group conflicts.

On the other hand, if the union of federated states is read through a neo-liberal lens then federalism is regarded as a form of political balance and a counter to the centralising tendencies of the State (Weingast 2005). The antidote to a centralising state, which is readily put forth, is decentralisation within a union, with its attributes of devolution of power and finance. The notion that a diffused system of control is more conducive to the advancement of individual freedom and that it can provide an effective basis for economic development within a federation, as opposed to a union, has found many supporters. Additionally, the federal structure of government is deemed to encourage competition, and therefore a shift from a centralised union structure to a more open federal form is seen to be market friendly (Sinha 2005).

Federalism and state power

Federalism as a form of union government creates a strong central state but has a divestment of finances and devolution of administrative and political power to

[20] Weber saw the formal legal system and rational state structure, accompanied by procedures to ensure predictability and calculability, as necessary to ensure modernity in Western Europe. Yet there the importance of society-based forms of rule-making continues to be attractive within the European tradition. See van Seters (2006) for a set of readings on the growing importance of communitarian approaches to the law.

the constituent states/provinces within the national polity. The structure can emerge from a variety of forces and there is no easy one-to-one relationship between historical past or current political ideology that can singularly explain the need for a unionised federal structure. Whether the legal structure of a nation is unionised federation, loosely controlling, or it is a diffused federation tightly administered, the refashioning of State–society relations happens continuously, across national and sub-national spaces. Refashioning may be deliberately directed by many agents but the result is without direction and such changes are unable to sustain a reform process. On the other hand, refashioning State–society relations can be based on mutual adjustments and manipulation of agents rather than through the consensus-building brought about by collective action. The State has an inherent advantage in refashioning relations through manipulation, for as the prime political power it has the authority to aggregate the political aspirations of the individuals.[21] The State also has the power to prevent conflict-oriented adjustments between groups and individuals within. Statesmanship lies in relating power of State to society in such a fashion.

Political statesmanship is similar to the inherent strength of capitalism as an economic aggregation of wealth of individuals. Capitalism or market reform or a new trading order comes into sharp focus as a dominant cause only in contrast to a previous inherently inefficient system, like barter trade or state trading with administrative allocations in distribution at administered prices. The redistribution of power among groups in societies through capitalism vis-à-vis power of State, exercised through bureaucracy and private sector in varying proportions, is central to motivations of individuals in ordering their lives.

Political statesmanship brings together group interests and channels their desires and objectives to a common national interest. This is a consequence of aggregation and is similar to the inherent strength that capitalism gains as an economic aggregation of the wealth of individuals. Capitalism represents a shift in society that gives greater prominence to the market and that results in the creation of a new trading order. Capitalism provides a sharp contrast to a previously inherent system of high-value trade within a mercantilist system and the redistribution of power, among groups in societies through capitalist institutions, such as the market and the firm, that is not exercised through the bureaucracy, and where the private sector provides an alternate route to the direct control of a centralised government. These tectonic shifts in the alignment between State and society create a new topography of social structures and institutions. The new relief maps cast by the rubrics that emerge within these institutions reorient the motivations of individuals and reorder their lives.

[21] The importance of historical movements in shaping the legal system is not regarded as relevant for the future. It is presumed that there is only one path to economic development and that legal systems will converge. See David Kennedy (2003) for a presentation of why historical differences continue to influence not just the present but also future legal developments.

State–society relations and federal arrangements

The nature of relations between the central State and its sub-national constituent parts is determined by historical trajectories that fashion the hierarchies of state and societal power. Developing countries entered the capitalist arena as independent nations because there were strong nationalist forces that had encountered and overcome divisive forces, both from outside and within. This coming together of society and State has played a fundamental role in the fashioning of national identity and has strongly influenced the constitutions and laws that were designed and approved by the independent governments. According to the constitution of the PRC, China is a unitary state and provincial and local authorities must adhere to the rules and decisions taken by the central government, though this occurs in consultation with these provincial and local governments. All provincial governments are local state administrative units and they must accept the unified leadership of the State Central Council and implement the administrative decisions and regulations made by the State Central Council. Where state provincial councils can make local laws these can be nullified by the State Central Council if it conflicts with national laws (Zheng 2006).

On the other hand, the Federal Constitution of Malaysia leaves substantial powers, particularly over land use and natural resource management, to the respective states. In addition, the constitution guarantees certain unique rights and privileges to the eastern Malaysian states of Sabah and Sarawak. The federal Parliament would have jurisdiction to legislate for the states only in those areas which had been explicitly identified by the constitution. The assignment of natural resource management and use to state jurisdiction creates problems for national governments. There has been a suggestion of partnerships between state and national governments. Recent court cases in Malaysia have consistently denied the *locus standi* (the right to sue) of environmental NGOs. In the Bakun Dam litigation, the plaintiffs argued successfully before the High Court that as residents in the affected area, they were directly and adversely affected by the inundation of the land caused by the construction of the dam. The Court of Appeal overturned the judgement of the High Court and ruled that the plaintiffs had suffered no injury, and that even if the word 'life' in Article 5(1) of the Federal Constitution were to include the right to a reasonably healthy and pollution-free environment, such rights may be extinguished in accordance with existing law. Second, the court was of the view that the plaintiffs should not be privileged over the majority of the indigenous group. The court responded that any injury suffered by the plaintiffs was not over and above the injury common to all others and that they were not convinced that the plaintiffs were championing the cause of the other 10,000 natives whose livelihood and customary rights were equally affected by the project. Third, the Court of Appeal felt that the High Court judge failed to consider the public and national interests involved, in particular the interests of justice from the defendants' point of view. Hence, arising from the courts' strict interpretation of *locus standi*, environmental NGOs have had to resort to a host of non-legal measures to bring attention to their cause.

The implications of decentralisation and an increasing devolution within a federal system has become more evident as there is increasing global exposure of domestic production systems to the world economy. The possibility of sub-national units competing with each other to gain comparative advantage to trade on the global market has brought to the fore forms of sub-national competition. The possibility of further capitalist gain through sub-national competition has not just pushed justice and redistribution into the distant background but has kicked it into the shrubbery and the props of the performance.

> [Regional] states in India have always been competing with each other; what has changed in recent times is the nature of competition. In the pre-liberalisation period, the primary mode of regional competition was vertical through the national state; now the primary mode is horizontal competition between the regional states themselves. This horizontal competition is more symmetric as it affects a wider set of states than before and encourages policy diffusion across many states.
>
> (Sinha 2004: 34)

The nature of competition between sub-national states does not only result in greater and more valuable market exchanges, but also reorders and influences the claims to resources and the access to and use of individual rights. The ordering and disordering that occurs when sub-national states, groups and individuals confront, coerce, cooperate and combat with the federal State is at the very origin of shaping State, society, polity and economy. These processes do not operate directly through the space of the market; rather, they redraw the market to suit their particular group interests.

The reading of engagements as being located within the market creates a model where the State is necessarily regarded as an evil so that human beings operate in opposition to the State. The notion that individuals operate despite the restrictions imposed on them with the possibility of the retraction of their privileges by the State does not take into account the fact that the State in turn has to respond to the demands that each individual imposes, so that there is at least a secondary contestation between sub-national regions in relation to fiscal and administrative matters. In addition, the process creates iterative forms, and the manner in which individuals and social groups perceive the State is through their local norms and the deflection of the state processes within this space.

The global sphere of trade and the increasing links between this level of exchange and national, sub-national and local production processes gives rise to an increasing clamour for decentralisation to be introduced as a competition-enhancing mechanism. In the case of Malaysia, the electronics industry in Penang was seen to be excessively influenced by the individual federal state laws that had a strong focus on the redistributive element in favour of the *bumiputera* Malays. It was when the king intervened to overrule state law and bring about a more equitable and productive solution that it permitted strategic state policy to overcome the obstacles to set up a redistributive policy. The growing use of constitutional powers by the king has not consistently been a force for good. In particular, the attempt to reform the judiciary and the government of the thirteen-state Southeast Asian federation has been undermined by charges of wasteful public spending, rising corruption and lawlessness and even has led to a constitutional crisis (Henderson and Phillips 2007).

The limited ability of national constitutions to bring about equitable treatment of sub-national institutions, particularly to permit the growth of non-state institutions, has led to charges of nepotism and corruption by ministers, bureaucrats and even judges. The refashioning of State–society relations to bring the power of capitalism into the national system is not a one-off requirement, but a repeated process. The continuous readjustment of capitalist institutions and the incentives that operate within them makes the job of a regulator no simple or single task; instead, it calls for a larger vision that encompasses both equity and opportunity.

> Liberal policies of States operate in a political–institutional context and are shaped by the historical legacies of institutions, resources and actor's choices. Yet, market reforms trigger new preferences and interests which rival actors interpret and deploy as they struggle with the new policy regime brought on by market reforms. Even as actors struggle with the existing regulatory regime, the reforms redistribute power and economic resources among rival actors. Reforms, moreover, may create new actors who acquire a stake in the results of the struggle. Policy changes brought on by market reforms, thus, transform the existing balance of power, but do so shaped by the preexisting institutional linkages, resources and skills.
>
> (Sinha 2004: 54–5)

The current rage for decentralisation is based on the assumption that there will be additional entitlement, benefit and gains to communities and individuals from such a move away from the central State. The possibility that the State could be an enabling environment that facilitates strategies and actions by benign rule is not entirely derisible.

Is a Leviathan a regulatory state?

Human beings, as individuals and in groups, live, cohabit and coexist by drawing on a set of social norms and legal order that does not correspond to the full legal framework of the State. Individuals and their social groups operate within society by deciphering the legal framework of the State through social norms, which, as customary laws have become embedded in everyday practices. There is the possibility that the resulting interpretations and readings generate versions, even mutations, of the legal order that are partial versions or even irregularities in the totality of the statutes. The resulting variations require the

State to adapt to these local versions or to rule out the resulting forms as unacceptable renditions that are illegal.

State–society interactions determine the form of legal order that operates in the local sphere. The citizen or economic agent is regarded as a rational player who responds to given rules. The manner in which social norms interact with the law gives rise to a *local legal system*. The laws created and approved by the federal government provide the *formal legal system* and the interactions between the local and federal levels generate an *irregular or transitional legal system*.[22] The possibility that the agent is not a rule-taker but an interpreter introduces a new dimension into the analysis.

The *local system* is symptomatic of many pre-modern ways of life adopted by local agrarian or pastoral societies. There was no great central source of power and the principles of reciprocity and morality prevailed. An accepted form of morality was the basis for valuing actions. The rewards and punishments for individual behaviour were meted out to reinforce the notions of morality, which were wholly functional to the benign organisation of the society.[23] In the *local system* there is a voluntary mutuality of interaction among individuals and their groups, where individuals adjust so as to conform to common moral norms and conventions.

This *local system* is also recognised within the local public sphere as a moral system that manifests mutuality of adjustment to another's needs by way of conformity through custom and mores or social conventions. Such mutuality makes personal liberties and rights of bodily freedom, movement, residence, speech, expression, assembly, etc., of the legal system merge into the mutual awareness and adjustment to one another's needs (Geertz 1963).

In the *formal legal system* there is an affirmation of rights of individuals by the State as laid down in its constitution and laws, which thereby gives the State primacy among the social groups among which individuals move. Such primacy gets expressed in the notion of 'rule of law' by the State as the prime identity of the State, whose other identities and embellishments could become secondary in certain situations. The *formal legal system* follows the established position that there is a separation of public and private and that the regulation of personal rights of movement, residence, speech, expression, assembly, etc., by the State becomes subject to interpretation of laws on such rights by courts of justice; the rule of law is left to be determined to a great degree at the discretion of the judges, on what is best in the public interest or interests of justice.

[22] Eggertson (1990) provides the new institutional view of how the State has a comparative advantage in violence as the sole authority in maintaining law and order. It is notable that the authority of the State to represent the interests of society has disappeared from the literature, through the increasing influence of the public choice school that has also influenced the field of law and economics.

[23] The notion of the 'irregular' comes as a response to working across social science disciplines, where historical renditions such as Weberian rational law and technical demands for a predictable, i.e. regular, market have pushed out the messiness of development in all its aspects.

In the *transitional system* observance of the remnants of personal mores and custom and failure to enforce the legal order of the State exist alongside. Enforcement of law is in the hands of those with legal authority and difficult to initiate for the oppressed, poor and weak. Equitable laws are not easy to enact and they are almost impossible to enforce in the face of absolute ownership of property and wealth asserted by many individuals and corporations. An *irregular transitional system* encourages a *fragmented multi-class* state, where ownership and identities contest repeatedly and ferociously.[24]

Changes in *local and transitional systems* towards the *formal legal system* come with growing centralisation of power within the State and its rising dominance over social groups. Feudal relations, binding individuals and groups at the local level, slowly get replaced by direct legal links with the top rungs of political power, mostly through the civil service and judiciary. There is an emergence of new forms of clientelism, as the State with its dominance as a neo-patriarchal figure binds individuals directly to itself. In such a situation the moral order and its associated economy begins to unravel and progressively settle into a legal order of the State. In situations and circumstances where vestiges of moral order remain, these are compacted into icons of extra-legal discretionary state favours or honours bestowed for moral virtues beyond the call of legal duty; to the faithful, the upright (Fennell 2003) and those regarded as good Samaritans.

The rule of law that supports the legitimacy of the State is the key to ensuring the modern legal order and yet is also the very essence of the quotation from Kautilya's *Arthashastra* cited at the beginning of this chapter. The emphasis on the rule of law is only as powerful as the enforcement of rights and duties of individuals and groups by the designated authorities of the State. Inordinate delay in enforcement of law erodes the power of the State and its constitution and laws, which live in enforcement and not on paper. As stressed by Kautilya, the legal system is not there for placing personal liberties and rights on a pedestal, or idolising an individual, but only for impartial enforcement of respect for rights of all (even against the ruler's son). According to him, mores as sacred law and history as custom are to yield to ever-alive human reason or rationality (which is imprisoned once for all into enacted laws of a formal legal system unless rescued by equity) underlying the rule of law, when there is a conflict between them.

The *local system* emphasises reciprocity and mutual recognition among individuals. Such an approach or attitude in no way detracts from the operation of commercial principles in the payment system, like wages and rewarding positions of hierarchy and social status or even measures of market value. What is received in excess of market measure may be viewed as what is to be held in

24 These systems are not merely a historical feature and a social form of the past: they were commonplace in local communities even at the end of the twentieth century. See Strathern (2003) for a heterodox examination of the anthropological 'othering' of societies.

trust for others under moral norms or conventions. In the formal *legal system*, the moral concept of holding wealth in trust may survive despite the dominant legal concept of absolute ostensible private ownership, as the equitable rights of others are what is viewed as held in trust. The centralised exclusive legal approach makes it impossible for anyone to access non-contractual moral equitable rights within the legal system.[25]

The twist by which historical wrongs are dealt with by market-based selection takes away the possibility of group-based equity. The allusion in Hobbes' *Leviathan* to the State as a large and powerful organisation is not about its inherent legal form and nature but its impersonal and cold or unfeeling bureaucratic attributes felt and perceived by the populace.

The irregular/transitional legal system creates a new set of economic, political and social aspirations in individuals and groups (De Soto 2002) where the local community ceases to be a reliable basis to earn income or gain a livelihood within the group. The State becomes, through its patriarchal and patrimonial development policies, the primary provider of resources and livelihood and imposes demands of loyalty and allegiances in return.

The shift from a local system to a formal legal system changes the nature of engagement between State and society. The contractual approach to human interaction takes people away from the reciprocal but hierarchical relations, such as the master and servant or well-wisher and dependent, to that based on contractual and seemingly non-hierarchical interactions (Deakin 2001). The change in regarding individuals as equal and no longer part of a moral order gives way to the central principle that rules are focused on providing rights that give rise to equal treatment rather than being based on responsibilities that preserve notions of equity. The shift involved in organising society away from existing social orders to that around the individual appears to move the focus away from a communal or even associational structure. In nineteenth- and twentieth-century Europe, there were shifts in State–society relations where the relative power of both varied on account of historical events. These changes have been set out as models where different combinations of weak and strong forms of both State and society show the effects on the polity (Jepperson 2002). The replacement of traditional forms of State–society relations by relations of State with new corporatist and collectivist forms of societal organisations within the State is a move away from a moral to a legal framework, providing a new basis for understanding how State and societies interact.

The local system is increasingly edged out, if not replaced, by the introduction of laws and even by the notion of state-administered rule of law. The move from a local legal system to a formal legal system is not a swift or inevitable shift and can result in a confused if not contradictory set of impulses under which many generations have to suffer, and their suffering has become

[25] People unable to exit the transitional/irregular legal system are caught in a vicious grip and use extreme language such as the law being an arena of the ever ongoing fight between good and evil

synonymous with today's transitional economies. There is the possibility that an introduction of rules could be undertaken through a bottom-up process, so that the local meanings and norms are not jettisoned nor catapulted out of the modern but retain their links to the growing levers of capitalism, but it is seldom examined by the distant state rulers. The prevailing system of remedying historical injustices appears to be to regard them as equal to market-based income differences, recently termed as a method of examining 'historical inequality through a form of equivalence' (Mongia 2007); injustices are not tackled by welfare or charity or by framing equitable local laws for a transition phase lasting for generations. The legitimation of an oppressive legal system and society by a dictatorial and controlling state can give rise to a rewriting of history that is more suited to the demands of global capitalism.

Legal systems, State–society relations and capitalist crises

The whole of society, as a support or insurance system for any individual or group in society, is a feature of the moral system and not of the legal system. The temporary shift to a *local legal system* in order to benefit clients who operate as immoral actors in the capitalist legal system and the manner in which these shifts are orchestrated to further the interests of these actors to acquire capital assets is a increasing cause for societal reprimand.

The existence of hierarchies in both society and economy can be remedied by a removal of the vertical axis of hierarchy for the analysis of State–society relations. Its ready replacement by the seeming flatness of the marketplace wiped clean any imprint of social groups in the economic sphere. This erasure of group identity from the market is a very clever sleight of hand that has been achieved by the proponents of capitalist enterprise. Denying access to the strength of the collective and presenting the market as the only reality based on profit, free trade and fair exchange belies the huge inequities that social groups have had to face on account of obstacles to access, acceptability and quality of provision of goods and services. The maintenance of the fiction that the market has effectively removed all traces of group-based activity is played out against the local public, but such a lie is closely guarded within the private domain of capitalist enterprises.

The mass production of cheap goods is based on strictly maintained laws of cost-cutting and the continual search for cheaper inputs. The growing prominence of the selfish individual, who can permanently disregard others in acts of exchange and consumption, tears asunder notions of communal use. It is the ability to commodify goods that cuts, even cauterises, the links between members of a group. The notion of rivalry and excludability that have come to be the signifiers of a private good have made collective and reciprocal behaviour appear alien, if not backward, in the modern marketplace.

Federalism provides a hierarchy of location that has the ability to remedy hierarchies of social and economic inequalities by reallocating power and finance to sub-national and local administration. This system of state power is the alternative to the de-linking between economic activity and distribution that is achieved by capitalist processes, with simultaneous disconnect of communal notions of morality, allowing for consumption devoid of any guilt or concern for the consequences to the group. Federalism and devolution permit local groups and sub-national polities to revoke the trajectory of development that removes the power of group commendation or opprobrium on private patterns of usage and to chart out pathways to regain control of the process of economic development.

The current trend to shift power from the central government to and within a federal system, to devolve power to sub-national and local levels, could be the recipe for a more responsive and responsible form of government. Fiscal, administrative and managerial decentralisation has implications for the legal system though the process of devolution is often instigated by the legislature. How the shift from a central government to sub-national levels affects societal groups and the State in the schema given in Figure 3.1 in the previous chapter is set out in Figure 4.1.

The dotted arrow going from the *central* to *sub-national authority* indicates devolution of power, the shifting of power away from the centre, thus making opportunities for the local community. The transferring of legal, administrative and financial powers and greater participation of the local community makes itself felt in a number of ways. The dark arrow from *sub-national* to *national authority* depicts the strong fiscal and political demands made on the federal government by the sub-national administration(s).

The community regards the sub-national government as less powerful than the national one in effecting legal change, and hence the arrow from *claims* to *national authority* is in bold while the arrow from *claims* to *sub-national authority* is represented by a dashed line. The community also looks to the market to gain access to goods and services but is restricted by local hierarchies, hence the arrow from *community* to *market* is dotted. The sub-national government has the greater ability to influence market prices and outcomes, and this connection is represented by a dark arrow from *sub-national authority* to *market* while the lesser impact of federal law on local and sub-national markets is indicated by a dotted line arrow connecting *national authority* to *market*. The market at the sub-national level is regarded as a site for exchange rather than a mechanism for social justice so the interaction between *market* and *community* is indicated by a pair of opposite dotted-line arrows.

Local social norms permeate local spaces and locals perceive reality through the subjective lens of these norms. Where there is distributional inequality in such spaces there is a demand for remedy. In such situations, local people take the view that market valuation should be the favoured method for making demands to the State, which would result in the creation of a welfare-based system of social support and subsidy. Where the established practice in the local sphere is to make collective claims the community would take the path of self-determination. The ellipses representing *self-determination* and *welfare* are now located in the left and right triangles of the expanded diamond framework and are identified with legal and market approaches respectively.

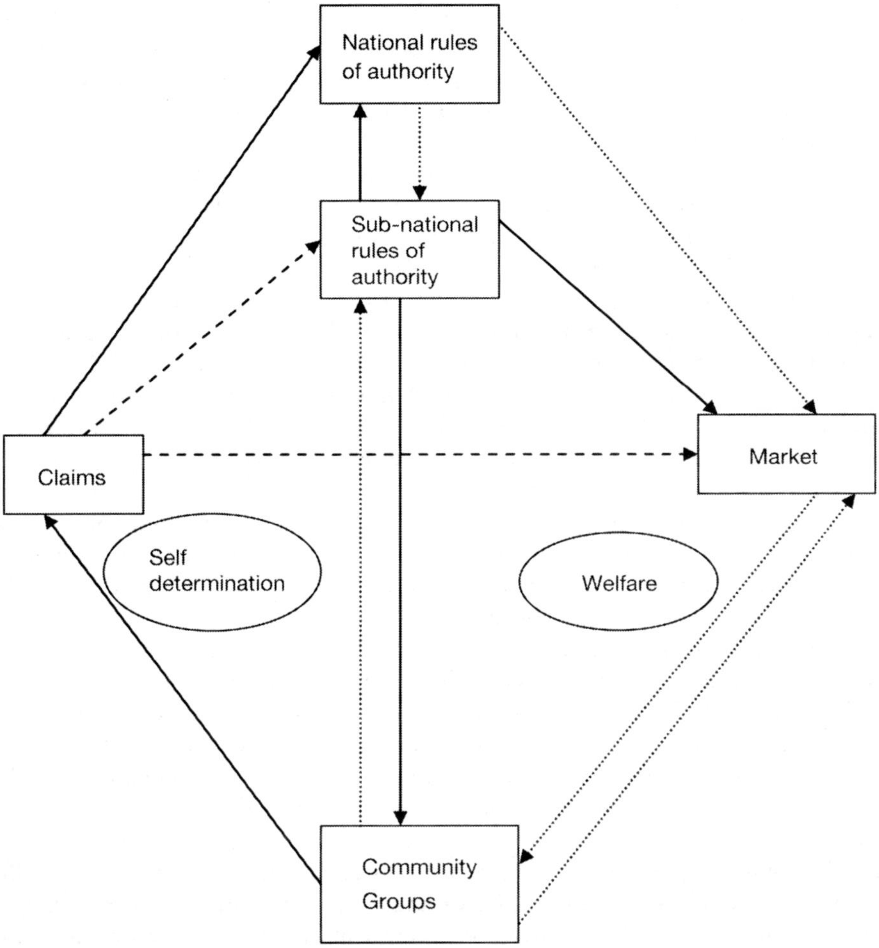

Figure 4.1 The effect of the shift from central government to sub-national

A world characterised by individualised consumption oblivious of the impact on the human and natural environment is the accepted face of capitalism. The characteristics of perfect competition and free trade are regarded as sufficient to ensure economic development. These criteria are highly vulnerable in the presence of the class of problems brought on by asymmetric information.[26] For instance, where the purchaser has more information than the provider of goods and services, the result is the withholding of information and non-declaration of

[26] The non-contractual moral right to hold property was inherent in the notion of trusteeship that still holds a central place in the creation of charities. Associated notions are those of stewardship that were commonplace in early modern societies – interestingly, these have returned in the literature on environmental sustainability but still struggle to get a foothold in neoclassical economics traditions.

relevant evidence, known technically as the problem of adverse selection. In the insurance market or the financial services market, where risk is purchased by companies or loans are provided against mortgages involving similar risk, buyers of services tend to withhold information – what has become widely termed as the moral hazard problem. Writers in the mainstream economic literature have taken to task financial analysts who only warn against moral hazard but who still argue that the paying out of monies indirectly from public revenues, for keeping companies such as LCTM alive, as was done in 1998, or keeping Northern Rock afloat, as was done in September 2007, is appropriate economic policy. The view of the analysts seems to be that unless there is contagion of massive asset devaluation, there should be no punitive action against financial companies that buy risky mortgage instruments (Summer 2007).[27] The reprimands of economic analysts are that the increase of risk in the financial and mortgage markets allows for greater gains as well as losses. Bailing out losers encourages the tendency to take risks which are bound to result in loss which some third parties, like the public, are made to bear.

A different view of capitalist markets begins to emerge when the market concerned is no longer that of private goods but one that generates services. Production in the service sector has traditionally been regarded as an anomaly in the economic literature. The literature represents service provision as an economic conundrum on account of the large indivisibilities of production that make it difficult to obtain an economically meaningful price (where marginal cost equals marginal return) for each unit of service consumed. Coase highlighted the difficulty of pricing of the radio frequency bands, in that the sale of a band width for a broadcast raises questions regarding ownership and the right to use, as well as cost of band width of various frequencies. The notion that 'the air is free' but that airwaves can be priced raises the possibility of public goods having different use value for different consumers, and therefore a difficulty arises in assigning a single price for their use or consumption. It remains no longer a simple matter of ensuring that supply meets demand at an equilibrium price, for there are now multiple prices based on differing notions of use and possibly a range of suppliers for final consumption.[28]

Provision and monitoring of services by State and regulators

The State is the central power that directs the path of industrialisation and can even operate as a super-firm in the provision of goods and services. The policies of the State are difficult to construct and even harder to implement, and the

27 See Arrow (1959) for a review of individual behaviour under conditions of asymmetric information.

28 A conversation with Professor Bhaskar Ramamurthi, an electrical engineer at IIT Madras and a leading researcher in telecommunication technologies, established growing irrelevance of a single price of production in the case of new telecommunications innovations, and how what was necessary was to be able to ensure that different communities had the financial wherewithal to make discrete payments.

services are not always provided in a non-discriminatory manner; often the poor end up subsidising the rich. Individuals in a society obtain goods and services by operating within a formal legal framework through contracts and prices regulated by market demand. Law is viewed only as a way of enabling internal regulation by players in the market to ensure that the flow of commodities is not disrupted.

Services have been treated as less amenable to market rules than goods, because of the technological, financial and social lumpiness that is characteristic of the production of services, ranging from utilities through to education and health, which creates monopoly conditions of production. The established solution for the problem of monopoly production in the post-war years was to award the production of such services to a national (state-owned) corporation to ensure fair prices and maximal access.[29]

The more recent approach has been to make service provision more amenable to the logic of the market by permitting private providers to operate under the supervisory eye of state regulators, who ensure fair competition and the absence of cartels. The role of the regulator was envisaged as having less to do with the Walrasian auctioneer and as having more in common with a judicial review bench (Cole 1999). The regulatory function was brought in to introduce an element of fairness in production conditions so as to reduce the injustice against consumers.

The institution of regulators can work to direct attention to the need to reduce the imbalance in market power, and also raises questions about how market inequality might be reduced with regard to provision of a service. What is less often made sense of is that regulation as an institution can also provide the means to track the economic nature of interaction between production and consumption of services, thereby making them transparent. For instance, when it is thought that investment in railway infrastructure imposes huge costs on private investors, then regulators become indispensable in order to bring in economic formulas that generate fair profits rather than arbitrary prices in the face of a huge consumer demand.[30]

The appointment of regulators through a judicial system rather than the market also emphasises the entitlement aspect of social life. The importance of local administration in the provision of services to the poor and marginalised has emerged as an important concern among international institutions[31] and yet this does not need to be achieved by privatisation but by regulatory frameworks that emphasise the centrality of an equitable provision of 'public goods' at the heart of social policy. Where there are groups which have experienced exclusion

29 See Prosser (1997) on universal access and how the principle of fairness inherent in universal access had been upheld in courts in the nineteenth century in Scotland.

30 The regulatory authorities in the United Kingdom in the 1990s saw a growing demand for additional rules to ensure the smooth functioning of the market. See Vogel (1996) for a review of the role of additional rules in making new markets.

31 See the World Development Report for 2003 (World Bank 2003) for a survey of ensuring provision of services to the poor.

from the market, and which are denied their collective claims (see Figure 3.1), an expanded rubric that permits us to analyse various levels of government can identify the problems of a national legislation that encountered resistance at the sub-national level due to considerable heterogeneity in social groups (see Figure 4.1). It is possible that an overarching legislation might not be sufficient for interpreting specificities, as in the case of provision of utilities such as electricity and water; infrastructure – both hard, such as transport, housing, telecommunications and the internet, and soft, such as education and health. The particular importance of an expanded rubric helps to understand how law and its regulators have a directional as well as monitoring role in ascertaining whether the specificities of the local situation require greater autonomy of local administration or more financial and legal support to the local community desirous of access to infrastructure and services. This is brought out in relation to the scramble that disadvantaged groups have to make in both urban and rural local spheres to gain access to hard and soft infrastructure.

Services and serving: making visible the link between production and distribution

From poorhouses to housing for the poor

The process and progress of industrialisation brings to the fore acute conflicts between the objectives of the capitalists and the conditions of work and life of labour. The need for a regular and large labour supply to work the new machines drew an aspiring workforce to the city. The amassing of industrial wealth in existing cities generated a demand for new and better houses for the rich, and a gentrification of the city followed. The civic amenities of roads, sanitation and water that were laid down to support this process did not automatically extend to all the denizens of the city. This is part of the twentieth-century model of industrialisation going back to the growth models of the 1950s, epitomised by the Lewis model of growth with unlimited supplies of labour.

The clash between the capitalists and the poor has a historical legacy. The city of London faced deteriorating housing conditions for the poor accompanied by a great property swell in the 1870s (Offer 1992: 231). Despite the gains of industrialisation, the conditions of the poor had not improved significantly during the nineteenth century.[32] It was the municipal corporation that was the foremost actor in the provision of physical infrastructure, building great aqueducts, broad thoroughfares, libraries and university colleges. During the property boom of the 1870s there was a squeezing of the lower classes to the very bottom of the housing market, and in 1876 there was a demonstration to Westminster, where 'the destitute women of Poplar, themselves stood up and pleaded for their sisters and brothers in despair. All told the same tale of want

[32] See J. Williamson (1991) on inequality during the nineteenth century.

of work, heart-rending poverty, miserable homes, and starving children' (Offer 1992: 251).

The preponderance of the municipal corporation was viewed by the socialists as the first stage to 'municipal socialism', and Fabians such as George Bernard Shaw and Sidney Webb accordingly welcomed the transfer of tenure administration (in residential places) from the private owner, the 'house-capitalists', to the municipal authorities. The pattern of industrialisation in Mumbai, India, displays a historical trajectory that shows considerable similarity to that witnessed in nineteenth-century London.[33]

The older tenements of the poor were termed the 'chawls', consisting mainly of semi-permanent structures,[34] both authorised and unauthorised, constructed by factory owners and land owners for low-income group workers between 1920 and 1956. Subsequently, the port authorities and a few other public sector units began renting out similar tenements to their workers.[35] While the chawls were originally built for single male migrants to the city, they later become family dwellings. The quality of the structures began to deteriorate by the 1970s and this has been linked to the rent freezes imposed under the Rent Control Act, which made the construction of new chawls an unprofitable option.[36] The inadequacy of rents to meet investment requirements for the maintenance of chawls and the possibility of mixed use has resulted in the severe dilapidation of many chawls, making them unsafe for living.

The limited ability of industrialisation to provide formal employment to the migrants to the city has resulted in the growth of a large informal sector. The newer exegesis of industrialisation, the self-employed and the unregistered sector, has resulted in a growing number of informal settlements built by migrant communities that continued to come to the industrial region from the rural hinterland of Mumbai[37] and from more distant poor regions of the country. The latest group of residents at the bottom of the housing stock became pavement dwellers in shanties built on footpaths alongside roads, as

33 See Patel and Thorner (1995) for a collection of articles on the historical development of society and economy in the city of Bombay (renamed Mumbai at the end of the 1990s).

34 Chawls are one-room tenements with small cooking spaces within each room and shared common sanitation areas, usually located on each floor at the end of a long corridor of rooms.

35 Study by Neelima Risbud (2003) undertaken as a part of the study of "Understanding Slums: Case Studies for The Global Reports on Human Settlements".

36 See Basu (2006) on the perverse impact of rent control acts on Indian cities.

37 The growing share of the informal sector in relation to employment and production has been a feature of most developing countries over the last half-century. This has been the subject of considerable work since the International Labour Organisation started a research agenda on migration based on the now classic ethnographic work of Professor Keith Hart (1971). The particularity of the migration that is interesting in relation to forms of inequity is that the informal sector continues to be treated as a marginal group even as its size approaches half that of the urban population. See Mitlin and Satterwaite (2002) on the obstacles faced by squatter citizens.

pavements. The living conditions of the pavement dwellers were worse than those of the slum and chawl residents, since they were not eligible for dwelling improvement schemes and often faced harassment and demolition of their shanties. A survey in Mumbai in 1985 revealed there were 125,000 pavement dwellers.[38]

The Mumbai municipal corporation did not regard the migrants as having rights to any of the city's resources, and the policy of the urban authorities was to remove the illegal settlements. Under the Slum Rehabilitation Scheme initiated by local municipal government in the 1990s, the municipality provided a scheme to build residential units for slum dwellers if they relocated from valuable real-estate land along the railway lines criss-crossing the city in a north–south direction. The intention was to ensure that the slum dwellers would offer the estate developers either the right to develop a proportion of the slum land for sale to others by them or a similar right on land to be developed in another part of the city. Such schemes have not come to much as yet since political interference and private real-estate developers have found it difficult to create, obtain and monitor contracts.[39]

The Malaysian government policy has been to maintain, and indeed improve, racial unity. This approach has been based on notions of preferential treatment of racial groups to correct historical socio-economic imbalances as well as on outward pronouncements that its policy firmly supports racial integration. In the housing sector this has led to policies of settling communities. While the strategy of the NEP was developed to prevent inter-ethnic strife, this strategy of preferential treatment has been held responsible for the continued existence of ethnic neighbourhoods and business practices.[40] The Malaysian development experience is evidence of the importance of addressing matters of horizontal inequality (see Figure 3.1) using the principle of affirmative action; yet an inadequate understanding of a single national law can generate unexpected though not unwarranted protests among sub-national administrations where there is a preponderance of minority groups. In the case of the poor and unemployed sectors of societies, the local governments and administrations are faced by increasing protests against a policy that is no longer viewed as ensuring ethnic harmony but where there is the breeding of hatred and violence.[41] The pressure on municipalities to control inter-ethnic tensions mounts as the lack of employment and education sets off a spiral of local violence. The challenge faced by the Malaysian State on how to evaluate the decades of NEP that has been the hallmark of Malaysian politics is still unmet and has resulted in a set of domestic social policies that have not ensured better State–society relations. The context of Malaysia's financial troubles since the late 1990s has

[38] Survey in 1985 by Nirmala Niketan for the College of Social Work and the Society for the Protection of Area Resource Centres (SPARC), both Mumbai-based institutions.

[39] See Appadurai (2002) on the possibilities provided by new State–society engagements of deep governmentality.

[40] See Gomez and Jomo (1997) on the opportunities and obstacles that emerge from a political process that has used patronage to ensure domestic profits.

triggered a decade of economic uncertainty and worsening interracial relations. A social housing policy to address inequity through a return to welfare-based policies might finally balance the ethnic-based claims approach that has been adopted by the Malaysian government. New initiatives that promote greater inter-ethnic interaction, within the framework of a government-sponsored resettlement programme in both rural and urban areas of high unemployment and deep poverty, could shift the development trajectory away from ineffectiveness with regard to the very primary and critical goal of racial harmony.[42]

The Chinese government has had the greatest challenge with regard to addressing the housing needs of rapidly growing migrant population when the economic reforms of the 1980s led to a move away from a centralised unitary model towards a more decentralised model of resource allocation and state responsibility. The rural household system has changed radically, with the dismantling of the iconic notion of the commune and the shift to a framework of production and employment where the State drew up contracts with individual households. The trend towards district and city-level decentralisation that was introduced in the late 1990s has shifted the levers of power to county and municipality with a rise of a contractual relationship between State and society.[43] The provincial State has been confronted by large waves of rural farmers seeking new lives and livelihoods in China in cities such as Beijing and Shanghai, which have seen millions of migrants who have urgent urban housing needs that are met inadequately by renting out single rooms in rundown apartment blocks within the poorest areas of the city. The restrictions imposed by the *hukou* (registration) system on migrants prevent them from being accepted as permanent denizens of the city and excludes them from the social services, housing, health and education provided by the municipal authorities.[44]

The municipal authorities in Beijing and Shanghai are responding to the challenge of migration that has accompanied their economic reform policies by looking to reorganise the provision of housing, with a particular focus on devising a system of low-cost social housing for urban low-income households.[45] The possibility that China will also face the turning point of being a predominantly urban society by the mid-twenty-first century presents a challenge of the highest order that will stretch resources of municipal authorities across China's prosperous coastal provinces.

41 The agitations of poor Tamil communities in the states of Penang and Sabah have based their grievances on their lower economic status in terms of income and education compared to local Malay (*bumiputera*) neighbours.

42 Jesudasan (1989) provides a useful survey of the impact of the ethnically constructed NEP-emphasised occupational segregation in Malaysia in the decades that followed.

43 See Tang and Parish (1996) for a commentary on the formation of a social contract in urban China under economic reform.

44 The current difficulties of the *hukou* system are set out comprehensively in Zhao and Li (2006).

45 The challenges of re-zoning and regenerating Chinese cities are presented in Zhang and Fang 2003.

rovision of housing goes to the very core of equitable development. The the migrant population is a physical measure of capital gains; they carry hemselves the potential of cheaper/better techniques and new products to further the process of capital accumulation.[46] The need for housing has been viewed as a social headache by municipal authorities since the 1970s, and yet a different rubric that sees housing as a social responsibility could turn housing solutions into the magic formula that generates local inclusive solutions.

The public–private interactions in the field of social housing expose the fundamental flaws that continue to vitiate attempts to increase the claims of migrants on the local State, notwithstanding the language of contracts and the market. The state regulators and private real-estate companies appear to evade the social obligations by pointing to the financial risks of working with the marginalised and excluded while they silently eye the huge profits that emerge from re-zoning the land of the chawl, shanty house or slum. Consequently, the public spotlight has not moved to designing mechanisms for ensuring the fair sale of houses, or rent and tenure administration by municipalities, state housing boards and county councils. They have continued to make the case for keeping out the demand for the *universal good* in social housing, while resisting attempts to bring in far more sweeping regulatory changes that would ensure competition within the private sector.[47]

Additionally, competition between the State and the private sector is more likely when there is ready recognition of the strength and ability of each sector. In particular, the established legitimacy of municipal delivery allows for a relatively smooth negotiation between the two sectors, municipal and private. Yet what must remain at the foremost concern of both state and societal organisations operating within the field of social housing is that the need for housing requires public action through collective and community initiatives, even social movements.

From education as human capital to educating capital

The central pillar of the model of 'education as human capital' is the assumption that there is a market for education that permits an individual to acquire human capital through investment in education. The model views education as an economic product that provides a comparative advantage in the labour market, ensuring the bearer of such human capital superior forms of employment. Even within advanced capitalist countries it has been difficult to ensure the provision of quality education for all, after two hundred years of the capitalist form of economic development. This led to the new forms of provision such as the introduction of public–private partnerships (PPPs) in education in Western Europe and the United States in the 1990s. In the United States, a

46 See De Soto (2000) for a powerful commentary on the power of the informal sector in the city

47 See Fennell (2007a) for a commentary on the need for soft forms of regulation.

'parent-spearheaded movement' resulted in development of the charter school model. It entailed contracting a school from the State for management by the parents in the community. It imposed a new form of accountability (on the community of parents) for quality of education in local schools. Charter schools began to emerge in 1991 and by the mid-1990s numerous states favoured the idea. The movement injected new life and content into teaching and learning within local communities, and the charter emphasised community-level entrepreneurship and accountability for quality (Hoxby 2003).

The difficulties of providing education for the underprivileged sectors of society is far more challenging in countries that are undergoing major structural transformation and where the State still has to ensure mass education while meeting the challenges of macroeconomic management (Fennell 2008a). The education of children of migrant workers in China is one such daunting challenge. With the easing of restrictions on internal travel and movement of people, Chinese cities faced a wave of new migrants, creating need for urban planning, security and social integration. One of the greatest challenges was equitable education for children of newcomers. Until 1998, the capital city did not allow public (state) schools to admit non-residents at all. Since then, migrant children have been permitted to enter Beijing's public school system (see Sun 2007 and Murphy 2007). Around two-thirds of them, in fact, attend public schools. However, many of these schools charge a hefty extra fee to enrol migrants, usually \$1000–\$3000, which is beyond the means of many migrant families and an intolerably heavy financial burden on others. Although government declared illegal the charging of extra fees for migrant children, the practice continues. Already stretched for resources, most schools simply do not have the budget or capacity to accommodate the extra migrants without supplementary fees.

The failure of government to provide quality education of an acceptable level and linked to the incomes of the parents has been identified as a major reason for the falling numbers of children in the schools in the state education sector in India (De and Dreze 1999). This inability of the state education system to retain children in schools has also been identified as a major reason for parental preference for private schools, even among the poorest sections, as well as the superior performance of children in the private schools operating even in low-income areas and poor communities (Kingdon and Muzzamil 2003). The inadequate and unravelling state education system has been increasingly supplanted by private, often unrecognised, schools that charge from \$10 to \$25 as fees from rural parents (see Fennell 2007b).

In Malaysia, the provision of education is made by the State, with education imparted through the medium of English and Bahasa Malaysia, the national language of the country. The formulation of education policy is in careful keeping with the stated objectives of the NEP. The need to ensure inter-ethnic calm has placed ethnic demands at the forefront of national policymaking across the development agenda. In the case of education, ethnic claims are met through the private provision of Tamil and Chinese language schools to cater to the particular linguistic needs of ethnic minorities.[48] The foundations of Malaysian educational policy continue to be closely aligned to the claims-based approach set out by the NEP, yet it has not moved much closer to its primary objective of ensuring ethnic stability.[49] The formulation of a national education policy that does not take into account the prevailing social norms within communities, risks returning to a narrow market-based logic among minority groups who feel left out of the claims-based process. It needs a three-way approach that brings into play welfare, claims and market-based instruments to ensure that education provision permits capital to enrich the full range of communities and ensure that human capital can be channelled into national wealth.

On society and State

The seeds of modern economic development that sprouted in Europe were based on the need to take risks. The legal enforcement of mercantile contracts required a new community – lawyers, judges and arbitrators – to permit reparations of loss arising from unavoidable risks, yet these professional classes have increasingly become part of the power elite and have come to regard the development process as requiring continuous refinement within an increasingly technocratic rubric. The economic and social structures of both industrial countries and late developers have been denounced for excessive dominance of central government ownership of national institutions, yet the replacement of a strong centre by an increasingly decentralised system of sub-national and local governments has not ensured that minorities and marginalised groups have access to the tools of wealth creation. Access to institutions at the sub-national and national levels and the option of drawing on both the market and the law have not been addressed adequately; rather, the market and law are used as simple, if not naïve, alternatives.

The difficulty of balancing national and local interests is particularly noticeable in the growth of wealthy commercial centres that have marked twentieth-century capitalism. This is accompanied by a rise in the share of wealth attributable to debtors and creditors which requires trust. However, trust is not a general feature in society but a characteristic that requires careful tending in the market. Yet people are not averse to working with social norms or to respond to calls for equity or reciprocity.

> People do not refuse to accept change even after the trauma of it. They want the change to enhance their inborn and cultural capacities. Leave them free to change the rules and the contents of change according to their own culturally defined ethics and aspirations. They were used to having someone who could respond to somebody else's suffering, finding

[48] See Gomez (2004) on the challenges to equity imposed by an ethnically based economic policy with the recent decades of economic reform.

[49] See Jomo (1999) on the consequences of the NEP for occupational segregation and educational achievements.

> comforting responses in the traditions of solidarity: the culture of gifts, hospitality and reciprocity which linked people together.
>
> Rehnema and Bawtree (1997: 378–93)

Communities are repositories of knowledge but such social groups are economically dependent on trading and commercial networks for the sale of their knowledge (Rosenberg and Birdzell 1986: 139–40). Some have risen to become economic powers which have been aided by their political rulers and have enjoyed their protection. The attraction of power and riches has spurred them on to accumulate riches using new rules and manipulation of the rubric of development. The acquiring of riches, pleasures of expropriation and exercising power of ruling over others has led to human creativity. It has also led to the State and society interacting in wealth creation and controlling power over others, and that has replaced the norms of reciprocity and equity. It is this contradiction that we currently face in the early decades of capitalism in the twenty-first century.

The shift of focus from groups to society, from local to central, does not reduce the role of government but increases its responsibility. Formal rules and legal systems within the national economy can be refashioned to look further than the formal and obvious, i.e. to current market concerns of wealth generation away from expropriation of wealth of State and the weak poor labour. What is more demanding, is to recognise the excluding tendency of capitalism, the exploitation that comes with its fruits being kept within the system of the privileged. This sensitivity to the damaging aspects of capitalism can only be acquired by looking at the counter-tendencies that manifest themselves in sub-national and local spaces. The process of working with and at the local level, of acquiring the willingness to redistribute, suits not only those who gain less, but also those who either remain within or are pushed out of the national economic sphere. Exclusive capitalism adds rapidly to their numbers. The importance of services is that they facilitate a focus on radical policies, such as in housing and education, that make capitalism more palatable, through the power of such services to neutralise inequalities and rework vertical hierarchies.

5 The interface between the global and the national

The ancient tree that towers above the river bank
The mighty king who rules over the kingdom
Both have lives that are limited
While he who toils, ploughing and watering the land
Leads a life that is beyond compare

All other lives are marred

(Avvaiyar 2008: 12)

The nation state sits at the helm of rule-making, yet it is not the rulings of the king that create an abundant life, as the above extract from Avvaiyar, a thirteenth-century wise woman and seer who lived during the Chola era in southern India, indicates. Wealth emerges from the work of the denizens of a state and it is consequent on their effort and enterprise. The law provides an umbrella for these actions, as the tree provides shade on the riverbank. At the core of a moral and just world is located the worker, and it is the long hours worked by the toiling farmer that make the munificence of the nation. These didactic words of Avvaiyar have been taught to many generations of children in Tamil Nadu, and are popular in school textbooks even today. Yet this moral world, within which work is valorised, is very far removed from the global market for trade, where cheap labour and an amoral approach to exchange drive the accumulation of riches. The power of the global drive for resources and commodities dominates international agendas, and from the vantage point of global trade, it is only the nation symbol of the king (and the tree) that can be seen, while the toiling labour disappears from view.

National agendas and the global gaze

International institutions, particularly the international financial institutions (IFIs), have adopted a neoclassical rubric to economic development and have consequently directed their attention to the flows of trade in international markets.[1] The low level of trade and the seemingly associated low growth rates of

[1] Between 1950 and 1980, 90 per cent of world trade took place between developed countries (Singh 1989) and this represented the golden age of capitalism.

developing countries have led IFIs to surmise that it is the inefficient nature of government actions associated with nepotistic rather than market (or Weber's meritocractic) principles that have denied these countries the fruits of economic development. The failure of national governments in the developing world pronounced by the IFIs in the 1970s has been followed by a growing interest in these international quarters to find an alternative drive to the nation state, to drive the process of economic development. The inability of local and sub-national governments to provide services to the communities that reside in their administrative regions has become justification for bringing in private forms of supply (World Bank 1996). The ineffectiveness of decentralisation of powers and the question of whether further devolution of power can continue to be viable has led to calls for a replacement of the State by the private sector (Bardhan and Mookherjee 1999). While decentralised supply was initially propounded as the key to equitable distribution at the bottom of the social ladder, it is often derided as a poor and inferior alternative to market-driven private initiatives (World Bank 2005). If there is a secret code to ensure development, then it is the learning of the sequence of how moving between the public and the private sector spells out new ways of delivering services and provides economic opportunities to those who are at the bottom of the societal ladder.

Understanding the nature of public and private provision to the under-privileged and disadvantaged requires an examination of how the nation state engages both within and outside the national economy. While the push within the national economy has been to devolve administrative and financial powers to sub-national and district authorities, thinking about these matters at the national level has also been influenced considerably by the international arena (Rose-Ackerman 1995). There is a preponderance of international policy guidelines that are based on the premise that sub-national and local authorities have greater ability to provide goods and services for the poorest and most destitute (World Bank 2006; DFID 2006). There are other international players who still openly express disquiet about the holding back of economic development by inefficient decentralised supply by state enterprises or the private supply of commodities and services (World Economic Forum 2007). Decentralisation is seen as a way to ensure a greater presence of the private sector and thereby enhance wealth creation in the national economy.

The international financial agencies appear to have forgotten the first lectures on development economics. They have not learnt the lesson that it is the State that provides a contour map of development that make possible any calculations about marginal returns (Khan 1996). Even very clever students who do not need any teacher need to know that constructing development within a country is different from trade between nations.[2] For instance, it is imperative to recall

[2] The context within which development was discussed by both the early development economists, see Nurkse (1953), and also in the older and more general sphere of economic growth, see Smith (1976 [1776]), is one which is guided by national government, and what was under review was the type of policies that should be followed in relation to savings/investment and production/trade.

that liberalisation, or opening up the economy to the international market, is not the same as expanding the market to economically, socially and politically disenfranchised sectors of the domestic population. There is no simple scale transformation that slides seamlessly between the international and the local sphere, where national production is located, and consequently the creation of a global value chain for commodities does not fall into place without concerted effort. It requires a refashioning of State–society relations within a nation and also demands reworking international capital flows by transnational companies. It is the national government that provides the directives for such a reorganisation and facilitates such reorientation of national economic production.[3]

The nation state and the fashioning of economic and social rules

The need felt in newly independent nations was to create a domestic environment that would allow their people to heal the wounds of colonisation and to create a set of norms in returning to a way of life that allowed them the restoration of their dignity (Chatterjee 1993). It was not only that a colonial law and government had been imposed on them, but also that fragmented local communities had been encouraged to operate within a racialised context that had been superimposed upon the existing and sometimes reconfigured hierarchies of caste and tribal identities (Béteille 1991; Bates 2005). The creation of wealth by national governments was a powerful lever for shifting the national identity from one of an 'oppressed subject state' to one of a dynamic independent economy. The nation state was the harbinger of the possibility of 'independent economy' and its role stood validated by its citizens and by international agencies (Jolly *et al.* 2004). In many countries, the opportunities for growth that were created within the new State were not made openly available to all, but were allocated to pre-selected organisations of the nature of firms. The right of the State to 'select winners' that has been so much acclaimed in the case of East Asia (Amsden 1989) was a nascent idea in the national plans of newly independent economies. The methods and instruments that were to be used for this purpose might have been poorly and ill devised, yet this does not detract from the universality of directed development that is evidenced in national plan documents produced by these countries. The inadequate set of economic instruments were not out of line; instead, they were based on the very instruments created by the colonial masters, such as the marketing boards in Kenya (Bates 1986). The selection of firms by administrative favour was undertaken to ensure that the low savings rate and purchasing power of the national populace did not become a barrier to expanding the scale of production.[4]

3 In 1998, Andre Gunder Frank published *Re-Orient*, in which he enjoined developing countries' governments to cease to regard Western models as the appropriate rubric on which to design their economies (Frank 1998).

4 Nurkse (1953) had pointed out that the low savings of low-income countries implied that there would be inadequate private savings. This made it necessary to bring in government investment, which keeps risks down by selecting winners from the private sector to whom the government distributes investment funds through financial or administrative institutions.

The selection of private firms was based on their past financial ability, a key feature in ensuring survival. The financial strength and staying power of firms was regarded as critical for entry into new markets. These were large players with diversified product portfolios, and it was this acumen that was recognised and valued by national governments and used as an integral part of the national industrial policies they devised (Chang 1994; Amsden 2001). This mode of thinking adopted by national governments is not inimical to promoting cost minimisation, for it was the financial fortitude of the firm that ensured dependable future production. Administered licences and contracts were preferred to market selection of a weak private firm that could undermine national growth (Price 1967). The early decades of national planning were guided by these principles, and the contribution of the private sector was sketched out to comply with national concerns regarding national unity and employment (Jolly 2005). This central concern with the economic progress of newly independent nations was also evident in the international order and the institutions that emerged after the Second World War.

The post-war consensus and the rise of the United Nations

The international order witnessed the creation of institutions such as the United Nations in a new post-war environment in which new states were trying to develop. The United Nations (UN) was founded on the principle of state sovereignty, with numerous UN organisations providing national governments with a forum where they could meet and discuss matters as equal partners. The UN conventions were drawn up to ensure the social, economic and political rights of individuals living in independent nations, which had embarked on the path of economic development (Jolly 2005). The frameworks of the UN and its organisations have been couched in the language of international law, and these laws are to guide nations in maintaining their due responsibility to their citizens and to prevent any unintended imposition of obstacles by other countries, or the international community of nations, in their path of development.[5]

The charter of the United Nations is a key component in present-day international law and its principles are meant to guide the community of states towards development. The sources of international law range from agreements, treaties and conventions to international custom and judicial systems which go to providing a 'common legal vocabulary' (Zacklin 2003: 22) for nation states. The various instruments and documents of international law that have been contributed by the UN system are intended to ensure various economic, political and social rights for individuals in all nations (Jolly *et al.* 2004; Rajagopal 2000).[6]

[5] Anghie (2002) regards the role of international law in the post-war period as imbricated with post-colonial intent by an unequal power relation between Western powers and the newly emergent nation states, where the former imposed greater contractual demands and sanctions on the latter group.

[6] The economic rights of individuals are regarded as the responsibility of nation states, and the UN charter is regarded as an international affirmation of the principle rather than a statement of intent to interfere in national policymaking or processes.

The United Nations organisations were regarded as supra-national bodies that would permit national governments to share their political concerns as they proceeded towards economic and social goals. These organisations were not located in a new sphere of the 'international' that was to operate over and above the authority of the national governments. The United Nations organisations were seen as a collective body of nations rather than a higher order and form of governance.[7] In this sense, there was an implicit sense of commonality of purpose and the treaties and laws were regarded as purpose-built, based on an agreed understanding of the world.[8]

The post-war understanding that international organisations would regard nations as sovereign was increasingly overshadowed by the creation of trading-based alliances between nation states.[9] The member states of the GATT held eight rounds of discussions from 1947 to 1994, and the last, called the Uruguay round, ended with the creation of the World Trade Organisation (WTO) on 1 January 1995. GATT was a treaty, not an organisation, and was based on the idea that there would be diplomatic negotiations in case of disputes and disagreements (Hilf 2003; Jennings 2004).

The organisations of the International Monetary Fund (IMF), International Bank of Reconstruction and Development (IBRD) and General Agreement on Tariff and Trade (GATT) became very active in the 1950s, with GATT functioning actively, even as a provisional agreement, and by the 1980s they had become key international players. The UN Food and Agriculture Organisation (FAO) and the International Labour Organisation (ILO) operated actively in arenas somewhat different to those in international finance and trade, focusing on food production and labour conditions respectively. The World Intellectual Property Organisation (WIPO) of the UN remained largely confined to the realm of legal interpretations of the UN charters and principles. The agencies of the UN did not direct their policies to national development plans until the 1970s, and it was only in the 1980s that the rapid expansion of national economic activities came to interest the UN agencies.[10] With growing awareness,

[7] Unterhalter (2008) argues that the first movement was one of the inter-national, which was followed by that of the international.

[8] The economic institutions set up immediately after the Second World War, following the Bretton Woods Conference in 1944, were the International Monetary Fund (IMF), the World Bank or International Bank for Reconstruction and Development (IBRD) and the General Agreement on Trade and Tariff (GATT). There was the intention to set up an International Trade Organisation (ITO) but this never came to fruition. These were intended to further garner the ability of national economies to access world markets and gain from participating in international trade.

[9] The level of trade between developing countries and advanced capitalist countries remains a very small part of international trade. UNCTAD has calculated that developing countries' share of world merchandise exports increased from less than one fourth in 1960 to one third in 2002 (UNCTAD 2006).

[10] Jolly *et al.* (2004) provide an excellent review of the trajectory of UN policies and its impact on international development. See Fine *et al.* (2001) for an analysis of how UN policies were increasingly replaced by the neoliberal agendas of the IFIs.

first, of national economic growth being closely linked to fluctuations in global markets and, second, of the negative impact shifting the growth pole from the West to other regions of the world (Chang 2004), there was a much closer scrutiny in many organisations, culminating in the creation of the World Trade Organisation (WTO). This body brought together under its domain all the earlier agreements entered into under the GATT (see www.wto.org.; Loibl 2003: 700).

The creation of the WTO catalysed the growth of the WIPO from a small legal outpost of the UN system to a large body of legal advisors to the members of the WTO, which were now freed from duties under the UN to frame equitable policies on intellectual property rights affecting the development of nations.[11] The increasing interest in the economic activities of late-industrialising countries led to growing skirmishes that exploded into full blown battles before arbitrators within WTO, between contending countries on gains and losses in the spheres of international trade and labour exchange. The tendency of the nations to try to adhere to stated principles of development within the UN system gave way to ascertaining whether any matter for contention and arbitration arose from unfair trade practices and the size of gain or loss for arbitration. The focus on the legal and financial dimensions of international trade has created a new and expanded focus on the role of the contract law (Anghie 2000) while also skewing the realm of political statesmanship guiding the spirit of the UN.

Examining the evolution of laws provided a way forward to understanding the international arena and also what countries do to acquire a more comprehensive and far-reaching legal framework so that their nationals could gain from exchanges in the global markets.

The role of international law in the new order

The centrality of maintaining peace after the Second World War overrode all other concerns; in a sense, therefore, the security dimension was the most sought-after aspect of the United Nations as well as other international organisations that emerged in the post-war years. The role of legal organisations was therefore set out as one of dispute resolution rather than rule-making or legal precedent and the ICJ was accordingly not awarded powers to interpret the UN charter or the legality of any decision of a UN body. It was meant to solely advise on disputes submitted to it (Thirlway 2003b).

The UN charter sets out that in the event of a conflict between the obligations of the members of the UN in the charter of UN and their obligations under any other international agreement, their obligations under the UN charter

[11] The growing role of the WIPO since the 1970s is associated with the growing role of global communications. See Chakravartty and Zhao (2008) for a review of how global communications have played a major role in restructuring the realm of state, market and society.

shall prevail. The aims and purposes of the UN, namely peace, security and promotion and protection of human rights, constitute an international public order. The understanding of the member states of the UN is that states which formulate and conform to international agreements and conventions take into account the political, economic and military rights of other states within a legal climate. The relation of the ICJ to the UN is that the ICJ presents a written report to the UN on its work where it makes clear where, in international law, the rules or norms come from, who is purporting to apply them and in what actual context. International law may be regarded as 'rules that restrain', 'a common language' or a 'normative guidance in the making of decisions' (Higgins 2003).

National strategies are formed within the prevailing international legal climate, and economic, social and political exchanges take place within that legal order. Late-industrialising countries situated in such a global framework of agreements have from the 1950s attempted to gain in economic strength and in international economic exchanges. Their thinking was that in a world governed by the Bretton Woods system of finance, economic growth would result directly, and solely, from national plans for industrial investment, and the gains from trade that would ensue.[12] The early models of industrialisation regarded new technologies and upgraded skills as natural components of industrialisation that would be put in place during development. Though the models varied in relation to whether the technology would be generated by the corporate sector[13] or by the administrative ability of the government, in a range of variations around the Feldman–Mahalanobis formulations of national plans the models adopted by the late-industrialising nations regarded appropriate technological prowess as a sufficient basis for industrial economic advancement through international trade. Economic performance of nations was measured by their industrial success rather than by the conditions under which they traded. In a world where trade flows were rising, the conditions of trade did not seem to matter as much as the type of technology.

In the golden age from the 1950s to the 1970s, economic growth was rapid, and 'Trade among the Western industrialised nations was the most dynamic element in this, with trade and output growth especially marked in manufactures' Glyn *et al.* (1990: 42). It would appear that advanced capitalist countries did not regard the share of trade as a problem, since they saw the

[12] The link between national growth and international trade was a consequential one. See Lewis (1954) for a discussion of the trade emerging automatically from industrialisation.

[13] The mainstream microeconomic models on economic growth did not make any particular comment on the ownership of technology (see the Solow model; Solow 1956); this was seen as a matter of no consequence. The macroeconomic models that focused on industrial development did address matters of ownership in relation to investment flows but the actual ownership of technology was still not taken up; the presumption was still that technology, once introduced into a national policy, would become available to all, either in the first round as industrial information or in subsequent rounds as new industrial products.

mainspring of capitalism as located in the advances in technology and they were maintaining their lead through these advances. Trade gave little cause for worry. In fact, the US administration regarded international trade as a necessary condition to ensure full employment in the United States (Glyn *et al.* 1990). It appears to be the case that international agreements are only a technique of domination, a coercive order to make less dominant nations behave. Many treaties concluded after wars were indeed such instruments. While a treaty is seen more as a binding international contract, allowing use of force to enforce it, international conventions are viewed as international laws.

Trade as an instrument of international dominance

Free trade is posited to be a natural outcome of industrial opportunity (Ricardo 1821) and yet the history of US trade policy is littered with instances of high tariff walls and large domestic subsidies to industry. The national state was a key player in creating the environment and the instruments for industrialisation, at huge costs and with very serious intent (Chang 2001; see Evans (2000). The 1970s saw a growing debate about the nature of trade as the share of already industrialised countries began to falter. The emergence of Japan was as a competitor to the US in some areas, with South Korea and Taiwan eroding US markets elsewhere, but the Eastern competitors protected their own markets for domestic producers, leading to a change in perception in Western economies, particularly in the United States. The rise of the Asian Giants was evidence that the state-led model (with high tariff walls and large domestic subsidies to industry, as was the case in the US earlier) was working even better in East Asia, where the nature of State–society relations appeared more amenable to ensuring industrial growth from the development of a national compact.[14] This superior ability of the East Asian economies to play the industrial game is what worried the industrialised world and instigated a series of critiques of inappropriate orientation, use of technology and, above all, a violation of the rules of the game of industrial production-based trade (World Bank 1994). At the heart of the plot was the painful revelation that the power of technology was uncertain, and could wield greater gains in the hands of a competitor. The ability of East Asia to leapfrog technologies and to cherry-pick the benefits of industrial growth has shaken the industrialised countries to the core. The dismay is particularly palpable in the realm of ideas and knowledge, where the developing world seems to have been able to emulate the West without the painful innovation of products while creating new knowledge of industrial processes. The possibility that intellectual property could be de-coupled from the industrial processes and technologies, in place in the advanced nations, and

[14] See Amsden and Hikino (2002) for a pithy commentary on how the evidence from late-industrialising countries that non-Western approaches to development did succeed was disregarded by international institutions, particularly in the rules that were set out within the WTO.

be replicated to give higher productivity in a new soil, was a realisation of the 1990s which was previously inconceivable.

The principles of international trading systems have remained relatively constant from the early years of the post-war period. The first principle formulated under GATT, and also followed by WTO, is the 'Most Favoured Nation' treatment (MFN) where every member is to treat every other member in such a fashion. Only non-members can be less (or even more) favourably treated or only they can be discriminatingly distinguished. Such equal treatment does not apply to products, since consumer tastes and habits affect the markets for different goods differently. The second principle is 'National Treatment'. A product imported from different members must be treated equally in relation to taxes, regulation, own product, etc. It is also referred to as the 'equality principle' of treating all traders of the same product as own nationals. The third principle is of 'Schedule of Concessions' and it binds members to tariff concessions given (the so-called bound tariff rate) contained in a schedule of each member of GATT. Save for differences in the rates in the schedule, products of all members must be treated no less favourably. The fourth is the principle of 'Quantitative Restrictions' which prohibits restrictions in any way on import or export by quantity, viewing them as being restrictive of trade. Restrictions can be imposed only in accordance with conditions set out under GATT. The fifth principle is 'Transparency', requiring all members to publish all trade and trade-related measures, to promote certainty, predictability and accountability of governmental measures. The sixth principle is 'Exceptions', allowing exceptions to liberalisation of trade rules, such as emergency actions to import particular products, safeguard balance of payments, protect public morals or protect human, animal or plant life or health. Exception could also pertain to national security or to free trade areas or customs unions allowing preferential treatment between members of such special arrangements as the EU. The sixth principle was a special provision for developing countries allowing them more favourable treatment, non-reciprocity in trade and an 'enabling clause'. The said clause allows developed countries to give a 'Generalised System of Preferences' on the products of developing countries, and its 'Global System of Trade Preferences' allows developing countries to exchange trade concessions among themselves.[15]

The UN forum set up for dealing with trade matters was the United Nations Conference on Trade and Development (UNCTAD), established by the Group of 77 (currently 131 members) to voice the concerns of developing countries. UNCTAD was the earlier inter-governmental forum for North–South dialogue and negotiations on issues of interest to developing countries, including debates on the 'New International Economic Order'. It identified the Group of Least Developed Countries (LDCs) in 1971 and became the focal point within the UN system for tackling LDC-related economic development issues. Its reports from the 1970s were critical of intellectual property rights (IPRs) in economic

[15] A useful summary of the principles can be found in Loibl (2003: 700–4).

development. UNCTAD was popular with developing countries for negotiating lower IPR norms appropriate to their standards. Because of its technical competence in going into IPR technologies and the developing-country orientation of its governing structure, UNCTAD was not found suitable for the trading objectives of the US, the EU and Japan. UNCTAD was deliberately marginalised in the 1980s and the US led a successful 'forum-shifting strategy', and transferred IPRs from WIPO and UNCTAD to the GATT through an agreement reached among many national governments on Trade Related Intellectual Property Rights (TRIPS) in the Uruguay round of GATT (Duttfield 2000). The interplay between UN organisations and international principles regarding the trade between nations reveals that the setting up of the WTO was an attempt to retrieve a system of international trade that would reassert the dominance of advanced capitalist nations.

The bringing together of a range of international laws regarding trade, to ensure world trade during the period 1950–80, was devised to uphold the dominant development paradigm (Rajagopal 2000) but these laws are not enshrined in the language of contracts. Rather, they bear strong traces of diplomatic negotiation, tinged with the language of security (Hudec 1970). This admixture provided the necessary ingredients to create the golden age from the 1950s to the 1970s.

The golden age gives way to dark discontents

The newly industrialised countries enjoyed considerable surplus in balance of trade with the US, and it was the result of reconfiguring the links between technology, industrialisation and trade. Further, UNCTAD provided technical assistance to developing countries in the Uruguay round of trade negotiations, up to the time of the setting up of the WTO. The procedure for resolving conflicts between nations in all these international institutions has been through the use of diplomatic avenues, hence the preferred choice of the route of dispute settlement in matters of trade (Anghie 2005). The framing of international contracts, particularly around trade, within a security framework has permitted the language of disputes to dominate within international institutions.

The Uruguay round of GATT came to an end with the setting up of the WTO agreement based on the Marrakech meeting in 1994 (Palmeter and Mavroidis 1998). The creation of the WTO saw GATT agreements subsumed into the WTO as a legally binding instrument on its members. There are currently over 150 member states in the WTO. The EU is an independent member, in addition to the European states, and the EU has as many votes as the number of its members.[16] GATT had a well-established dispute-settlement mechanism, albeit flawed in the view of the developed nations.[17]

16 Figures from the WTO website, www.wto.org (accessed 25 August 2007).

17 The international trade negotiations that preceded the WTO were the Tokyo round (1973–6) and the Uruguay round (1986–94).

The dispute-resolution approach has been the lynchpin of the international system since the Second World War but the arrangements lack power and discernment. The Dispute Settlement Understanding (DSU) has been reviewed by scholars in international law to unearth the legal basis in its laws as deduced from the language and use of the DSU (Busch and Reinhardt 2000), and it shows a move away from 'diplomatic jurisprudence' and towards a rule-based system with more judicial procedure and documentation (Hudec 1970).

It is the Appelate Body of the WTO that deals with disputes between governments on trade undertaken by their nationals, and Hilf suggests that the system is closer to that followed by the European Court of Justice (ECJ; Hilf 2003) rather than encompassing the full body of international law. The role of disputes is indicated in Article 3 (2) of the Dispute Settlement Undertaking, which states that the dispute-settlement undertaking is provided to ensure that rights and obligations are 'in accordance with customary rules of public international law'. The patchy use of the principles of international law within international organisations has become more apparent since the 1990s (Crawford 2002), particularly with the increasing presence of environmental disputes between nations (Rajamani 2006). The mismatch between the principles of free trade enunciated in the key principles of the WTO and the implications of dispute resolution raises a number of questions regarding consistency of the underlying conceptual framework. The WTO framework draws on the language of 'contracting parties' and works to ensure a transparent and equal footing for exchange, yet it does not make full use of the articles of the ICJ (Palmeter and Mavroidis 1998).

First, if the WTO is all about ensuring trade which does not create barriers then the procedure of 'suspension of concessions' (i.e. the creation of tariff barriers) against the appealing State, which is stated as an 'equivalence principle', is inimical to advancing free trade. The nub lies in the fact that a country that is being induced to move towards market-based principles is deterred from tariffs. If, however, the penalty for appealing for the use of DSU is the de facto imposition of tariff, such a sanction creates a perverse incentive to use rather than shun tariff-like restrictions. The use of a simple tit-for-tat rule to trigger a suspension of concessions is based on an economic logic that is actually devoid of any equivalence in a legal or substantive sense, notwithstanding the application of the term 'equivalence principle' to such tariffs. The simultaneous profferment of free trade and tariff as tools for the operation of the WTO presents nations with conflicting signals. Second, it is not clear how, within an economic understanding of the WTO framework, the suspension of concessions can be an appropriate response rather than the payment of monetary compensation (Davies 2006). Third, the increasing gap between actual negotiations under GATT and the model advanced by economic theory identifies an inability of the WTO framework to work with economic principles (Page 2001)

Further weaknesses of the WTO framework are revealed in the way the trade-related actions were used to ensure the protection of intellectual property rights (IPRs). For instance, the unilateral action of the United States which brought

Japan into the Uruguay round of talks could be regarded as a positive feature, yet the Uruguay round (and the WTO rules that followed) is regarded as being biased against developing countries and unduly favouring developed countries (Khor 2002). There is also disquiet regarding the different treatment given to trade and to IPRs; while there is a tight ruling with regard to trade there is a much looser arrangement with regard to the protection of technological power and knowledge, described increasingly as the IPRs.

Supporters as well as critics of economic globalisation believe that WTO agreements are reducing the significance of national economic boundaries. This is evident in the increasing adoption of market-based procedures in the WTO. The WTO has perceptibly shifted the arena of interaction from one of national power to the rule of the market. This shift is at odds with the dispute-settlement mechanism which still retains traces of the national sovereignty model of diplomacy (Anghie 2000). The undermining of national authority by placing sole emphasis on trade has sparked off responses within the UN system institutions, such as UNCTAD, which are increasingly advocating the principle of equality of nations and the introduction of the language of rights and responsibilities to reconcile differences and disputes (Rajagopal 2000). The increasing reliance on rules to create market-like conditions in international trade and thereby encourage contract-based instruments for dispute resolution is intended to create a level playing field. However, it also reduces the room for manoeuvre among nations, as they are now required to operate using economic principles rather than calling on changing power configurations that give greater leverage to developing-country configurations such as the BRIC countries (Brazil, Russia, India and China).

Exceptional rules: the setting out of TRIPS and TRIMS

The agreements of the WTO are multilateral and binding on its member states[18] and the 'agreements regime' of the WTO is highly restrictive so that any violation of an agreement brings into play the redressal mechanism of dispute settlement. Waivers are permitted under exceptional circumstances through the granting of exceptions to certain obligations for a limited period of time, under specified terms and conditions to be reviewed on a regular basis. However, these tenets do not sit comfortably in a global world where national security, even sovereignty, has become subservient to the interests of international capital and transnational corporations.

An exception is with regard to international commodity agreements where there are special rules governing primary commodities and raw materials. As

[18] The agreements deal with reduction of technical and tariff barriers to trade, agriculture, sanitary and phyto-sanitary standards, textiles and clothing, Trade Related Investment Measures (TRIMs), customs valuation, pre-shipment inspection, rules of origin, import licensing procedures, anti-dumping measures, subsidies and countervailing measures, and safeguards. The agreements limit members' discretion in these areas.

there are extreme price fluctuations in the global trade of primary commodities, these regulations override free trade in commodities like wheat, coffee, cocoa, olive oil and tin. Instead, the regulating mechanisms are buffer stocks and export quotas, and councils containing all member countries oversee commodity agreements.[19]

The Agreement on Trade Related Intellectual Property Rights (TRIPS) covers a wide range of principles – trading, protection of rights, enforcement of rights, settlement of disputes, special transition arrangements. The rights have to be registered in order to receive protection and the description given for registration is regarded as 'public information'. The TRIPS agreement of the WTO requires developing countries to introduce intellectual property rights, copyright and related rights, trademarks including service marks, geographical indications, industrial designs, patents, layout designs (topographies) of integrated circuits, undisclosed information including trade secrets, to a level similar to that in developed countries. However, copyrights and trade secrets need not be registered and the period of protection varies.[20]

The WTO was set out as a framework that opens markets of developed countries to the exports of developing countries, at the time WTO succeeded GATT, on 1 Jan. 1995 (Duttfield 2000). The IPR and trade agreements were taken together in the Uruguay round to achieve the aim of plugging any leakage of IPR-linked profits. However, the TRIPS agreement introduced trade retaliatory sanctions in instances of breach of agreement, which is a provision that is regarded as restrictive and unattractive to developing countries.

The WTO framework also makes stipulations on the investment that countries can undertake by insisting that there is equal treatment of foreign companies with domestic companies, in both goods and service sectors. The Trade Related Investment Measures (TRIMs) Agreement stipulates that foreign investment should be accorded the 'national treatment' principle and that foreign investors should not be required to employ local factors of production to ensure a minimum 'local content' requirement or to meet a requirement for imports to be kept to a certain maximum percentage of exports, i.e. the 'trade balancing' requirements.

Both TRIPS and TRIMS are regarded as part of the 'covered agreements' within the WTO convention. These rulings are regarded as facilitative for the contracting parties under the GATT framework. The language of contract that has been used to push the trade boat further out is intended to promote

19 Such commodity agreements are in decline, with producing countries increasingly coming to an understanding among themselves, and UNCTAD launched the 10th Commission on Commodities and Trade to address the global biases in the magnitude and conditions of commodity trade.

20 Computer programs are literary works under the Berne Convention on the Protection of Literary and Artistic Works. International copyright rules cover rental rights. Authors of computer programs, sound recordings and films have the right to prohibit commercial rental and unauthorised reproduction and performance, for no less than fifty years. Service marks like trademarks and geographical indications for wines must be protected by member states. Industrial designs must be protected for fifty years, inventions for twenty years, integrated circuits for ten years.

commodity and service flows between countries. What is missing in this representation of international trade is the understanding among national governments that trade flows should primarily improve domestic economic performance, rather than international prosperity. The simple notion of comparative advantage that sits behind the neoclassical model of trade does not allow a more sophisticated reading of a nation state that is using absorption and adjustment considerations to better locate its domestic resources.[21]

The expanded Figure 5.1 sets out the impact of these processes on national and local levels. The international organisations advocate the benefit of trade to the nation, as it will bring more goods and services to its nationals. The focus on improving the lot of ordinary people is powerful, but the manner in which global institutions operate in a new conjoining of the global and local into the *glocal* draws the gaze away from labour contributions by these individuals. The thick line from the *global* to the *national* indicates these trade flows. The thinner solid line indicates the manner in which the *national* moves to the *global*, as in the case of the flow of labour across national boundaries. The many aspects of international trade and labour movement that impact on the everyday lives of individuals generate political concern at the national level.

It is not the realm of interpretation of law but the realm of everyday politics, which affects people. Figure 5.1 shows how the introduction of a global level of rule-making can reduce the power of the nation. The demands from the international trading forces oppose actions that are regarded as inimical to free trade changes, even when these emerge from actions to strengthen the production of goods and services within the nation state. Though the WTO is explicit that national sovereignty is a principle of utmost importance, this does not get reflected in the chastisement that nations receive for supporting growing industries and propping up fragile livelihoods within the national economy.

The rulings by international conventions such as the WTO that are established to regulate international trade and property rights cannot remain impervious to the international political consensus in the UN with regard to framing laws. Laws governing contracts of trade should take regard of the notion of public interest within member nations. The lines that go from *global* to *national* to *local* (where the current push is strongly hierarchical) need to be further investigated and interrogated. The manner in which the global sphere is currently driving agendas militates against national sovereignty even as global claims are being made for a more equal (even flat) world. If one looks at the institutions of trade that are being advocated as the most powerful methods of bringing about a horizontal world, this contradiction is further revealed to be another manifestation of the amnesia regarding hierarchies while fixating on benefits of competitive exchanges.

[21] Trade theory has used Keynesian thinking, which emphasises the interlinkages between the conditions in the domestic sector and the commodities that are exported by an economy, since the 1950s. It is an oddity to find a reversion to the early pre-war neoclassical trade analysis, which looks at prices alone, in recent decades.

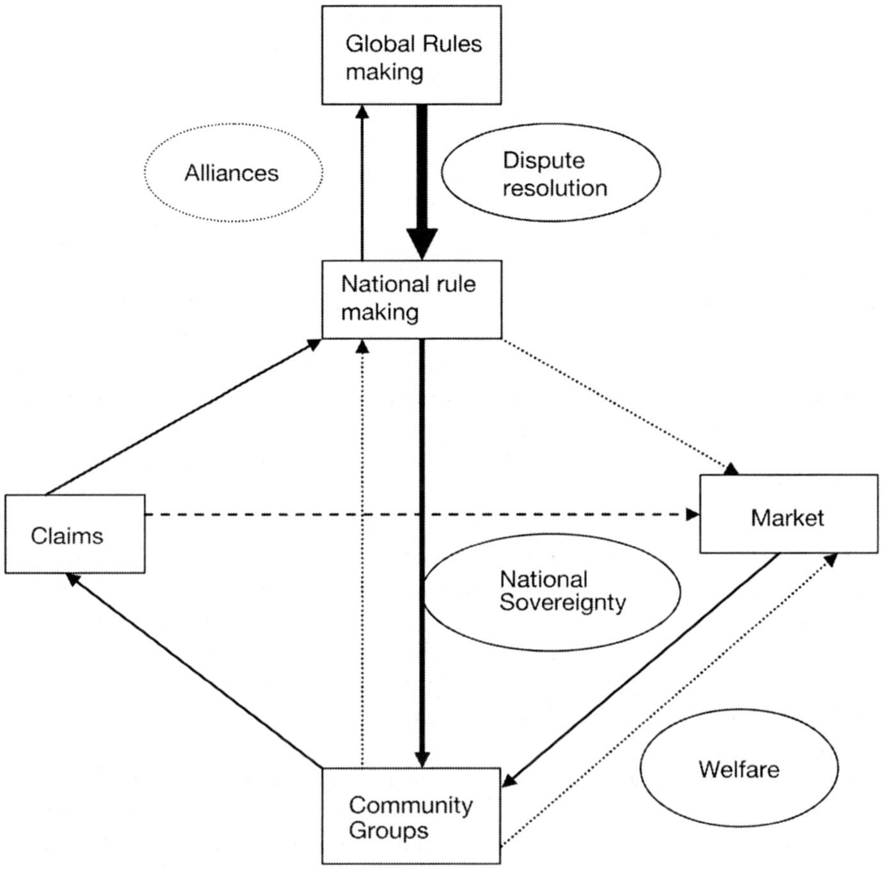

Figure 5.1 The impact of global rules at national and local level.

The dispute-resolution mechanism that has increasingly permitted the priority for admittance of market principles over national direction of trade is represented as a dispute resolution ellipse that emerges from a *global* to a *national* rule-making process. The response of national governments to the undermining of principles of national sovereignty through the building of alliances, such as the BRIC formation or the groups around the Doha round, are indicated as an alliance ellipse that emerges from *national* to *global* rule-making. The increasing interference of global trade rules in national development plans and processes is visible.

In the aftermath of the WTO

With the WTO providing access to more markets in more countries there has been an increase in international financial flows. Such an opening up of markets was designed to encourage foreign direct investment (FDI) flows to become a major component of global free trade. Though seemingly laudable, this move has also led to concerns that the greater openness has contributed to an increase in financial instability and volatility within and across countries, spread both by shifts in manufacturing investment and variations in exchange rates (Singh 2003).

A case in point is that of China, which applied to join the WTO in 1987 and entered the trading system in 2001. The move towards adopting the WTO framework was mooted by the Chinese government, as the objectives and conditions of the WTO were in line with the desired domestic economic policy (Qin 2007). There was intense debate within the government as to the level and speed of entry, with the final decision being that the country would join at an enhanced level of 'agreement plus' to signal to both the external economy and domestic companies that it had serious intent with regard to reforming institutions and incentives in the economy (Qin 2003) and also use of the framework as a possible mechanism for bilateral or multilateral free trade agreements (ICTSD 2008a)

The official position of the Chinese government was that, in joining the WTO in 2001, China has spared no efforts to improve its IPR legislation, and now the legislation is in full accordance with WTO rules. There have, however, been cases where other countries, particularly the United States, have accused the Chinese authorities and their national companies of unfair trading practices. In a response, in 2005 the Chinese mission to the WTO submitted the view that the United States is actually trying to change the WTO's legal structure on IPR protection, with an attempt to impose extra obligations on developing members.[22] The Chinese government is regarded as radical, as it had taken the initiative to go for 'agreement plus' conditions and exceeded the minimum requirements of the WTO convention. The Chinese position was that China would continue to pay much attention to IPR protection, as it is necessary for China's economic development, but would not accept obligations that go beyond what is prescribed in the TRIPS agreement among the 151 WTO members, which covers trade-related intellectual property rights.

The contradiction between the Chinese view of their compliance with WTO rulings and the current position of the WTO authorities indicates the conflict caused by different positions regarding views within the world economic system. The WTO currently classifies China as a non-market economy (NME) and expects it to move to market principles (Qin 2008b) while China on its part regards itself as different from the Western market economies as it considers development to be a right that has higher value than social and political rights (Potter 2001). This is not a problem exclusive to the Chinese position within the WTO, arising in external categories that essentialise countries, but one that faces economies which are regarded variously as emergent, transitional or post-socialist.

[22] These matters are listed under DSB 362. Commentary available at Xinhua News Agency, 14 August 2007.

The case of Malaysia is instructive. Malaysia was one of four countries that had a Trade Policy Review Measure (TPRM) in 2001 to evaluate its performance within the WTO framework. While such procedures are to be welcomed to advance the principle of free trade, the report seemed to indicate a much greater concern with tariff rather than non-tariff barriers (Athukorala 2002b). Their narrow focus on current trade balances and associated rush to remove current barriers to trade so as to further the volume of trade by the WTO is matched by the hurry evident in developed countries to ensure that there is no erosion of their trade shares in world markets.

The announcement by the US Trade Representative (USTR) that the USA was moving towards a free trade agreement (FTA) with Malaysia in March 2008 is indication that developed countries are keen to expand trade even faster than the provisions of the WTO have permitted to date. The USTR, Collins, made the case that this would ensure that Malaysia no longer gave preferential treatment to national companies such as Proton and Perodua over 'non-national' autos, even those that were manufactured in Malaysia by foreign-owned companies. The Malaysian government has already eliminated some local-content requirements and has cut its tariffs for autos having at least 40 per cent ASEAN content. However, it has imposed excise taxes on autos to compensate for the lost tariff revenue. 'The high tax rates continue to overburden automakers and discriminate against foreign-owned manufacturers' by giving Proton and Perodua a 50 per cent rebate on the excise taxes, was the view of the USTR. There was also official commentary on another Malaysian barrier, the issuing of permits for importing and distributing imported autos. Besides restricting the number of auto imports, capped at about 10 per cent of the domestic market, the system also allows sale of the permits for profit, with the higher costs passed on to prospective imported-auto buyers. Yet it did not appear that trade flows were uppermost in the mind of the USTR as his comments were directed towards the 'opportunity to open Malaysia's market to more imports' rather than any expansion of the national economy. It would appear that this analysis uses a neoclassical rather than the more advanced Keynesian model of trade (ibid.) and understands far less about the nature of local procurement policies within the industrial production system (McCrudden and Gross 2006).

Alarm bells begin to ring equally when looking at Indian government interactions with the WTO, and the manner in which transnational companies (TNCs) have drawn on this system to impose further restrictions on production within the Indian economy. India joined the WTO in 1995, and as a developing country was awarded a period of ten years to bring its patent laws into line with those of other WTO member states. This period ran out at the end of 2004 and India declared itself to be fully compliant with WTO standards as of 1 January 2005.[23]

[23] At an international conference on law in November 2004, the chairman of the Indian Planning Commission, Montek Singh Ahluwalia, began the session on product- and process-based distinctions in intellectual property by declaring, prior to inviting the panellists to present their papers, that India was going to be fully compliant on 1 January 2005.

The strong intention of the Indian government was unwavering, even in the face of considerable opposition from many quarters within the national economy and polity. This clear-cut position was based on considerable negotiation and deliberation on the part of the Indian WTO delegation. In particular, the Indian government, on the advice of the negotiating home team, made changes in the Indian patent laws to make them compliant with WTO requirements. The modifications to the patent laws were called into question by the global pharmaceutical company Novartis when it launched a case against the Indian government in the High Court of Chennai in early 2007 for refusing to give it a patent for its cancer drug, Glivec. The reworked Indian patent law had made a provision within Indian patent law under section 3(d) which excluded 'incremental innovations' from patents, i.e. where there was an existing product extant in India, prior to the introduction of patent laws, new patents would not be awarded for incremental tinkering and minor variations in processes. The case was dismissed by the High Court and the company has decided not to take the matter up to the next level of judiciary, the Supreme Court of India. It has instead chosen to take up the matter in the international arena, particularly in Switzerland, where there is active interest in the matter of patents for pharmaceutical companies. It is noteworthy that Novartis has claimed that the court decision is opposed to innovation and thereby advances in public health, but that the refusal of a patent is a consequence of the Indian government's violation of intellectual property rights requirements of the WTO. The ready manner in which the TNCs draw on the language of the WTO to stake claims for new patents is a tendency that pushes legal debate away from the *sub-national–national* space into the *global–national* space. The repeated use of the WTO framework with regard to the national level of the judicial system as the only platform for negotiation and its complete lack of consideration for the domestic policy framework would result in a further reduction of engagement between national legal frameworks and time and deliberation needed to listen to and speak the language of the local sphere. This in turn pushes forward the international agendas and their attendant language, and forces national governments to devote more of their time to deciphering the legal contractual aspects, taking precious time away from the more difficult but ever pressing task of interpreting in the local sphere the effect of translations between the official and the vernacular that are indicated in the bottom half of Figure 5.1.

The intended objective of the WTO framework, to ensure that all partners are on an equal footing, is based on the notion that all countries have the same economic structure, one that as closely as possible approximates to an economic textbook model, and consequently assumes that actions within these countries should be dealt with in an identical manner. Such thinking occludes the reality of the very different starting conditions of developing countries, the very distinct positions to which they were relegated in the high period of colonialism at the end of the nineteenth and early twentieth centuries, and the various and diverse pathways that they have chosen to get on to the high road to industrialisation.

The implications of WTO rulings

Where countries are of the view that there has been a violation of a trade principle, regarded broadly as a broken promise, they have the right to raise the matter at the WTO. Complaints made by one country against another are regarded as disputes, and if the parties to a dispute are unable to agree on resolving the dispute within sixty days it can be referred to a dispute settlement panel. There have been 378 disputes that have been referred to a panel during the period 1995–2008. These disputes do not show staunch support for upholding free trade; rather, they indicate the shifting of rules and standards, a reordering of priorities as well as a reworking of the weights accorded to different aspects, particularly to the relative valorising of product and process distinctions within panels.

There are also concerns that the WTO is expanding its coverage to take on new commodities that are entering the international trading system and that it is successively entering jurisdictional spaces where it has little experience and even less knowledge. One area of particular concern, where disputed matters have received increasing attention, is that relating to different environmental concerns between countries. These cases show how the trade interests become subordinate to other concerns in decisions.

The case of the environment

Environmental provisions in the WTO agreements are designed to take into account the impact of environmental constraints on trade. The WTO has greater provision for taking into account exceptions to free trade, in relation to the protection of other matters, than was the case under GATT, where only Article XX permitted exemptions from free trade to ensure environmental protection. In the case of the WTO, there are numerous provisions that come under a variety of agreements and get highlighted through particular disputes, as discussed below.

Tuna–dolphin case

The tuna–dolphin case was initially raised under the GATT regime in 1991. There were two General Agreements on Tariffs and Trade (GATT) involving tuna–dolphin disputes (1991 Tuna–Dolphin I and 1994 Tuna–Dolphin II) which were the first to test the legitimacy of using environmentally unfavourable foreign process and production methods (PPMs) as justification for trade restrictions. Tuna–Dolphin I revolved around a US primary embargo on Mexican tuna caught using purse-seine nets that incidentally trapped a high number of dolphins, while Tuna–Dolphin II centred on a secondary US embargo against countries who re-exported tuna from nations under the US primary embargo.

While the import of Mexican tuna fish, which were not certified as dolphin-safe, was banned, the United States was simultaneously purchasing export from many intermediate tuna-processing countries. The dispute panel did not agree to the ban of imports from intermediaries as the latter demand was regarded as a matter relating to process issues, while the Mexico case was seen as a product matter. Mexico did not press for enforcement of the decision of the panel after bilateral talks with the US. The dispute panel upheld the US practice of labelling tins of tuna as 'dolphin-safe' so that customers could make the choice of whether to boycott processed tuna tins that did not bear a label of 'dolphin-safe' in domestic retail outlets. These labels were regarded as a mechanism that prevented any deceptive advertising regarding tuna products.

The tuna–dolphin cases under GATT have remained the signifiers for environmental concerns under the later WTO regime. The increased environmental obligation that the US has had to face from domestic groups could be interpreted as a move to reduce the hierarchical relations between the national State and its groups (see Figure 3.1). The ability of the US to transfer the costs imposed by these environmental groups indicates that the nature of flows between national and global operate in a powerful manner in the US compared to that in developing countries (the arrows from national to global are much bolder than set out in Figure 5.1). The US administration has persisted in transferring these environmental costs to other nations that had not yet been subject to such pressure groups in their own economies, rather than merely internalising these costs within its national boundaries. The ability of the US to use environmental measures as a way to control its trade policy lends credence to the view that developed countries are increasingly using these measures to impose on exports from developing countries (Maskus and Wilson 2001).

Shrimp–turtle case

The WTO was drawn into this case in 1994 when India, Malaysia, Pakistan and Thailand complained against the US demand that their shrimp imports needed to be certified for the use of turtle-excluder devices (TEDs). The matter was initially instigated as a matter of domestic law when the US Environmental Protection Agency (EPA) was sued by a US environmental group, Earthjustice, in the mid-1980s for negligence in saving the lives of turtle species due to inadequate monitoring of national and international crafts at sea. The courts demanded a rewording of the laws of the EPA, and the US was to comply with the requirement for TEDs and by 1995 had only done this with relation to the countries in the greater Caribbean region.

The United States imposed a ban on the import of shrimps caught at sea without using turtle-excluder devices to protect endangered turtles, in 1994. This ban only covered shrimps from four South and South-east Asian countries. On 8 November 1996, the four countries, India, Malaysia, Pakistan and Thailand, requested consultation with the US through the WTO Dispute Settlement Body (DSB). The US lost the case on grounds of discrimination and the decision was not based on a negation of its rights to raise environmental issues (in fact, Article XX on Trade and Environment has been used by the US in the case of tuna–dolphin as well). Though environmentally valid, the ban was held to be discriminatory for not being applied to all shrimp imports and so it was held to be invalid by the dispute-settlement panel.

The matter was then taken to the Appelate Body, which reversed some of the original judgements in the case and moved away from the interpretation in the tuna–dolphin case. The Appelate view was that it was not the environment that should be regarded as key under Article XX, rather the focus on the need for multilateral rather than unilateral negotiations. In the subsequent case of Malaysia raising the matter of certification on a shipment-by-shipment basis, the Appelate body ruled in favour of the US on grounds that their action was within the rules of the GATT. The case underlines that countries are allowed to have national regulations on protecting the environment as long as they comply with the rules of the WTO.

The ruling created considerable interest, particularly in relation to the blurring of the distinction between process and product with regard to identifying grounds of discrimination (Bhagwati 2002). Such cases raise the important difference between standards and rules that have not been adequately differentiated by the WTO framework (Trachtman 1999). The distinction between these two aspects (process and product) of an innovation has been regarded as a central tenet in economics, at least since the industrial revolution, and in recent decades has become a keystone in dealing with matters relating to intellectual property. The re-weighting of the importance of process and product, with a view in favour of process in such rulings going in favour of developing countries, has been interpreted as a form of judicial activism within the WTO dispute resolution process (Howse 2005). The dominant tendency was favour towards commodity and product approach in trade matters, but a preference for process in relation to intellectual property matters gave an indication of the schizophrenic approach to goods and services in the international sphere. It would be logical and consistent to argue that goods are product-based and services are process-based. Yet while it is argued that trade in goods should be based on product description and prices, when new products are to be patented there is an emphasis on process to show innovation in need of patent. Equally confusing is the treatment of intellectual property, where the logical approach seems to be in relation to the process of creation, yet disputes seem to focus on product characteristics and so do the TNCs which draw on the framework of the WTO to bring products into service patents.

Rules on copyright

The violation of intellectual property rights, particularly in relation to not meeting copyright rulings and requirements, show this disturbing polarity of thinking (product and process). The United States raised the matter of copyright infringement with China in April 2007 and through June, and consultations conducted under the aegis of the US–China Joint Commission on Commerce and Trade, set up for such purposes in September 2006 'did provide some useful clarifications' (ICTSD 2007). On 4 April 2007, the 1422nd Meeting of the Adjudication Commission of the Supreme People's Court of China and the 75th Meeting of the Supreme People's Procuratorate adopted an interpretation of the Law in Handling Criminal Cases of Intellectual Property Infringement where the interpretation of Articles 1 to 7 was read so as to incorporate 'reproduction and/or distribution of materials' and 'penalties' for such actions. The USTR made the decision to complain about the infringement of copyright and trademarks on manufactured goods by the People's Republic of China, on 31 August 2007.[24]

On a complaint by the US, the Appellate Body of the WTO in 1998 upheld the dispute panel's finding that India's filing system for patent applications for pharmaceutical and agricultural chemical products was inconsistent with TRIPS. The system did not provide the 'means' by which applications for patents for such inventions could be securely filed, as a patent application filed under administrative instructions could be rejected by a court under the contradictory mandatory provisions of the existing Indian law. Legitimate expectations of the parties to a treaty (TRIPS) are reflected in the language of the treaty itself. Its interpretation should not include the imputation into a treaty of words that are not there or the importation into a treaty of concepts that were not intended. So, there was no mechanism in place in India for grant of exclusive marketing rights for the products covered by TRIPS.[25]

Whether demanding amendment to Indian patent law, the view taken by the WTO on limiting by law the justiciability of individual patent rights in superior Indian courts, which are courts of 'justice and equity', would also have been the view taken in superior US courts is anybody's guess. Copyright infringements concerns have been raised more than once by developed nations, and most often and readily by the United States.

The cases illustrate how the WTO legal framework adjudges contentions thrown up between members narrowly, where the rules of trade are concerned about legal protection of the rights of holders of IPRs, rather than openly, ruling out interference from national courts. The importance of even competition in trade appears to be downplayed by the WTO where there are greater gains to be made from reducing rather than increasing the flow of goods and commodities, through secure legal protection.

The contrary logic of devaluing global trade is also evident where there is a unidirectional increase in international trade, with more trade between developed countries than trade going into developing countries. It would appear that the contracting parties voice complaint when there is indication of less than fair treatment in relation to the flows between countries, particularly when there is a dispute between developed and developing countries. There is also the case where a small developing country grows its share of the world market, as in the

[24] China – Measures Affecting the Protection and Enforcement of Intellectual Property Rights (WT/DS 362).

[25] WT/DS 50 INDIA – PATENTS (US)1(DS 50).

case of the share of textiles and clothing accruing to Bangladesh, which is regarded as unfair practice (Consumer Unity and Trust Society International 2007). This has led to accusations of price-cutting, permitting the dumping of goods in developed country markets.

WTO and government action

Anti-dumping duties

Anti-dumping measures are to be applied only under Article VI of the Agreement of 1994 under the Uruguay round and after very detailed investigations thereunder. The injury of 'dumping' is not considered as criminal and is treated only as an injury in tort. There is neither any duty to care nor a strict liability for any type of injury by dumping that invites exemplary damages. The quantum of damages is appealable, by a nation against the nation causing an injury by dumping, to the WTO panel. In effect, the country suffering dumping, by traders of another country can impose anti-dumping (AD) duties, but only after a detailed investigation and calculations, and consultation with other governments, to be able to defend its AD duties. Though dumping is done by traders of a country, its government has no liability. However, the onus of the action, consequences of delay and payment of costs for such an action are all on the injured country and not the persecutor trader, who is innocent until proved guilty and cannot even be arrested.

Dumping is not a criminal offence, unlike the infringement of intellectual property rights. Subsidies to meet export targets or to promote domestic goods in place of imported ones are 'prohibited subsidies'. If imports are subsidised they are deemed actionable subsidies and a countervailing import duty can be imposed as a correction. Temporary import restrictions are regarded as a safeguard that could operate as a short-term measure against unilateral dumping action, but not so the providing of subsidies, as this is opposed within the WTO framework since they block trade flows. There are other measures in the framework that are permitted to reduce trade levels in furthering the interest of countries to maintain a minimum safety in the production of food. The health and quality of animal and plant products traded between countries is one such measure where the requirement to meet international health safety standards is regarded as an acceptable basis to ban the trading of goods on the international market.

Phytosanitary measures

Under the Sanitary and Phyto-Sanitary Measures Agreement (SPS), adopted under the Uruguay round, trade can be regulated by measures for ensuring food safety and animal and plant health and safety. It is required that these measures should be based on scientific principles that are drawn from sufficient scientific evidence. Where relevant scientific evidence is insufficient, measures should be based on evidence from the relevant international organisations as well as sanitary or phytosanitary measures applied by other members of the WTO. The difficulties of inadequate scientific knowledge has been a growing concern among international jurists, who point to the procedures of the International Court of Justice where there is a prerequisite to ensure that the opinion of scientific experts is available prior to adjudication procedures getting underway.[26]

The consequences of uneven use of jurisdictional authority and of inadequate availability of scientific evidence came to the fore in 1995 in one of the first cases at the WTO, known as the Beef Hormone dispute. In this case the United States opposed the ban by the EU of meat and meat products from cattle grown by injecting natural or synthetic hormones. The evidence that was drawn on by the United States in this dispute was taken from the body of FAO/WHO codes and standards of the International Animal Health Organisation. The conventions of the FAO appear to support the US stand that the ban was unfair practice by the EU. Yet the different approach taken by the European Union, drawing on its long-standing use of the precautionary principle, emphasised the point that the risks associated with importing US beef were large, particularly as there were limited – as well as a variable quality of – scientific materials on the ill-effects of hormones, highlighting the need for further research and tests to be conducted before the magnitude of risk would diminish (Josling *et al.* 2006). The different regulatory regimes regarding meat production in conjunction with the varied understandings of standards between countries that emerged before the Appelate council in the Beef Hormones case raise doubts about whether the WTO has a sufficient and well-rounded understanding of the manner in which standards for trade should be set out and negotiated.

The ban by the EU in the Beef Hormones phytosanitary case had been in force for ten years when the DSB of the WTO allowed retaliatory action by the US, implying that the ban imposed by the European Union on hormone-treated meat and meat products was anti-trade action. The ruling, which overturned an important consumer health law, caused outrage throughout Europe. Supported by a growing body of evidence suggesting that certain natural and synthetic hormones are linked to rising incidences of cancer, the European Commission decided not to lift its ban, despite the WTO ruling. The decision in the dispute over hormone beef was the first ruling based on the three-year-old Sanitary and Phyto sanitary Agreement (SPS). WTO decided against the scientific evidence of the EC and in favour of the scientific view behind the FAO standards in deciding that the hormones were safe.[27]

Another agreement in the WTO, the Technical Barriers to Trade Agreement (TBT), is designed to ensure that regulations, standards, testing and certification

[26] Crawford (2002) sets out the challenges before the ICJ in dealing with states and what is considered national and what is regarded as foreign,

[27] WT/DS 26 and 48 for the initial set of disputes in 1996 and WT/DS 320 and 321 for the attempts at continued suspension at the end of the decade-long ban. In DS 39 the responding country requested the DSB to suspend additional measures by the panel. See Ortino and Petersmann (2004).

procedures do not create unnecessary obstacles to trade. It is distinct from the SPS agreement as it applies to risk assessment undertaken by members, based on scientific evidence regarding barriers and the underlying measures drawn from environmental science. The first case under this agreement was raised by Canada in 2001 against France, against the latter's decree to ban the import of asbestos and all products containing the substance. The WTO dispute panel initially regarded non-asbestos and asbestos goods as 'like products' and upheld the right of the French government to uphold human life or health concerns in the Asbestos case. The Appelate Body reversed the decision regarding like products, emphasising that all evidence about the product should be considered, including its physical nature, rather than a mere analysis of the end product (Wirth 2002). The panel had also pointed out that the case did not come under the TBT agreement as the dispute was not one of technical standards since it did not set out product-performance criteria for permitting market access; rather, it imposed a complete ban on asbestos and asbestos-related products.

Bringing government procurement under the WTO regime with its 'national treatment' principle (TNCs treated like national companies) will help TNCs get contracts as locals. TNCs would be able to bring the national governments into the dispute-settlement system of the WTO on charges of discrimination, through the intermediary of their own government, and claim compensatory and retaliatory measures using the power of their government. The notion of equality in the treatment of countries is partial, and at times contradictory, in its usage. The intention to give 'national treatment' to TNCs sits uneasily with the insistence of developed countries that their farmers should receive support to maintain their traditional way of life, an advantage they do not wish to share with farmers in other nations.

Friction in agricultural trade

The US and EU countries have a long history of subsidising their farmers through tariff as well as non-tariff (Ricardo 1821) measures. This has worked to bring value to their produce and keep down the international price of food. The role of subsidies and tariffs has been a source of concern in the Agreements on Agriculture (AoA). It is clear that subsidies create price distortions by creating a different equilibrium price to that produced from a market exchange. Tariffs, on the other hand, are a shield from the competitive market and protect the producer.

The difference between market compensation and protection needs to be maintained. It has been argued that it is difficult to comprehend the meaning of 'subsidy', given that it is based on a model without government, to which there is little correspondence in the real world (Sykes 2003). If we wish to start with the political economy of the real world, the taxation is the true measure of the legitimacy of a government, and if a subsidy is viewed as the flip side of a tax, then it can be regarded as a legitimate and universally recognised tool of government policy. As a negative tax is the true character of a subsidy, it achieves the task of affecting the incidence of economic activity.[28] It is therefore akin to producers' version of an incomes policy. The reason for confusion in the world of trade is the readiness of governments to replace tariffs by subsidies when faced with international pressures to open up the economy. Subsidies are less aggregative but they also consequently have a much lower element of the public good and associated positive externalities for production.

Subsidies and countervailing measures

Subsidies and countervailing measures (SCMs) were introduced in the Uruguay round of the GATT in 1994. The agreement was brought into the WTO in 1995, and subsidies that are contingent upon export performance or upon use of domestic rather than imported goods are prohibited under the SCM agreement. Other subsidies are permissible (actionable subsidies), but where a country has evidence that a particular subsidy has an adverse effect on a particular trade flow the matter can be raised within the WTO framework having a provision for the imposition of countervailing duties if damages can be calculated and shown.

Under the WTO framework there was a gradual reduction of tariffs on agricultural products during the six years 1995–2000, as all developing countries that joined in 1995 were awarded a ten-year period till 2005, to become fully compliant in agriculture. The ban on import of agricultural products was also eliminated over this time period. Commitments were made by members on (a) market access (substantial reductions in import ban and tariffs), (b) export subsidies reduction (with a view to phase out totally) and (c) domestic support reduction (reduction of supports).

The WTO did recognise that farmers need to be shielded from effects of swings in weather and prices, and that farming as a way of life deserved support. Agricultural support under the three categories of prohibited, actionable and acceptable subsidies are classified into green, amber and blue boxes. The framework places domestic support for agriculture in the amber box, signifying that it is a 'temporary' measure. The amber category has in practice stretched over many years. It is only the measures that are deemed to have a minimal impact on trade that are placed in the green box; they could be services like research, disease control, infrastructure, food security, payments made directly to farmers that do not stimulate production, direct income support for restructuring agriculture, environmental and regional assistance programmes.[29] It is

[28] The first principles of public finance deal with the importance of the incidence of tax of changing production. In an identical fashion, the role of subsidies is a direct impact on the costs of production. That subsidies are current, not 'smart', is a matter of a different dimension and should not be collapsed into a simple in-or-out prescription for subsidies.

[29] There is a tendency to use the make hidden concessions to products so that they appear as green box commodities, but where an amount equal to double the subsidised price of the product has been transferred.

interesting to note how these classifications are made. Direct payments to farmers to limit production (as in the US) are currently in the blue box. The logic of this categorisation is that such actions reduce the payment to US farmers arising from economies of scale associated with large-scale agricultural production. The logic of income lost is not accepted in the case of farmers in developing countries, who are affected by large-scale changes in agricultural commodity prices. It would appear that trade-induced efficiency losses can be compensated, but this does not apply to trade-induced agricultural risk.

It is also significant that it is developing countries that have raised objections against the developed countries with regard to agriculture, rather than the other way around. The developed world view is that agriculture is a declining sector and so objections raised are solely on account of aggrieved interest groups who are opposed to economic development (Anderson and Martin 2006). There is little or no concern expressed regarding the huge challenge faced by developing countries in maintaining livelihoods and domestic economic stability in the face of global agricultural fluctuations where a majority of the population is located in rural and consequently agricultural occupations.

Developing countries have also increasingly become pro-active in taking developed countries to task where they have found trade barriers raised against their agricultural commodities. The most talked-about disputes in recent years have been those initiated by the Brazilian government. In December 2007, five years after Brazil first requested a consultation, a WTO panel issued a report, known as Article 21.5, upholding Brazil's claim that the marketing loans and countercyclical payments that the US offers its cotton farmers violate both the Agreement on Subsidies and Countervailing Measures and the General Agreement on Tariffs and Trade.[30] The DSB's ruling, which confirms Brazil's view after several years of disputes and appeals, marks the first time that a developed country's agricultural policy has been successfully challenged at the WTO. Furthermore, the Appellate Body ruling allows Brazil to retaliate by imposing more than US $1 billion worth of sanctions on US imports each year. The WTO has suggested that this could take the form of a suspension of intellectual property rights.[31]

The US appealed against said ruling in February 2007, maintaining that its cotton payments fall outside the scope of Article 21.5 and that they do not significantly suppress global cotton prices. The panel rejected the US appeal, stating that it was convinced by Brazil's arguments that even a small drop in prices harms Brazilian producers, given their narrow profit margins, and that US cotton producers' 'artificially high' market share reflects the impact of these subsidies.

This case follows in the footsteps of an earlier case where Brazil and Australia raised consultations in the WTO in opposition to EU subsidies on sugar

[30] WT/DS 267.

[31] ICTSD reporting. 'Brazil Claims WTO Cotton Victory', BBC News, 27 July 2007; 'US Loses in Cotton Dispute at WTO', BBC News, 2 June 2008; 'US Loses WTO Brazil Cotton Appeal'.

on 27 September 2002.[32] The two countries made the submission that the EU subsidies are trade distortive and that Brazil particularly targeted exports of the so-called C *sugar quota*, that covers sugar produced above domestic production quotas and which cannot be sold internally during the year it is produced, but was nonetheless sold on the global market, using export subsidies, at below the cost of production. The panel concluded that the European Community, through its sugar regime, had acted inconsistently with its obligations under Articles 3.3 and 8 of the Agreement on Agriculture, by providing export subsidies in excess of the quantity commitment level and the budgetary outlay commitment level.

Both the cotton and sugar disputes have widespread implications for other major traded food crops, particularly rice and wheat, as farmers receive considerable subsidies for these major cereal crops from their governments in many developed countries (Powell and Schmidt 2005).

The Doha round

The European Commission, with the support of Canada and Japan, and the US, have an ongoing agenda for continuing negotiations regarding the WTO framework, popularly known as the Doha round. It covers agriculture, intellectual property rights, services, investment, public procurement, competition policy and other areas. The November 2001 declaration of the Fourth Ministerial Conference in Doha, Qatar, provides the mandate for negotiations. In Doha, ministers also approved a linked decision on implementation problems that developing countries face in implementing the current WTO agreements. Southern governments are resisting negotiations on new issues, afraid that they would impact the ability of national governments to regulate FDI flows needed to support national development objectives and priorities. Therefore, they demand that the investment issue be discussed within the framework of the UNCTAD.

The area of agriculture has been much debated in the various Doha rounds, but significant headway is yet to be made. One reason for the inability of talks to proceed is that the core issue continually flagged by the developing countries, regarding the need for adequate instruments within the WTO framework to protect vulnerable sections of farming communities from the uncertainties of global agricultural markets, has never been addressed. The sole consideration of trade-distorting supports by the US and EU has not taken into account domestic rural livelihoods. Also the offers that have been made by developed countries have not been sufficient to ensure real cuts in the actual or planned future levels of domestic support. This became strikingly evident in the latest round, in the summer of 2008 when an offer of a 'July 2008 package' was proposed by the WTO. The US had made an offer, conditional on other countries making concessions, of restricting domestic agricultural subsidies to the value of $15

[32] WT/DS 265.

billion, which was rejected by India and China with strong support from all developing countries. This seemed like a prelude to the US strengthening the demands it would make on the developing countries, in agricultural market access as well as non-agricultural market access (NAMA) and services.

The tendency within the WTO for the United States administration to dominate disputes and debates relating to agriculture is indicative of the long-standing investment which its government has made in supporting its influential farmer lobby, a matter that could be dismissed as merely a matter of domestic concern, and yet such consideration is not given to domestic concerns of others, particularly of developing countries. There is also the need to recognise that the growing inclination to accord the United States administration the leader status is foolhardy, and it 'shows the folly' of 'negotiating' with the US administration when it has no trade authority. Even in private contract negotiations, no one will negotiate unless the other party has the power to negotiate and sign (Raghavan 2003).

The green box can be expected to be the major category of domestic support in future, as this constitutes an escape from having to really reduce overall subsidies. The developed countries can continue to use the green box subsidies without limit, as the August 2004 Framework and the Hong Kong Declaration do not put a cap on these. Some of these green box subsidies are actually trade-distorting (as the cotton dispute decisions have shown) and should have been allocated to the trade-distorting boxes such as amber or blue or *de minimis*. As long as the green box category of subsidies is not disciplined and capped, it would not matter what the US offers on capping its 'trade-distorting support', since it can then operate more of its subsidies through the green box, which has no limit and hardly any discipline at present As Das (2006) has pointed out the opportunity provided by the green box is to the tune of US$ 50 billion and 22 billion euros in 2000 in the US and the EU respectively, particularly its window of 'decoupled income support' (paragraph 6 of Annex 2 of the AoA).[33]

There is also the matter of Article 13 on due restraint, known as the 'peace clause' in the Agreement on Agriculture that exempted WTO members from being taken to a dispute settlement panel if they were in violation of certain agricultural subsidies. The clause was introduced in 1993 as part of the Uruguay round of negotiations. The peace clause expired in December 2003, thus opening up these non-actionable subsidies to countervailing measures and the possibility of dispute procedures[34]

The growing disquiet around the implications of the WTO framework for the state of domestic agriculture in developing countries (and a majority of their populations reside in the rural economy) is a reaction to the imposition of

[33] A list of possible criteria could be devised around the eligibility of farmers in terms of their lower economic status, a ceiling on payments to individual farmers in a year, and exclusion of companies from such payments.

[34] The considered opinion among developing countries is that the US will bring in some way to restore the peace clause (or some version of it) as part of the outcome of the Doha negotiations.

global hierarchies on national production and trade policies. The attempts of developing country governments to ensure that the enforcement of WTO procedures and the penalties for infringement are equitable, including the procedures for getting evidence, injunctions, damages and penalties that form part of the WTO agreement, is a new feature that works to reduce the power of global agendas and reinforce the importance of national sovereignty. This phenomenon of developing countries taking the initiative in refashioning trade relations is gaining momentum in the rapidly expanding realm of intellectual property rights for genetic materials, as new natural, particularly biological, resources increasingly enter the global commodity market through agricultural and also industrial trade.

Trade-related IPRs and biodiversity

The increasing entry of the market into the realm of natural, particularly biological, resources has overwhelming implications for developing countries which contain over 80 per cent of the world's biodiversity. It is this large store of biodiversity that provides products for many pharmaceutical and agricultural patents, and 40 per cent of production worldwide is currently anchored in the exploitation of biodiversity.[35] Patents are the most common form of protection used by companies to protect their economic products as well as processes.

Currently, the US, supported by the EU, Canada and Japan, is pressing hard for the expansion of the product arena covered by intellectual property rights using the intellectual property rights provisions in the WTO framework. The industry-dominated US delegation to the WTO, with 96 out of the 111 members from the corporate sector, called for everything to be patentable, including plants and animals. Developing countries appear determined to stand firm against US and industry pressure, proposing among other things to definitively exclude biodiversity from TRIPS. The compromise was a so-called 'biodiversity provision' in the TRIPS agreement which allows countries to exclude plants and animals (but not micro-organisms) from patentability, provided they develop a similar system of protection (a so-called *sui generis* system). The imbalance, coupled with concern about the ethical implications of the private ownership of life, prompted some Southern countries to fiercely oppose all types of life-form patenting, during the TRIPS negotiations.

The current conflict over intellectual property rights has long roots in the UN system. In 1981, the FAO had called for a legal convention on 'plant genetic resources' and faced opposition from the US, the UK and Australia (as well as from global seed production companies). Despite this setback a non-binding undertaking was agreed to by over 100 countries with a commission set up

[35] The Convention on Biological Diversity was created at the 1992 United Nations Conference on Environment and Development (also known as Rio 92). A separate Biosafety Protocol was agreed by the parties in 2000 which operates its own clearing-house system. The Cartagena Biosafety Protocol (CBD) entered into force in September 2003. See http://www.brad.ac.uk/acad/sbtwc/gateway/TRADE/CBD.HTM

within the FAO to monitor the undertaking. It has come to be known as the International Undertaking on Plant Genetic Resources (IUPGR). The monitoring commission met in 1985 and, despite a continued boycott by the United States, 93 countries attended the meeting. Currently it is the largest commission in FAO with 161 members and the EU, in it. The creation of these international bodies has not prevented matters regarding biodiversity being brought to the DSB by member countries. The different perspectives on biodiversity, in terms of both opportunities and risks, have given rise to a new area of disputes.

The five-year EU moratorium on genetically modified (GM) crops in response to European fears about the negative human and environmental effects of introducing GM cereals and other foods into their markets came to an end in 2004. In the run-up to this date, the US announced that it would request consultation in the WTO about the legality of this ban as it violated its stated trade laws.[36] The dispute settlement panel found that the EC had acted inconsistently with its obligations under the SPS agreement with respect to approval procedures because there were undue delays in the completion of the approval procedures for each of these products. Additionally, the panel noted that with regard to the EC member state safeguard measures, the EC had acted inconsistently with regard to all of the safeguard measures, as these were not based on risk assessments satisfying the definition of the SPS agreement and hence could be presumed to be maintained without sufficient scientific evidence.

Convention on Biological Diversity

Concerns of civil society relating to life forms and genetic material get discussed in two international fora. One is the Conference of the Parties (COP) to the Convention on Biological Diversity (CBD), along with a Commission on Plant Genetic Resources (PGR) for Food and Agriculture, of the Food and Agriculture Organisation (FAO). The other is the Commission in FAO on the International Undertaking on Plant Genetic Resources (IUPGR). Both the CBD and the Commission on PGR aim to ensure the conservation of biodiversity and the sustainable use of plant genetic resources for food and agriculture. The Convention was opened at the United Nations Conference on Environment and Development (UNCED) in Rio de Janeiro in 1992 and came into effect in 1993. There are currently 187 country members as well as the EU. The United States is not a signatory to the CBD.

The CBD provides for the transfer of biotechnology between parties on fair and most favourable terms, for conservation and sustainable use of biological diversity and use of genetic resources and preventing damage to environment. The implementation of the CBD is reviewed in the COP composed of all contracting parties, and it is in this forum that IPRs get discussed in relation to access to genetic resources, benefit-sharing, technology transfer and knowledge innovations and practices of indigenous and local communities. This process helps to focus

36 WT/DS 291.

on injuries in the public domain from monopoly elements in each IPR. The national delegations to COP are civil servants from environment ministries. They focus on conservation, sustainable development and food security.

In November 2001, a revised IUPGR became the legally binding international treaty on Plant Genetic Resources for Food and Agriculture (PGFRA). The Treaty recognises sovereign rights as well as interdependence of countries over their PGFRA. It establishes a multilateral system for access and benefit sharing by standard agreement for material transfer between members and with third parties, applying also to subsequent transfers. The recipient shall not have any IPR as will limit access to plant genetic resources for food and agriculture, or to their genetic parts and components. The US and Japan abstained in the voting of the treaty. If a DNA sequence or chemical is isolated and patented it becomes the property of another and not of the sovereign owner of plant material from which it was isolated. The treaty allows only access and benefit sharing among members and not any property in what is isolated. Anyone else is equally free to isolate and use it, if access or benefit is withheld to him (Duttfield 2002).

Developing countries have introduced measures to regulate IPRs to support the CBD objectives and have pushed for a move to revive old UN forums and create new forums on IPRs, in order to dilute the WTO regimen of TRIPS. Where technologies represent the IPRs of a particular country, any transfer of such technology must be on terms which recognise and are consistent with the adequate and effective protection of the IPRs. The importance given to recognising access, benefit-sharing, traditional knowledge and biosafety under the CBD has provided powerful ammunition to developing countries to counter the trend of exploitation and smuggling of national biological resources. Currently, Costa Rica requires application for protection of IPRs, to contain the certificate of origin and consent from the provider of biological material and traditional knowledge relating to it, from a government (Duttfield 2002). This in effect is aimed at preventing bio-piracy masquerading as an original invention meriting right to patent as an IPR. An Andean community has baulked against the global trend and will not allow life forms to be viewed as inventions.

Organisations in the international sphere have been brought into the fold, such as the Consultative Group on International Agricultural Research (CGIAR), founded in 1971, which was sponsored by the FAO, World Bank, UNDP and the UNEP. CGIAR supports sixteen international agricultural research centres (IARCs). The CGIAR network holds the largest collection of plant genetic resources (PGR) as an international trust of FAO. IARCs distribute germplasm to plant breeders and they cannot get IPRs on materials transferred. The push towards a more open and inclusive discussion has resulted in the CGIAR calling for a moratorium on grants on IPRs on all plant germplasms in trust with the FAO.[37] Even the US has indicated its willingness

[37] A report by the International Union for the Conservation of Nature and the Natural Resources 2005 calls for closer interaction between the WTO and CBD frameworks through the operation of a disclosure procedure.

to accept the goal of reversing the current decline in biodiversity (pressed for by G77) by the year 2010.

Security, safety and the Cartagena Principle

The difficulty of measuring risks associated with genetically modified organisms (GMOs) has also been taken up by developing countries. Many of these countries do not have any legislation governing the use of biotechnology, and lack effective control over compliance with security norms and measures. The CBD reiterated the centrality of the principle of national sovereignty over biological resources and instituted a legal framework that required bilateral market-like contracts between the holders of biological resources and the users. The emphasis in the CBD is on institutionalising the right to exploit resources within national jurisdictions.[38] The Cartagena Protocol, which was only brought into the remit of the Convention in the very last month of the legal drafting process, is important in terms of its reaffirmation of the 'precautionary principle', which states that, in the absence of full scientific certainty, a country can limit importation of GMOs on the grounds of their potentially damaging effects. The centrality of the precautionary principle in the CBD provides an additional rationale to national governments to take a risk-mitigating approach in the face of new and inadequately tested technologies. The importance of ensuring national sovereignty in improving the legal rights in trade of biological species was driven by important concerns about bio-piracy as well as biosafety. The issue of biosafety was taken forward by the adoption of the Cartagena Protocol on Biosafety in January 2000. The international pressure, particularly by the US, the EU and private corporate interests, was keen to focus on improving the international legislation on cross-border movement of biological resources, and the consultations on the precautionary principle only emerged in the later months of the negotiations (Bail *et al.* 2002). It is the first international treaty to recognise GMOs as a separate category of organism that requires its own specific regulatory framework. The Cartagena Protocol on Biosafety came into force on 11 September 2003. The strong emphasis on biosafety in the Cartagena Protocol is strongly oppositional to the position of the WTO that challenges the right of any country to take measures to protect its environment and its people to the detriment of free trade. Additionally, when countries have turned to the dispute settlement panels on environmental matters the panels have not possessed the necessary competence to make the decisions that can adequately take into account the full implications of the 'precautionary principle'.

When Sri Lanka decided in 2001 to ban GMOs in food and agriculture in order to protect its biodiversity and competitiveness in world markets (given the increasing consumer demand for GM-free food), the US embassy in Colombo threatened it with economic retaliations, including a WTO dispute

[38] See the official documentation Secretariat of the Convention on Biological Diversity (2005).

settlement panel. The thought of being condemned by the WTO and having to pay a fine for compensation is a considerable threat for a small country like Sri Lanka, and the Sri Lankan Parliament was forced to 'suspend' the law against GMOs. The threat of WTO sanctions against environmental measures has had a chilling effect on the development and ratification of major environmental agreements, most notably the Kyoto Protocol on climate change and the Biosafety Protocol on GM Organisms (Mulvaney 2002).

The WTO framework and the shape of agriculture

In the case of agriculture, there is a general view that domestic subsidies in agriculture are structural flaws that should not be permitted at all, as is the case for industrial subsidies, which are already banned in the WTO. Yet the call for a removal of subsidies must be initiated by the United States and the European Union, for it is their intransigence that has stalled progress of the Doha round on agriculture.

The relinquishing of subsidies by these nations is required to provide the appropriate signal for developing countries to reduce their domestic protection of agriculture. It must be a reciprocal action that facilitates mutual negotiation, a strongly Coasean point that has been forgotten within the WTO while being strongly reflected in the legal framework set out by the CBD (Boisvert and Caron 2002). The extreme shift to a narrow language of contract has written out these more embedded aspects of the process.

A radical, yet feasible, solution would be to permit agricultural subsidies in developing and developed countries not exceeding the level of direct and indirect subsidies in the US and the EU from year to year. This would help developing countries to copy the US subsidies, and also help the US, for the question has been asked, 'Where would American business and labour be, if food was imported below the real price of local production in the US?' US farmers would go bankrupt, the tractor and machinery companies would go bankrupt, and millions of people depending on these jobs would be without work, as would be those providing products and services to them (see Smith 2005). If the policy focus were to shift from no subsidy to employment generation, the remedy of participative welfare schemes for generating rural assets benefiting agricultural production would be suitable to augmenting existing purchasing power in rural areas, in all nations.

Agriculture needs to go out of the regimen of the WTO, in order to allay well-founded fears of food insecurity and restore to people, as producers and consumers, their food sovereignty, in all nations.[39] If agriculture goes out of the WTO regime, there will be a rise in agricultural prices and a revival of tariff in

[39] There was a joint agreement signed by International Federation of Agricultural Producers and the Secretariat of the CBD on 22 May 2007 to ensure the maintenance of biodiversity within agricultural practices. Joint agreements entered into by CBD, referred to as Partnership Agreements, are available at http://www.cbd.int/

developing countries to the level of agricultural subsidy in the US and EU, covering, direct, indirect, red, green, amber, blue, *de minimis* and all. The rectification of prices through reallocating incentives in the global agricultural markets is a more equitable and sustainable solution to that of the current WTO procedures of forcing unequally placed nations into a façade of free trade.

WTO and laws and agreements of other bodies

The growth of free trade agreements (FTAs) and bilateral agreements in the WTO regime indicate that advanced capitalist countries are now concerned that they cannot make adequate economic gains even within this regime (see Oxfam's website at http://www.oxfam.org.uk/). The difficulties of ensuring that trade provides the wherewithal to accumulate riches are compounded by growing labour power and the formation of labour unions. Labour power did not manage to gain a foothold in the international sphere to create a movement of proletariats of the world through their governments. The alternative was the creation of the ILO that helped governments to agree on a balance between labour rights and political stability in nations, even though in some nations political power of government was pro labour.

In its time, the WTO understood the power of international pressure of capital and also the gains to be had with a balanced approach, and recognised the need to balance its power with the power of the ILO. Labour standards are not a part of any multilateral agreement in the WTO, but they have been discussed extensively by members of the WTO in their meetings. The key phrase is 'core labour standards': that is, essential standards applied to the way workers are treated. The term covers a wide range of things, from use of child labour and forced labour to the right to organise trade unions and to strike. In 1996, ministers from member countries, meeting in Singapore, declared their commitment to observance of internationally recognised core labour standards. The WTO identified the ILO as the competent body to deal with labour standards and affirmed support for its work in promoting core labour standards, while expressing its belief that increased trade promotes core labour standards.

Additionally, while the WTO rejected use of the standards for protectionist purposes in trade it agreed that comparative advantage of countries, particularly low wages in developing countries, must in no way be called into question in matters of trade by reference to perceptions on labour or wage standards (implying that any conceivable change on free trade agreements applicable to low-wage countries will be opposed in the WTO, but the same governments could disagree on the wage standards in the ILO). Countries of the North use their skilled diplomats to decide on issues in both the ILO and the WTO, without having to subordinate the WTO to the united political power of states in the UN on any issue. The debates by members of the WTO outside the WTO agenda have posed three issues. A legal question is whether trade action is to be permitted as a means of putting pressure on countries considered to be severely violating core labour standards (commonly referred to as the weapon of human rights to reduce competition). The second, an analytical question, is whether, if a country has lower labour standards, for protecting rights enjoyed by its labour, it gains an unfair advantage by its exports (in practice more a dilemma for labour living by exports and unable to lose livelihood by demanding better standards). The third, an institutional question, is whether the WTO is the proper forum to discuss labour in trade (a political plea for mutually agreed hands-off approach in the ILO and the WTO on trade and labour-related political matters). The WTO is getting used to its 'divide and rule' powers in the political arena, to prevent the build-up of a united political power of states in the UN on trade and trade-related labour issues.

No DSB of WTO has addressed the restrictions on trade imposed by the Convention on International Trade in Endangered Species, the Montreal Protocol on Ozone Depleting Substances and the Biosafety Protocol to the Convention on Biological Diversity. The WTO's dispute settlement panels have only found unilateral trade measures taken by members of the WTO to be legally contrary to the WTO obligations.

The world summit on sustainable development (2002, in Johannesburg) seems to lean towards favouring free trade regimes over environmental protection. It suggested reconciling the conflicts between the two objectives of free trade and environmental protection, and that safety through international regulation should be decided within the WTO bodies rather than by the UN environment programme or a general forum like the UN General Assembly. This would appear to be an attempt by dominant players in the WTO to avoid a political ruling by the plenary body of the UN, whose charter empowers it to override all other international agreements like those of the WTO.[40]

The dominant voices within the WTO, and its associated bodies such as the WIPO, have whipped up a tornado regarding the need to protect IPRs while being extremely tardy in dealing with counter-claims that emphasise the centrality of the *public good* in the creation of new technologies and processes. Those who campaign for IPRs have been so completely caught up with the concerns of international trade and the benefits of technology to national economies, often through the offices and actions of corporate companies, that they seem to have entirely forgotten the primary reason for the state-led model of development which is the need to provide universal access. Today, these arguments of bringing the larger public into these debates about the public nature of knowledge are even more crucial than they were in the nineteenth century. Though it would appear that at present the right of national governments to determine the public national good is being consigned to the dustbin of history, the bout of amnesia regarding the defining and directing role of the nation state in ensuring development, is foolish at best, and dangerous at worst.

The contractual language of the WTO does not ensure that there is equal treatment of countries. The creation of wealth from increasing trade flows does

[40] Boisvert and Caron (2002) raise these concerns in their paper. Also see Loibl 2003: 164–5).

not seem to have been free; rather, it has created de facto political neo-colonisation while using trade agreements, not guns, *de jure*. The creation of the WTO has awarded political power to an international body that has increasingly taken a partisan view, that fairness should be measured by equal conditions of trade rather than greater integration in the world trade system. The developed nations, particularly the United States, have pushed their trade agendas through the creation of new branding and labels, whether these are the consequence of domestic environmental lobbies demanding 'dolphin-safe' products or political pressures to enhance 'human rights' to identify an increasing number of trade processes adopted by late industrialisers or emerging economies as unacceptable, as in the case of dumping.[41] The superficiality of contracts and the increasing strait-jacketing of developing countries will continue to create friction between trading nations until the fundamental disagreements in paradigms are understood and addressed in a manner that is more robust than the introduction of additional parameters in the current system. We need to look at the prevailing rubric in a concerted and discerning manner to identify its conceptual limitations and intellectual presumptions, rather than blindly pursuing ways and means of bringing in more rulings to reel in the riches.

[41] The inability of domestic civil society to counter the state framework on trade is one major reason for the increasing twisting of legitimate domestic concerns into international rules to hit developing countries hard. See Hadden and Tarrow (2006) for a sharp rebuke on the falling level of activism in the United States on global justice issues since 1999.

6 Dissonances and discordances

From deaf ears to inclusive development

What is seen is not the Truth
What is cannot be said
Trust comes not without seeing
Nor understanding without words
The wise comprehends with knowledge
To the ignorant it is but a wonder
Some worship the formless God
Some worship His various forms
In what way He is beyond these attributes
Only the Knower knows
That music cannot be written
How can then be the notes
Says Kabir, awareness alone will overcome illusion
(Kabir (15th century CE): 'Illusion and Reality')

Introduction

The poet Kabir, a wandering seer in fifteenth-century India, points out that the truth cannot be seen, it cannot be heard. His exhortation that music is experienced not by the external senses but within the soul appears contradictory to the ways of the modern world. The spiritual exhalation of a Sufi mystic could be regarded as having no bearing on the matters of this world. It seems even less likely that the views of a wandering mendicant could provide a framework for understanding the contradictions and conflicts that appear at every twist and turn of economic development.

Looking hard at the many challenges of achieving national development plans, it is the demands raised by local people in the face of directives of national and international decision-making that appear to be difficult to decipher and even harder to resolve. It sometimes appears that the needs of people are oppositional to those set out by nation states and international agencies and that people and professionals continue to fundamentally oppose each other (Chambers 1997). It is not just those engaged in the world of policy that are faced by confrontation: academic disciplines also display this loggerhead approach as they battle for intellectual supremacy in conceptualising international development.[1] The friction of competing ideas and the ensuing battle for supremacy over a concept, problem or dilemma through a brandishing of academic tools has gained the intellectual centre ground. This scramble to claim a disciplinary advantage has also become visible in the answers given to how and why countries grow economically, socially or politically (and fall by the wayside), that continue to trouble those engaged in the world of international development. At the same time contradictions have emerged within the process of development and the claims of people who have been inadvertently marginalised or even consistently denied access to rights and resources.

Additionally, the power of these disciplinary traditions and tools lies in their ability to teach us to view the world in particular ways, yet seeing is not the only way to make sense of the complex interplay between economic, social, political and cultural claims in local, national and global arenas. Indeed, in human terms, it is our other senses that permit the identification of auditory, tactile and olfactory signals that may belie visual signals. The preponderance of the textual over the oral stems from such a privileging and is commonplace in the harder social sciences, particularly in economics. In many cases the written (documented) word or model takes on much greater power than its oral equivalent. Though the softer social sciences have explored the text in greater depth and detail there remains a deficit in our understanding of the oral in economics.

This bias that weights the text and oral differentially also manifests itself strongly in the legal system. A code of law is the context within which the testimony of the witness is understood. Judicial rulings use the text of the legal code and the record of past cases to arbitrate on the oral and written statements of the concerned parties. This is based on a rubric which fashions rules that privilege text over the oral. Such a rubric projects a partial reality based on the letter of the law rather than on listening to the voices of those affected by inequity and immorality.

The development models that were drawn up and analysed in Western academic spaces were applied to the newly independent nations of Asia and Africa and such academic exercises were regarded as legitimate vehicles for devising development policies based on blueprints from the capitalist world.[2] It was regarded as appropriate for these countries to follow the models of the West, with the West firmly in control, and guiding the process. The model builders

[1] See Majid Rahnema for a critique of the power of development theories to distort the dilemmas of development (Rahnema and Bawtree 1997). The contradiction between the importance accorded to Western development theory, and its growing irrelevance in explaining the difficulties of development, is the subject of a powerful exposition by Gilbert Rist (2002) on the rise of Western theories as the sole repository of knowledge on development,

[2] The process of development was regarded as a linear process and nations emerging from the colonial yoke viewed as benefiting from the power of industrialisation. See Lewis (1954) and Huntingdon (1968).

and paradigm proponents were happy to take their notions of development and its associated sets of models and techniques to regions outside Europe, even as these were receiving criticism for their ill-conceived thinking and faulty wares within their own academic institutions (Trubek and Galanter 1974). The inappropriate use of Western development models and the hasty dismantling of domestic and indigenous institutions have together led to the brewing of numerous and considerable conflicts due to the imposition of Western rules to design the rubric for economic development through the second half of the twentieth century.

> During the nineteenth century several 'laws' were laid down for the leading industrial countries. Having been proved wrong by the unfolding events in every instance, the law makers then migrated to warmer climes, that is, to the less developed countries. And here they really came into their own. For the less developed, dependent countries have long been the objects of history ... soon we were witness to a veritable deluge of paradigms and models, from the vicious circle of poverty, low-level equilibrium traps, and the uniform stage sequences of the economist, to the tradition and non-achievement-oriented or status-hungry personality of the sociologist, psychologist or political scientist.
>
> (Hirschman 1970: 335)

During what was regarded as the golden age of capitalism during the third quarter of twentieth-century development, it was acceptable to discuss redistribution through legal mechanisms and to focus on the ability of the government to use both legal and economic tools to bring into play a countercyclical force to contend with the fluctuations generated by capitalist tendencies. In contrast to this period, which corresponds to the first movement in the field of law and development, the 1980s saw the rise of neoliberalism ushering in a rubric of unfettered capitalism where it became appropriate to create rules that gave primacy to the creation rather than the distribution of riches, and it led to the second movement in law and development (Trubek and Santos 2006). The second movement further advanced the ascendancy of the market, which reached a new zenith at the end of the twentieth century with a feverish search for new commodities to trade, for new resources to acquire. The institutional and structural fetishisms that dominated society in the late twentieth century prevent us from comprehending the possibility of a different societal frame with its attendant set of social norms; instead, they make for an 'unwarranted denial of our power to change society, and ourselves' (Unger 2000: 26). Consequently, the rich are completely unable to register the demands, complaints and pleas of the underprivileged, poor and marginalised sectors of society, in the absence of a sense of community and given the lack of norms of morality and obligation (Rosser 2007).

The growing deafness of dominant groups in the international, national and local spheres to the objections and complaints of those who were excluded from the development process is a consequence of the 'winner takes all' attitude that had come to be regarded as the norm in late twentieth-century capitalism. The growing consensus among the top dogs is that opportunities must be grasped without any undue delay and therefore questions of equity and redistribution are treated as inappropriate or even unnecessary, which sharpens the discordances between the rich and the poor.[3] The discordant forms of development that have been produced by the impervious and impenetrable societal structures that support capitalist accumulation have come to be regarded as part of current societal forms of exclusion and inequity. The combined push of neoliberal economics and the directives of the second movement of law and development, to further capitalist growth through new laws, particularly in relation to property rights, has given vent to systemic dissonances between the words and agendas imposed by the major capitalist players and the demands of excluded groups and communities for the acknowledgement of, and remedy for, their unmet needs.

Exclusion becomes an inherent part of the dominant rubric of late twentieth-century economics as it seeks uniformity while denying the existence of any differences in ideas and understandings regarding the role of the market. The attempt to incorporate all reality into an existing single theoretical framework is a glaring instance of intolerance and is accompanied by an unwillingness to accept that historical specificity and the 'feeling of experience' play an important role in the development of societies (Hirschman 1970). Where theoretical analysis does acknowledge that other methods of analysis do exist, it still regards them as lesser and inferior (Glenn 2004). The admittance of equality between systems of belief and analysis is hard to come by. This singular paradigm that all human beings operate using the same set of principles and propositions generates a widespread failure to consider equality at anything other than the individual level.

The dominant rubric in the realm of economics and law is unable to identify dissonances and discordances, for it is unable to hear, far less heed, the voices of the marginalised and oppressed. The complete insensitivity to the auditory realm arises through having lost any predisposition to comprehend the complexities of sound, and to understand musical composition. An ear that can hear notes, identify chords and distinguish between melody and accompaniment is necessary to distinguish between harmony and discord produced by voices. Discordance arises when chords jar and prevent harmony from being achieved. The root of the word 'chord' is the heart, and the inability to perceive the feelings, emotions and passions of others blocks communication between those at the centre of capitalism and those thrown onto the rubbish heap by benign neglect or conscious exclusion. The heartlessness at the core of capitalism permits it to

[3] The separation of allocation and distribution is a central aspect of neoclassical economics that permits the study of efficiency to be undertaken. However, this separation is a pedagogical tool rather than a policy prescription. The tendency to regard production as separate from distribution has not only remained in economics but has also become commonplace in the field of law and economics. See Heckman (1997) for a review of the consequence, particularly the shortcomings of such thinking.

deepen accumulation by pushing for longer hours, greater effort and higher productivity at the expense of the moral and the cultural.[4]

This imperviousness to the dire consequences of exclusion and inequity hardens into an immunity, among the well-placed, against claims, calls and castigation by the marginalised. Such immunity becomes a justification for pushing harder and faster for further capital accumulation and authorises the blind, deaf and unflinching pursuit of these riches in the face of increasing conflict within and between oppressed and discarded communities. The presence of a cacophony of discordant voices cannot be identified if the prevailing rubric denies the possibility of disagreement in the ideas that are lodged in individual minds. Where a single framework with hidebound rules which single-mindedly searches for and acquires riches, guides a rubric, it does not permit social dimensions to enter its arena nor bring with it characteristics of a relational world, with its norms of reciprocity and codes of morality (Hodgson 2001).

Attempts to bring in social norms of reciprocity have been consistently warded off by both large international and national institutions as they have propagated and perpetuated the myth of a flat world. There is a refusal to engage with the questions people raise about how and whom such a paradigm of development of wealth accumulation will affect in society, and a reluctance to reorder the paradigm to shift and refashion political power. The total inability of development institutions to create 'concordance', i.e. an agreement and thereby an accord regarding the patterns of development, or to respond to the ideas and voices commenting on development is a telling consequence of the growing insularity of those amassing riches, who continue to use rules that alienate many groups and communities in a late twentieth-century rubric of capitalism.

If the powerful base their strategies and actions on their own reading of a situation and do not regard it necessary to listen to the dispossessed, or to endeavour to create opportunities for the excluded to speak in their own voices and vernaculars, then dissonance seems unavoidable. The consistent shutting out of dissenting voices that has accompanied the certainty of those in power, in the belief that wealth creation can be isolated from social structures and community pressures, is both short-sighted and faulty. This shutting out of the unwanted, unacceptable and unpalatable dimensions of capitalism occurs not only within national and at the international levels, but also at levels in between, as evidenced in the re-emergence of supra-national regional formations, with the established European Union undergoing expansion and the emergence of new formations assigned to other geographies, such as the East Asian, South Asian and Sub-Saharan African, and lately Central Asian, formations, that amalgamate nations while emptying them of national histories and economic specificities. The consideration of an Asian model of development and

4 The criticism levelled against late twentieth-century capitalism increasingly focuses on the lack of the moral, historical and cultural. It would appear that the human aspects of development are being stripped of all aspects of the broader context. See Folbre (2002) for a critique of economics for taking away the elements of the familial.

its relation to a distinct system of law in the region permits analysis in Asia that has followed a different path to be regarded in its own terms. This is positive but could become suspect if there was a fundamental distancing of these societies from the Western model of development. It is one thing to recognise the importance of history but quite another to look down on non-Western models as lacking in some way (Jayasuriya 2000).

Wealth accumulation and political power

The importance of history is particularly telling in the creation of nation states where past struggles over forms of political, and sometimes colonial, oppression, fashion the new dimensions of power-sharing and structures of State and society (Mamdani 1996; Chatterjee 2003). Government power and preferment is used to create individual wealth with little regard for community or nation, and these get reflected in the gains made by wealthy individuals. The rules of the nation are formally set out to protect and uphold the rights of the individual, sometimes even against the interference of the State. Developed nations might wish to cast their development path in terms of the paradigm of free trade but the reality of their development is closely linked to state support, through economic instruments as well as through political power, even military manoeuvres (Hobsbawm 1968).

National polities are not equitable either. The power of the corporate is replacing the power of labour. In the 1972 US presidential elections, of the $500 million spent, only about $13 million came from trade unions; the rest came from big business and wealthy individuals. In the 1956 elections, the contributions of 742 businessmen matched those of the unions representing 17 million workers, at a time when workers' unions played a considerable political role in the national production system. In Britain, the New Labour government, from 1997, in the main followed the policies of Conservative governments and saw its main funding switch from unions to wealthy businessmen. Significantly, New Labour's success was in part dependent on support from the right-wing media empire (Kivel 2004).

The notion of efficiency requires a horizontal form of competition which is presumed in the term 'a level playing field'. The existence of horizontal competition presupposes that there are no existing hierarchies. However, the world of business encounters many forms of hierarchies. Elite groups, in both the business world and government, recognise that they have to influence attitudes and opinions. The presence of hierarchy is necessary to ensure order. In fact, the manner in which elites configure society and create an environment where trade is permitted permeates the work of Vifredo Pareto, regarded as a leading figure in the marginal economic revolution (Medema and Samuels 2001).

The creation of bureaucratic, political and industrial hierarchies by elites has the objective of collective capture and control of wealth accumulation processes. The club-like structures that are set up by these elites to control labour practices and maintain their power draw on various financial as well as social markers, so as to play as important a role in industry as it does in the old boy network in the clubroom. The intention in each case is to keep out newcomers, and the vertical controls within the economy seek to pin individuals down, making them subservient to the market through contracts: a society-wide mechanism that mimics the processes operating within the Coasean firm (Fennell 2003).

The growing ability of elites, domestic, international and transnational, to create organisations and clubs to consolidate control over corporate riches makes redistribution more difficult, as these growing corporate forms take notions of equality and competition into the more aggregative sphere of companies and financial institutions, while differentiation of pay and individualised contracts operate at the individual level. The discordance between accumulation and distribution remains unheard, and where perceived is ignored. The dissonances that permeate through society when such discordances are experienced create waves of sound that buffet the underprivileged, but there are no longer frequencies that are heard by the affluent and acquisitive sections of society.

The dissonances created by the discordant clashes between the rich and the poor, the winners and the losers, the capitalist classes and the excluded groups, can begin to explain why it is neither socially acceptable, nor politically expedient, nor economically viable to allow the market to lead and the law to follow. Where the second movement in the 'law and economics movement' would seem to advise that the role of the law is to be the servant of the market, older thinking within law and economics would advocate calculating the transaction costs of exchange to ascertain whether there should be intervention by government, and what role government should play (McChesney 2006). At the other end, the third and latest wave of movement in law and development advocates that there is a need to allow judicial reform and social redistribution to take the upper hand (Trubek and Santos 2006).

Coercive forms of equality vs demands for public equity

In contrast to the corporate world, the forms of organisation within which human beings grow up are the social contexts of families, schools, playgrounds and neighbourhoods. The differentials, rewards and punishments that they encounter become the basis of the motivations that are learned and developed over time. Learning to craft rules that attract and encourage individuals who share norms of reciprocity and trustworthiness, or who can learn them over time, is a fundamental skill needed in all democratic societies. The positive side of law is that 'rules are the tools that fallible human beings can use to try to change situations to achieve better outcomes' (Ostrom 2005: 132–3).

The absence of any sense of obligation among the wealthy corporate and political elite triggers confrontational modes of action from the deprived and dispossessed sections of society. As traditional forms of redistribution have now been phased out, if not made completely obsolete, by the new and fast-growing strata of the elite, confrontations shift away from traditional forms of organised protest, such as trade union actions, to new forms. The new forms manifest either as extremely violent opposition that spills over into local movements, or as organised protests that are inspired by new international legal movements (Rajagopal 2003) which have generated a new shared language of global rights. The emphasis on personal liberty, and the right to speech, assembly and association are common to both types of movements from below, but the forms vary considerably between the local and the global spheres. The possibility of cross-engagement between local and global movements is a characterising feature of the new twenty-first-century forms.[5]

When the illusion of legitimacy wears thin, people organise themselves, and yet such organised groups are perceived as a threat to the security of the State. If the State is blind to injustices, such as those of unfair wages or inhuman ostracism of the poor, then discontent breaks into violence that spills over into the actions and strategies of social, political and economic group structures. The subversion of law by irate groups is viewed as a crime by the State rather than a form of legitimate protest. The State does have the authority to wield discretionary powers that override the life and liberty of its people, yet its exercise does not result in a curbing of violence but in a further fomenting of unrest into violent acts of rebellion.

Historically, the power of the absolute monarch has been appropriated by the legislature and the courts. Consequently, the right of contempt lies with the people of a sovereign republic. In nations with a monarchical head, the court retained the power of contempt as it remained the court of the monarch. Only the people, by their constitution or law, can share that power with the court or the legislature. But in republics the power of contempt that lay with the king, as the absolute monarch, would seem to have been appropriated by the judiciary, overlooking the people. The elections are a check on the legislature; as is the judiciary on the executive. Judicial independence is a functional one and not absolute independence. The function is to subserve social values that are in the constitution and the laws. The law should be accessible to all and the judiciary should not be above the law.[6] This is a shift away from the judicial right to use the power of contempt in its decision.

The adversarial legal culture, which is extremely competitive and in which the courts function, tends to be impervious to social mores and social purposes (Kannabiran 2003). Judges are products of their contemporary society, of its culture and norms, and though they are seen to be objective arbiters of the truth, they are not above and beyond social influence. Their perception of themselves may well differ from the reality of the influences they are under, because that reality

[5] The movement that led to the creation of the World Social Forums was one such attempt to create an alternative world.

[6] Chief Justice of India, K.G. Balakrishnan, raised the matter of whether the judges of the Supreme Court of India, should be subject to the Right to Information Act, in relation to whether they came under the purview of the law of the land. His current thinking appears to be that, though it is a matter of interpretation, it is clear that judges and public servants in that capacity can be above and outside the reach of the law.

gets hidden in the process of judicial decision-making. There are systematic differences in judicial decision-making, which can be attributed to race, gender or ethnicity. However, judges behave differently from legislators who make the law, in the context of both the influences of social norms and values on them.[7] In the United States, Congress and the president constrain the judiciary through the appointment process, impeachment, budgets, the executive enforcement of judicial decisions, and Congressional control over jurisdiction.[8] The problem with 'appointment and removal power' relating to both the presidential and the senatorial roles in the selection of justices had been the availability of basic information about nominees. The Senate maintained its procedure of handling all nominations in closed sessions until 1929, when nomination sessions became public unless they were to be closed by majority vote.

Conflict is indeed a characteristic of pluralist market society that has come to the fore with remarkable persistence. It is the natural counterpart of technical progress and of the ensuing creation of new wealth for which market society is rightly famous. Conflicts are associated with newly emerging inequalities and sectoral or regional declines and are the counterpart of precisely those various dynamic groups and regions that have been able to avail themselves of new economic opportunities and align themselves with new hierarchies and rules (Knight 1991).

Rules that support wealth-creating methods through reconfiguring ownership rights, thereby conferring legitimacy on the strategies and actions, come from the legislature while remedies for justice denied to languishing victims of development come from judicial decisions. The role of law-making in ensuring equality for citizens has been expanded and the judiciary has been brought into line as an equal player. On the other hand, the meting out of justice with regard to fair play is still a matter of considerable concern and debate. There is debate in the United Kingdom about whether the legal profession should continue to consider 'ethical' matters as its professional basis or be 'seen to administer justice' in an efficient and market-oriented manner (Grout *et al.* 2007). The capacity of the law to deal with ethics, morality or the market are all up for discussion, even criticism, and this is not restricted to a particular political system or level of economic development. In the case of China, there has been a rapid increase in the filling out of the legal system, in terms of both amendments to existing statutes and its application in the provincial and local sphere, but this has raised concerns about the institutional capacity of the State to ensure a uniform rule of law in the country. In the case of Malaysia, there are still concerns about the close proximity of the judicial system to the political process and cases are still pending against senior judges in the country. There are also objections raised about judicial and legal processes that are marked

[7] Lawrence Friedman, 'Judging the Judges: Some Remarks on the Way Judges Think and the Way Judges Act', referred to in Drobak (2006).

[8] John Ferejohn and Larry Kramer, 'Judicial Independence in a Democracy: Institutionalizing Judicial Restraint', referred to Drobak (2006).

by ideological rather than objective motivation and those that concur with religious rather than secular conceptions of the law.

Ideologies, beliefs and norms

In the social realm there are instances where the power is derived from social status. It can emerge from a sense of respect or from the ability to coerce others. Power that is not based on reputation discriminates between superior and inferior status and generates a desire in the lower power group to acquire the characteristic that signifies the higher power group as superior. Sometimes discrimination is overt, but most often it is covert, enabling claims that behaviour is fair and equitable. The discriminatory rules are sewn into the hierarchy and become beliefs, powerful and difficult to change (Sidanius and Pratto 1999: 20, 303).

The role of religion has long been present in the legal system and Lord Denning pointed out that, in England, it was only in the early twentieth century that the offence of blasphemy was abolished and that freedom of religion was permitted. It was the safety of the State that was paramount in taking a view on religion, and not the doctrines or metaphysics of the professed religion. In England, because the State remains religious, freedom of religion is maintained. The Church was there for making the State religious. The Church itself was not political (Denning 1949). The US Supreme Court favoured accommodation of religious faith and held that the US Constitution did not demand a callous indifference to religious groups. Separation of Church and State does not mean that public institutions can make no adjustments of their schedules to accommodate the religious needs of the people, as indicated in the permission granted to New York City state-run schools to allow students to visit religious centres for instruction during school hours, on the written request of parents.

The US Supreme Court upheld, as a law of libel, a statute prohibiting any publication portraying 'depravity, criminality, unchastity, or lack of virtue of a class of citizens' of any 'race, colour, creed or religion' and thereby exposure of such class to 'contempt, derision or obloquy'. It thereupon upheld prosecution of a group which published a petition attacking the 'negro' race and asking for local segregation laws, even in the absence of 'clear and present danger'. The dissenting view was that the statute was unconstitutional, since the constitution requires tolerance of the intolerant, where freedom of speech is involved (in the absence of 'clear and present danger'). The group charged for libel would have sympathisers in many states and the law could equally serve them (if they attacked) to charge them (the blacks) for advocating equality and non-segregation as an attack on such sympathisers in their imagined libel of them (the whites). If the minority ('negros') sought to be segregated by the racist group, viewed in the majority judgement as a victory for them, an ancient remark would apply to them; 'Another such victory and I am undone'.[9]

[9] Beauharnais v. Illinois, Supreme Court of the United States 1952, 343 US 250, quoted in Williams (1956: 402–6).

The power of group differentiation in maintaining a polity and society and the role of the law in creating these distinctions has not received a great deal of thought. The focus on equality before the law has made considerations of equity of justice across groups marked by differences of race, class, gender and ethnicity, a lesser area of concern. The ability of legal argument to split hairs and to unpick the threads of an argument not only wins the case, but also sets in motion ideas about differentiation and discrimination that demand a greater attention to matters of equity.

The veneration for the economics of efficient production presumes that the market has become superior to the law, but it is indeed the case that *efficiency of production* is intimately linked to the property rights regime for national resources (Libecap 1989, 1999). In particular it is the laws regarding ownership that award an owner of private property the right to exchange, buy, sell or even destroy a resource. In the case of common property, not only do individuals only have some form of user rights, but they are also unable to cash in the value of their common property unless all users agree to exchange property. Obtaining a full value for common property entails a communal agreement to assess its true price rather than accepting the estimated price, as well as ensuring that the commons has the legal approval to be dealt with as a joint property. If law gives that right to a small number of joint owners, they may effectively function as the board of management of a joint stock company. Without such legal right to property, the law of contract will not empower users as owner/s to exchange property resource or to transform the production (resource with value addition) under a contract. The law governing a company or corporation follows this precise method, by the separation of joint ownership of assets of company as a body corporate, from management of its assets. The public concerns about parcelling out broadcasting waves raised by Coase occurred in a milieu where commercial and amateur operators were sending out signals on many frequencies and jamming others, which led to regulation of the use of airwaves in the *public interest* after the World War I. There was a shortage of frequencies in the UK at the time, and consequently the government placed a legal obligation of impartiality on broadcasting on the BBC and on others accepting public service obligations (Grade 2005). The growing acquiescence to the economic logic of the market and its implication for moral behaviour are also found in the United States where the Telecommunications Act 1996 was passed in order to increase competition.

If the law makes provision for an equitable share in the taxed incomes of the wealthy, even indirectly by state transfer of GNP for welfare, it will empower the marginalised and discarded sections of society. There is also an incentive to judicial officers to restore equity into law, for the just interpretation of law will increase the legal knowledge of empowered groups of people and unjust advancement will become more difficult.

For developing equitable mortgages, the equity, i.e. the value of property after deducting the charge on it, that is the balance of loan outstanding and interest not paid should be the focus of equity. Similarly, when capital is advanced to the company by shareholders and it goes up in value (as the appreciated book value), because the value of the share fluctuates over time it is termed the 'equity share'; and players in the exchange market determine the value of that share invariably at a price higher than the appreciated book value. Fears of flight of capital, foreign and domestic, may not arise if equitable capital continues to get revered, welcomed and worshipped, and corporate capital and their dividend payouts get exempted from bearing the burden of welfare. It would be only the direct and indirect tax revenues that would then bear the costs of welfare by transfer of GNP for reparations of historical inequity.

Rules, responsibilities and reciprocity

In England, judges created the rule that every man has a negative duty (prohibition) that he ought not to injure his neighbour without just cause or excuse, in the area of torts. This notion of duty has both negative and positive aspects, and is particularly pertinent to those engaged in a public calling or in providing essential supplies and services, It is not acceptable for those employed in these professions to carry out activities simply for their own private profit, but they must also provide adequate and efficient service at reasonable charges for the good of the public, or what is regarded as a positive duty. This duty rests not only on public servants, but also on private providers of goods and services. The country requires every man to do his duty not only in times of war, but every day (Denning 1949).

Duties have an explicit interpersonal dimension and call for a commitment which could be based on a set of convictions, principles or faith. Social norms, on the other hand, do not always have a significant duty to other individuals. Safety-oriented conduct, like the use of seat belts or not smoking in public places, is made up of norms or legal rules applicable to all. The duty of one to get another to conform to such norms is generated by interpersonal interaction and is not based on a generalisable principle of a form of social monitoring.

Reciprocity and trust also, like duty, arise from a conviction of the need to make interpersonal commitment. They are present in members of self-governing groups where learning problem-solving skills in a local context generates citizens with more general problem-solving skills which enable them to reach out and more effectively examine far-reaching problems that affect 'all peoples living on this earth' (Ostrom 2005: 287–8). The institution of family has been looked at as a commons, which all human beings need and necessarily must replicate as a duty to incomers of the future into the world.[10] The norm of reciprocity is the key to trust and cooperation (Cárdenas and Ostrom 2006; Drobak 2006). Ethical norms and social norms (as persuasive conventions), as also legal rules, operate from outside, yet abidance in them also requires an inner conviction of duty. Individual choices are based on past actions and there

[10] Robert Ellickson, referred to in Drobak (2006).

is continued interaction with those whom individuals trust, referred
economic rationality 'embedded' in social relationships (Sunstein 2003

Norms and law may work together, or in parallel, to influence behaviour in society, guiding legitimate interaction and deterring anti-social interaction. Reciprocity and its positive reinforcement of individual duty appeals to the heart and an inner understanding, as in the sentiment that 'it is necessary to feed a starving supplicant' (Drobak 2006). A social norm often operates as a soft law and promotes adherence to contractual obligations and fairness in business dealings. It is regarded in such cases as an alternative route to formal laws and lends itself to ensuring a lesser need to resort to judicial enforcement of contractual and business obligations (Fennell 2008a).

The dissonances and discordances of wealth accumulation will find considerable remedy from the establishment of equitable principles at the heart of institutions. The belief systems valued in society that are reflected in social institutions; the property rights regimes that are defined by political institutions, and the reduction of uncertainty and management of risk that characterise the working of economic institutions, jointly reconfigure the path of human development. The key to evolutionary change is the intentionality of the players, and economic change is shaped by their perceptions about the consequences of their actions, their beliefs and their preferences and experiences. Soft laws provide a way of working with societal structures, and they also abound in international agreements, since nations interact with each other in a manner similar to self-regulating guilds, as in the case of the G-8 and South–South alliances within the WTO. While technology does hold the key to new possibilities of wealth accumulation, new opportunities are shaped by developing new organisational forms and systems of production within a particular society. The ability to harness technology is a product of the skills, knowledge and enterprise that resides in a society, and it provides the larger societal context within which corporate institutions work to manage risk and accumulate capital.

The current capitalist preference for creating a single focus, a uniform skill set, and a monolithic outlook may not ensure a strong and stable society. Motivations to use laws as the weapon of political power and economic motivations as the weapons of wealth cause discordances such as the hardening of hearts against historical injustices and the loss of morality and collapse of a realm of ethical duties and prohibitions, which work against fashioning current remedies through state and societal processes such as welfare or reciprocal arrangements.

The developmental experiences of China, Malaysia and India provide fertile ground for examining the varied manner in which the mechanisms of the market, legal claims and welfare policies have been drawn upon in the pursuit of economic development. The oddities that have emerged from a narrow understanding of the market as the only instrument to ensure wealth accumulation, without regard to the social structures and norms that fashion the lives and livelihoods of families, communities and sub-national territories, are not just matters to ponder over but are warnings of the dangers that lie in continuing to adopt such a restrictive rubric. The ability of national governments to engage with these levels of human life, within the nation state, is beneficial, rather than harmful, to its negotiations in the realm of international organisations and global trade. Gazing at Figures 3.1, 4.1 and 5.1 provides a clue to the way forward, for developing countries to regard international development as a set of opportunities by which they can move away from the straitjacket of existing models of development foisted on them by narrow academic vision, purposeful international agencies and impatient national ministries. The role of the law permits a return to an older, more inclusive form of intellectual rubric, that embeds current economic exchange within a historical context, and it permits development trajectories to be examined and understood, not as a failure of their particular institutions and beliefs in advancing economic productivity but by regarding social and economic spheres as jointly reconfiguring the path of human development (North 2005).

The legal systems that have prevailed in many countries have been widely regarded as major obstacles to their economic advancement. The challenge that faces us in the field of international development is to shift the framework that has reduced the power of economics and law to a simplistic use of markets and contracts, to one that sees the conundrums of development as a consequence of a limited vision, that has excluded and marginalised; to no longer be deaf to dissenting voices and claims from below. It is only in this broader rubric of social science analysis that heterogeneity of class, gender, race and ethnicity can be regarded as a major source and potential for wealth creation. The ability to hear other voices, to refashion social structures, to empower individuals with greater and more nuanced understanding provided by a more inclusive rubric, works to create new incentives in the market. It fashions new methods to make claims and expand welfare arrangements to ensure that wealth works to reorder laws and norms which will reduce conflicts, disorder and exclusion.

* econ & law → market & contract

* heterogeneity

* export-led industrialization
[sectoral differences
macroeconomics]

7 Reclaiming law and development

Ensuring equitable rules, inclusive rubrics and sustainable riches

The pen and the paper of the enemy
Imprisoned me
As an arm has yet been using
The pen as a weapon
As a mind has been employing
The paper as a front

Not for inciting the people to get armed
But for not getting armed myself
(Varvara Rao 1973, 'The Jail')[1]

We are one weak-hearted generation
Made immature by one domineering generation
We know nothing much about justice;
No one taught us about politics
Or the rule of law
(Rendra 1974, 'State of Emergency')

The draw of the market

The power of the market and the violence that it contains is exposed every time it imposes its rules on communities and peoples across the globe. W.S. Rendra addresses his Indonesian compatriots in 'State of Emergency', exhorting them to shake off their placidity and to act collectively and claim their rights in society. The concerns of academia, non-governmental organisations and development agencies are often latecomers in the imposition process and faint in protest volume. Also, the potential power of a market without social or cultural dimensions is attractive to national governments and international agencies since they are eager to grasp the spoils of development. These institutions are increasingly seeking to use market rules that permit them to insulate themselves from socially constituted movements which oppose their directives and programmes within domestic contexts. The revolutionary poet Varvara Rao protests that the rules laid down in national laws by the Indian governmental

[1] From www.varavararao.org (accessed 31 July 2008).

pens imprison their own people, in their headlong pursuit of market-based development.

These rules that have established the capitalist world are indeed powerful in their ability to ensure wealth accumulation, and it is this feature that acts to reinforce the virtues of those who do gain riches. Capitalist institutions operate within a rubric that regards the market as the primary mechanism for ensuring value creation through competition between firms and between individuals. Social forces are deemed not to have any influence, yet these very institutions covertly draw on the power maintained by social hierarchies and the value accorded to rank and status. It is these same market rules that work to both shore up capitalist institutions and tacitly reinforce social institutions that privilege the economic over the social dimensions of production, exchange and distribution.

Neoclassical thinking still maintains that the current rubric of capitalism ensures that the market is completely removed from the social dimension, is devoid of moral sentiment and is completely disjointed from culture or tradition. This ruling rubric has directed the past two centuries of capitalist development and imposed a very particular and restrictive straitjacket on the contours of wealth creation and accumulation. This rubric of economics followed today has moved far away from Adam Smith's concerns with the moral and deems that the market is able to separate the social system from the economic sphere. Within this rubric, any intrusions by social, moral and affective concerns are viewed as irregularities in the economic system. Yet prices do not emerge instantaneously, nor is there always an efficient pricing mechanism. The cost to players in engaging in market transactions is the deciding trigger for choosing between the market and a contract through bilateral negotiation, in order to agree on the price of exchange.

While economists regard contracts as assistance to the parties, lawyers have regarded them as a mechanism for balancing the private interests of parties with the public interest. Notions of public interest do not appear on the economic radar screen but they do become visible on the legal screen. Judicial and regulatory power to control the market is shunned, yet the use of legal rights and rules to keep costs of exchange low remains incontrovertible within economics. Such notions of law serving self-interest have also been transported into the field of law and economics. For instance, marginal costing principles are used to evaluate compensation for death based on 'foregone income', by reference to the earning capacity of the deceased before death. Such a perspective militates against a moral and legal understanding of equality of the lives of rich and poor who, say, die under the wheels of a motorist. The delinking of wealth accumulation from the distribution of assets in marginal analysis has found its way into legal thinking, with the effect of effacing the political implications of legal rights that are awarded to individuals. Voices located in the many worlds have enunciated concerns that the current rubric of development has a limited understanding of individual equality and denies any place for demands of equity. These dissenting voices demand that rules that impact social structures and institutions, adversely affecting the everyday lives of people, be dismantled, and yet dissenters continue to face violence and imprisonment.

Law, institutions and development

Laws create institutions to reduce the attempts of human beings to manipulate behaviour, in order to facilitate practices that advance the accumulation of wealth in society. Coasean analysis showed that property rights are a historically constructed set of rules that affected distribution in an economy, yet neo-classical economics has continued to regard institutional development as a function of economic forms in the market, rather than changing forms in the law. Wealth distribution rules follow an established tradition and history, and where these wealth rights are created with an exclusive focus on equality in relation to individuals they overlook the legal concept of equity.[2]

Economic development which does not contend with historical inequities is in danger of being upstaged by social movements. The current rubric advances the view that countries should adopt a range of political ideologies with associated legal systems where the market provides economic development, yet the view does not provide remedies for historical inequities. The instability and violence that emerges from ignoring equitable and inclusive forms of capitalist development cannot be countered unless new rules are devised from an expanded and richer rubric, where riches can be directed to remedy inequity and injustice.

Why rules and rubrics for riches?

The ability of humankind to conceive of ideals opposed to self-interest, such as notions of the *universal good*, provides an alternate rubric that could change the relationship between riches and rules in the realm of economic development. In contrast, the rubric of efficiency that is central to economics is based on marginal principles. It is not linked to reduction of inequality of wealth in society. The Gini coefficient remains simply a measure of income disparities; it does not point the way to improving the effectiveness of economic policy for reducing inequality. A needs-based equity coefficient would serve that purpose better; as for example the subsidy provided by the State to satisfy the minimum economic needs of all its citizens, as a ratio of the GNP.

Inequality in access to the market, or educational institutions, may get redressed by addressing unfair restrictions imposed by existing institutional rules, but historical injustices need redress by law enforcement to refashion the mores of society. Equity will not result from financial or other compensation in

[2] One reason that the New Institutional Economics failed to address the drivers of economic change was that it initially regarded individual advancement as the sole motivation for economic growth.

the form of affirmative discrimination related to social identities outside the rules of the market; it demands reform of social relations, moral framework and affective attitudes, which individuals engage in. The legal rubric of 'equity' is seen in opposition to the rubric of 'equality', for equity moves the focus away from the rights of an individual.

The market, household and ownership

In political philosophy the notion of public and private spheres has held centre ground since the seventeenth century, with the public sphere being deemed as a male domain while women are relegated to the private sphere of the household. The collapse in feudal labour relations and advent of industrialisation which heralded the rise of capitalism sharpened that distinction of public and private. Yet the patriarchal social construction of gender, devaluing work of women in both the spheres, is not acknowledged in the economic rendition of the processes of capitalism and development.

Economic trajectories are invariant with regard to gender, and understand the labour market to have the same drawing power on men and women resulting in an identical impact on both. Economic development models have been 'gender blind' till the last quarter of the twentieth century, by regarding labour as a factor of production rather than a consequence of gender relations. That gender relations and economic conditions for development are mutually constituted and that economic principles might have a role in the household is not taken into consideration, whereby gender relations, as a social feature, are not seen to affect economic development.

This myopia is also evident in the way family law has long been treated as a matter occurring within the private sphere and the modern State has seen it appropriate to restrict itself to matters that are deemed to be in the public sphere of the market, such as, property acquired in marriage, laws of marriage and divorce covering economic rights, i.e., to matters limited to the concerns of the capitalist world. This creates an anomaly, where state legislation on women is more advanced in relation to labour markets than in matters of the family and its disputes.

In some societies, the marriage contract continues to be closer to that between a serf and owner rather than that between the employee and employer. The husband has an unlimited claim on his wife and also children who do not have recourse to any compensation or redress. Those passing laws relating to marriage and divorce are presumed 'gender-neutral'; they are slow to recognise the unequal treatment of men and women within the household and slower still to understand how marriage and divorce affect, differently, the lives of men and women in a family environment. An exception occurs where a radical ideology modernises society by the ushering in of, say, socialism into the family, as in China. National and local contexts, within which gender relations are played out, call for an understanding of gender that does not fall into the trap of regarding the non-Western world as a single entity or ideology.

Gender equality is often regarded with distrust and an imposition is hoisted on nations, and their legislatures, by Western gender theory. While there are reasons for genuine concerns regarding Northern imposition on gender relations in the non-Western world,[3] an obfuscation of gender inequity, arising from resistance to the cultural dominance of Western models of the family, household and gender politics, results in contradictions between the global demand for gender equality and the manner in which national governments put forward gender laws to facilitate economic development. The contradiction has shifted the focus from gender and other inequalities in patriarchal regimes to decrying any move to a single historical trajectory of Western-style liberal democracy. This shift is an obstacle to directing patriarchal national governments to look closely at the relation between household hierarchy and individual human welfare.

In many countries it is not appropriate to regard marriage and divorce as solely the consequence of individual decisions, for they are often the outcome of mediated action by the household and community. A wife who leaves the husband's home bears a loss of investment that is husband-specific, but she suffers an even greater loss from the withdrawal of status and the support of the larger familial network that has been gained by her over the years of marriage. Further, divorce is accompanied by a social stigma that is inordinately weighted against women, who are thereby rendered outcast. Equitable justice could emerge from family courts that ensure reparation in relation to duties and obligations, rather than from state laws which present a set of mutually exclusive legal concepts in the matter of awarding compensation in divorce settlements, which do not automatically flow from mere promulgation of new state laws on women's property rights.

Where the law is silent on the gender-based inheritance of family assets, in the context of cases of marital breakdown there is need to introduce an equitable determination and division of properties which do not have specified shares. In marital laws the matter of divorce throws up divergences in law as well as in approach to equity across cultures, and the most important variable is the State.[4] Women bear a 'triple burden' of work, namely production, reproduction and caring, but have little economic security or empowerment over their own lives; yet the duties and obligations under family law are increasingly unavailable to them as forms of recourse under law. A few relationally sensitive laws emerge out of cultural contexts which privilege equitable social norms over legal rules in gender conflicts. Yet the local sphere of community is dominated by groups of households, where lives are lived and gender inequalities are experienced, and it is this important local interface between the

[3] See Connell (2007) for a powerful exposition on the unequal power relations in North and South with regard to the conceptualisation of gender relations.

[4] The Shah Bano case introduced the difficulties of dealing with maintenance rights for Indian Muslim women in regard to divorce cases as seen in the passing of the Muslim Women (Protection of Rights on Divorce) Act, 1986. See Mullally (2004) for a very useful commentary on how seemingly secular perspectives of the law can create inequality in relation to divorce settlements under religious laws.

individual household and the state system that fashions lives in a gendered world.

Group rights, distributional conflicts and the making of unequal identities

The economic view is that groups only form when individuals join together in the pursuit of a common objective or good which is not attainable through individual action. Collective action is regarded as acceptable behaviour within this rubric when the market is unable to provide a commodity, since the cost of production to be met by the private producer far exceeds the price that society is willing to pay. The historical reading is that collective action was primarily about establishing the right of labour to make claims against the aristocracy, and then the capitalist, when trade unions were established to obtain a greater share of wealth as equitable shares were not automatically proffered by the market. The different understandings, within economic and historical perspectives, of collective action expose the basis for contestation across schools of thought and academic disciplines on the role of collective action in ensuring group identity and mobility.

Additionally, there are different understandings of the most effective methods to be deployed to ensure successful collective action. Groups, and the collective action that they embark upon, have a considerable bearing on individual identity, as individual preferences and boundaries are shaped within the context of a set of group rights. Group identity consequently plays a central role in understanding individual decision-making, which in turn lies at the very heart of the capitalist system. Understanding the role of social norms, morality and reciprocity, and redrawing the economic terrain, in the creation, maintenance and ownership of common property rights, provides the possibility that the affective and communal dimensions of social life might be reflected in, rather than refracted out of, the market. There are also different types of resources and demands around which collective action is undertaken. In the case of common pool resources (CPRs) the resource in consideration belongs solely to a group and is therefore different from open access resources which are available to all who have the right to pass through a locality (Vira 1993). The greater the heterogeneity among the members of a group with regard to income, the more likely it is that there will be success in creating a common pool good (Olson 1965).

The challenge for economic development is to ensure that wealth creation does not continue to clash with the many historical claims from groups and not to believe that the simplistic remedy of a 'trickle-down' solution will continue to satisfy claims for ownership.[5] Where colonial administrations drew

[5] The trickle-down approach to distribution is associated with the Lewis model of development, which propounded that the benefits of industrialisation would pass to the agricultural sector. However, this is a misrepresentation of the main mechanism in the model, which was a drawing in of labour from the agricultural to the industrial sphere, an early form of the inclusion process.

on visible social markers such as race and caste to classify a subject population, the newly emerged independent nation states have had to confront these markers as they attempt to create an equitable political solution. The processes that have worked effectively in Asian societies over the second half of the twentieth century are not provided by the foundations of law that draw on Western notions of individual equality; these notions remain either a distant dream or a disreputable hangover from a colonial past. In the early decades of development planning the dominant political ideology adopted was that individual liberties were weighted lower than that of the group. Such a perspective permitted the redressing of historical injustices, and such privileging of the group over the individual also has the ability to promote the maintenance of natural resource use and management. The principle of equity that treats individuals in relation to where they are vertically located in the hierarchy and group allows social and economic inequalities to be addressed where they are most acute and disturbing, that is, within a group context rather than looking at individuals in isolation and bereft of their social context.

The notions of equity and equality originate in tradition and modernity respectively, and are based on very different considerations. Equity has a strong association with fairness and is located within the realm of interpersonal comparisons, while equality advances individual rights, autonomy and enterprise, leading to the ideal of absolute rights to act according to one's will, especially over one's possessions. Any furtherance of the ideal of 'equality before law' and 'rule of law' contradicts the parochial demands of dominant groups. The ability to overcome objections of dominant groups who are opposed to change is a conundrum for national governments (Knight 1991; Khan 1996). In the case where laws are a set of rules created to ensure the economic advancement of the nation, its laws need to protect as well as constrain the economic decision-making power of the autonomous and enterprising individuals in the society towards that end. In England, the courts of common law and equity as well as ecclesiastical courts were combined into the higher courts named as courts of justice and equity. This led to the dominance of enacted laws and the devaluing of equity by the courts.

The failure to distinguish the principle of equality before law from the application of the legal principle of equity results in the concept of equity getting viewed as a legal principle of the second order, employed to make pragmatic corrections to adjust for inequalities. Equity is also wrongly viewed as having subjective elements, overriding an ideal of 'legal equality' instead of recognising that the latter is also a subjective ideal based on historical development and not based on objective determination. Legal equality does not prevent the formation of perceived inequalities based on economic or social differences. Additionally, the emphasis on individuals in the role of the judiciary in the changing of social norms to enforce individual equality leaves out the dimension of influence of social groups and associated concerns of class and equity.

Social groups, inequality and political lobbying

While inequalities and heterogeneity within and across groups have emerged as a key aspect of the management of resources, this has been unable to gain ground in the broader economic literature on economic development. The option of using community-based solutions is rarely used as it requires a longer time horizon within which communities need to be engaged and their views taken on board. National governments have tended to prefer market-based approaches to rectify distributional conflicts in the economic arena. Yet any remedy for inter-group inequalities (IGIs) and within-group inequalities (WGIs) that arise from a subjective sense of grievance cannot emerge from a market-based approach.

Group claims which demand the attention of the government or result in petitions to the court can amend the rules to ensure that a measure of equity is brought in. In contrast, economic development within a globalising world of production and trade has increased the emphasis on the need for legal rules that are increasingly oriented towards ensuring equality within markets, and are opposed to processes that differentiate between players, or privilege particular groups.[6] The direct-action approach adopted by social movements influences the market, and their demand for avenues of empowerment that facilitate self-determination of group identity change the values of goods and services currently available in the market. There is a dislike of such movements within established economic institutions as they question, even undermine, existing systems of production. The State prefers the use of welfare policies to remedy failures in economic production as these policies channel financial flows at existing prices and do not upset the apple cart by questioning the valuations decided by the market. While the welfare approach does guarantee greater participation in economic exchange by other excluded groups by granting greater access to the beneficiaries, it falls short of ensuring greater forms of self-determination. In the case of participatory policies that emphasise ownership and action, there is a greater possibility that the group motivation to create an asset instils a form of empowerment over and above that of a welfare provision which remains a simple transfer of income.[7] Through concerted citizen actions,

6 This importance of investment for development has accelerated governments to push for local economies to be attractive to foreign, even national, investors. This has legally devalued acquired assets of local communities instead of allowing the market to fix prices, resulting in opposition to corporate investment on a horizontal plane of administered prices, while the reality could be that the local community was to be involved in a process of negotiating its interests in relation to new market values (i.e. moving upward along the vertical axis) as a result of incoming investment. The Indian company Tata signalled its interest in investing in Singur, without letting equity of market forces supplement law in fixing compensation viewed by the majority as a fair expectation or the State acquiring land in Special Economic Zones (SEZ) without transparent fairness, in the view of the majority. This illustrates the ease with which misrepresentation of equity and fairness can take place in democracies.

7 This does require that participation should be substantive rather than seemingly present, where it is not the external agenda of donors or governments that is driving access, but the concerted action of a social movement. See Cooke and Kothari (2001: 1–15).

as well as social movements, the market can also be manipulated into providing equitable relief to disadvantaged communities, as in the case of use of price subsidies and fair price shops.

If more equitable rights, like opportunities for housing, sanitation, safe drinking water, electricity, education and health care, were written into laws, then many group claims for acquisition of assets could be successful. While the annual budget of a nation is in effect a financial law to ensure the financial wherewithal to provide goods and services to its citizens, benefit is often denied to many groups on the grounds that state funds are insufficient. Despite, this gross form of inequity in the budget (Finance Act) there is little attempt to enforce equitable treatment in the use of state funds by the judiciary, at least in relation to the satisfaction of the minimum needs of all getting priority in allocation of state funds. Additionally, as the financial disbursement occurs at the national level it is distant from the struggles at the local level, and is not readily a matter over which social movements could have particular influence.

The struggles that emerge in discourses at sub-national level, to demand equity for disadvantaged and marginal groups, cannot be comprehended within the legal framework and language used by courts at the national level. Equitable justice becomes complicated when there are contradictory equitable claims which push courts into a difficult position regarding the provision of equitable justice so that the focus of courts shrinks to ensuring individual equality, often a euphemism for historically legalised forms of inequality. The tendency of allocating budgeted funds to supplement the efforts of some groups to advance their development objectives without having first met minimum needs of less privileged groups should be a matter of concern for national audit offices constituted in most central and sub-national governments, who do examine the expenditure patterns but do not raise questions about the inequitable annual financial law on allocation of funds in the budget itself.

Asserting group identities and affirming resource rights

Group and class discriminations have been tackled in India, Malaysia, USA, China and South Africa and highlight how equitable demands were enacted into laws and were upheld by the judiciary. In these cases, the discriminated groups successfully came to power in legislatures, and the historically discriminated majority gained from new economic policy to their advantage by ensuring that the erasure of inequity to discriminated group identity or grant of privilege became a high priority for the State. The redressing of group inequalities has become a central pillar for an advancing development path where the convictions held by the judiciary and their deliberation on the letter and the spirit of the law have radicalised legal systems in some parts of the world, with the judges begetting a verdict of 'judicial activism'. These legal interventions provide a valuable resource in ensuring social transformations that is distinct from the market-based approach to law with availability of law enforcement to the highest bidders, and in fact the demands of community-led groups have attracted both activist judges and lawyers. The shifting balance between the market-based and claims-based approaches is beginning to address the different dimensions of inequality that are evident in current-day development approaches.

Capitalists and state-led development

Capitalism is a powerful force for development, providing more and better goods at cheaper prices, yet it is bound by the type of state and social structures present in a society. Whether state structures for fiscal, administrative and managerial functions are set out in a unitary or federal framework has particular implications for the provision of goods and services within capitalist markets. Societies operate through social norms, and the laws are refracted through these norms. The legal system does not directly enter the lives of ordinary people who reside in marginal worlds. Additionally, demands made by excluded and dispossessed groups are expressed through local channels and address local and sub-national institutions rather than the national players. The interaction of social norms at the local and sub-national levels with national laws is critical in understanding how these laws are received and responded to within these social contexts.

Fashioning State–society relations and federal structures

The hierarchies of the State command a central place in the organisation of society and political and economic power flows along these lines of hierarchy. Society is constituted by those realms of existing hierarchy that do not legally constitute the power and hierarchy of the State. It is the search for and acquisition of wealth, power and status, together, which determine and direct the actions of groups and individuals as they seek to rise through the hierarchies that dominate a society. While hierarchies create distance they can also work to create momentary homogeneity, unify a nation and bring about consensus formation. Identities fashioned to create national unity create a sense of belonging to the nation state but do not dismantle sub-national or local distinctions or differences.

The system of sub-national territories with the right to decide the economic and social policies for their constituents permits the existence of identities within the national State that do not have to contend with the other sub-national entities at the national level. This containment can successfully diffuse large-scale group conflicts. Whether the legal structure is that of a unionised federation that is tightly administered or a diffused federation that is loosely controlled, the refashioning of State–society relations, the federating activity, happens continuously across national and sub-national spaces. While a federal structure might appear attractive as it permits an easier refashioning of State–society relations through incorporation of the demands of many local stakeholders, the result might well be a demand for a reform process either without direction or that is not sustainable.[8] On the other hand, where the State is the prime political power, it is enabled to prevent conflict-oriented adjustments between groups and individuals, to bring together group interests and channel their desires and objectives to a common national interest, in pursuit of wealth accumulation.[9] The ability of capitalist institutions such as the firm to redistribute power and to reconfigure rubrics of exchange and engagement does succeed in reorienting the motivations of individuals and reordering their lives, through both state and societal initiatives.

State–society relations and federal arrangements

State–society relations are primarily fashioned by nation-specific hierarchies at national and regional levels that construct national identity and strongly influence the constitutions and laws approved by the independent governments, as has been witnessed in the case of China, Malaysia and India. The federal structure, notwithstanding its level of tautness or looseness, redraws the market to suit particular group interests. The State responds to the demands of individuals and there is a secondary contestation between sub-national regions in relation to fiscal and administrative matters. Individuals and social groups perceive the State through their local norms, and the extent and angle of deflection of the state processes within this space, with decentralisation, acts as a competition-enhancing mechanism.

The power of capitalism to refashion State–society relations emerges from an iterative process where the continuous readjustment of capitalist institutions and the incentives that operate within them makes the job of a regulator no simple or single task. Instead, it calls for a larger vision that encompasses both equity and opportunity. The underbelly of this process is that, under the guise of equitable treatment of sub-national institutions, there are attempts to use channels of nepotism and corruption by ministers, bureaucrats and even judges. While the increasing fad for decentralisation assumes there will be additional entitlement, benefit and gains from such a move away from the central State, yet the State could become an enabling environment that facilitates strategies and actions by benign rule. The State can become a context rather than a creator, but this feature has been ignored by the reigning rubric as it increasingly focuses on the preferences of the individual rather than the relational world within which wealth creation takes place.

Is a Leviathan a regulatory state?

The idea that the State is in itself a regulatory space and does not simply provide a regulatory environment adds an additional and important dimension to

8 See Singh (2007) on the difficulties of decentralising financial systems in a large federal state.

9 There is a new literature on 'policy space' that emphasises the central role of the national State in discerning and defining the contours of development policy (Chang 2006).

understanding the relationship between legal reforms and national as well as international development.[10] If one begins to examine State–society relations and how they influence development processes, then it is the social norms interacting with the laws of the land that are seen to give rise to a *local legal system*. At the other end of the spectrum, the laws created and approved by the federal government provide the *formal legal system*. Finally, the interactions between the local and federal levels generate an *irregular or transitional legal system*. The *local system* operates on principles of reciprocity and morality, yet the prevalence of these norms in no way detracts from the operation of commercial principles or market valuation. Furthermore, local rewards and punishments reinforce functional forms of morality to ensure the benign organisation of society. They aid and abet the observance of voluntary mechanisms of mutuality of interaction among individuals and their groups so as to conform to common moral norms and conventions.

Social norms are undermined within a rubric that regards individual forms of wealth creation and accumulation as privileged over social forms of interaction and consequently social mores. Consequently customary practices have increasingly given way to rubrics that place a higher value on human reason or rationality. In the *formal legal system* the State affirms the rights of individuals laid down in the constitution and its laws, interpreted by courts of justice, and as a neo-patriarchal figure binds individuals directly to itself. Consequently the moral order and its associated economy begin to unravel, and the remaining vestiges are transformed into icons of state honour that uphold moral virtues that can be pinned onto Good Samaritans.[11]

The moral concept of holding wealth in trust has continually and more rapidly yielded to the modern individual concept of absolute ownership, so that equitable rights of others are legally lost to the winner in competition among equal right holders. This later and exclusive legal approach denies all non-contractual equitable rights to their historical holders. The *irregular transitional system* encourages a *fragmented multi-class* state, where ownership and identities contest repeatedly and ferociously by the clash of remnants of personal mores and custom with legal order of the State not enforced fully or efficiently, and no exit option is available to anyone. The local community ceases to be a reliable basis to earn income or gain a livelihood within the group, leading to a dependence on the State for livelihood and pledging loyalty and allegiances to it

[10] The development literature has not paid adequate attention to the latent possibilities provided by a regulatory approach. The limited understanding of the State as the umpire through a regulatory framework differs from state activity, where the government holds as custodian private companies, such as Freddie Mac and Fannie Mae, by claiming a right to 'conservatorship', selectively, on mortgaged titles to private assets by treating them as national assets.

[11] The desire and commitment of the State to confer favour on faithful officials and incorporation of Good Samaritans to the state system was important in early modern societies (see Fennell 2003 for a commentary on the official recognition of elites by the Chinese imperial State).

in return. Replacement of the *local system* by modern rational laws or even by the notion of state-administered rule of law is not swift and results in generations leading a confused life moved by a contradictory set of impulses and deemed to the directionless categories of 'transitional economies'.

A shift of power from the central State to the lower levels of government places people, both as individuals and groups, closer to the levers of power. It is the attraction of power and riches that spurs them to accumulate riches using new rules and manipulation of the rubric of development, and it has led to human creativity. Communities and social groups are repositories of knowledge and work within social norms, yet they are not averse to working within a market context that recognises their existing rules of equity and reciprocity. As a result, State and society interact in wealth creation and in having controlling power over others, replacing the norms of reciprocity and equity by market-friendly laws. It is this contradiction that we currently face in capitalism in development. The excluding tendency of capitalism, and resulting exploitation generate, as a reaction, the counter-tendencies that manifest themselves in sub-national and local spaces of society. The ability of housing and education to become radical policies, that make capitalism more palatable, comes from their power to neutralise inequalities and rework vertical hierarchies.

The interface between the global and the national

The power of the global drive for resources and commodities dominates international agendas and from the vantage point of global trade. Yet it is the national government that provides the directives for reorganisation and reorientation of national economic production without which there is no exchange possible in international trade. The post-war understanding that international organisations like the UN and its agencies would regard nations as sovereign was increasingly overshadowed by the creation of trade-based alliances between nation states. The International Monetary Fund (IMF), International Bank of Reconstruction and Development (IBRD) and General Agreement on Tariff and Trade (GATT) became very active in the 1950s, with GATT functioning actively even as a provisional agreement, and by the 1980s they had become key international players. From the 1980s, the fluctuations in global markets, and shifting of economic growth from the West to other regions of the world culminated in the creation of the World Trade Organisation (WTO) in 1995. It brought under its domain all the earlier agreements entered into under the GATT. The legal and financial dimension of international trade governed by agreements in the WTO has created a new and expanded focus on the role of the contract law while also skewing the realm of political statesmanship guiding the spirit of the United Nations, with each nation supporting their nationals seeking gains from exchanges in the global markets.

The aims and purposes of the UN, namely peace, security and promotion and protection of human rights, constitute an international public order. International law may be regarded as 'rules that restrain', 'a common language' or a 'normative guidance in the making of decisions'. In the early post-war decades the late-industrialising nations regarded appropriate technological prowess as a sufficient basis for industrial economic advancement through international trade, ignoring the way they traded; trade did not seem to matter as much as the type of technology. Advanced capitalist countries regarded international trade as a necessary condition to ensure full employment, using coercion in trading agreements with less dominant nations. A trade treaty was seen more as a binding international contract, allowing use of force to enforce it; in contrast, international conventions are viewed as international laws.

The framing of international contracts, particularly around trade, within a security framework has permitted the language of disputes to dominate within international institutions. Dispute settlement in the WTO is to ensure that rights and obligations are 'in accordance with customary rules of public international law'. The simultaneous proffer of free trade and penalty tariffs as tools for the operation of the WTO has presented nations with conflicting signals. The simultaneous existence of market conditions in international trade and of contract-based instruments for undertaking dispute resolution reduces the room for manoeuvre by developing nations and works against any initiatives to change the power configurations with the institution. At the present juncture, the increasing interference of global trade rules in national development plans and processes, and the undermining of principles of sovereignty of national governments, has resulted in the formation of alliances such as the BRIC (Brazil, Russia, India, China), or groups as in the Doha round.

In the aftermath of the WTO

Globalisation designed to encourage foreign direct investment flows as a major component of global free trade has contributed to financial instability and volatility across countries and shifts in manufacturing investment and variations in exchange rates. The WTO framework places all its members on an equal footing based on the notion that all countries have the same economic structure, or bring their structures as closely as possible to an economic textbook model. Such thinking occludes the reality in developing countries, with economies which were relegated in the high period of colonialism and are, currently, developing in diverse pathways on the road to industrialisation.

The 378 disputes that came before the dispute panel of the WTO during the period 1995–2007 do not show staunch support for upholding free trade; rather, they indicate the shifting of rules and standards, a reordering of priorities as well as a reworking of the weights, particularly, relative to valorising of product and process distinction before the panel.

Advanced capitalist countries are increasingly using environmental measures to impose on exports from developing countries. Member countries of the WTO are allowed to have national regulations on protecting the environment, but only to the extent that they comply with the rules of the WTO. Commodity and product are traditional trade matters, but a preference for process as a trade matter is noticeable in relation to intellectual property matters affecting goods as well as services in the international trade.

Copyright and patent infringement concerns have been raised more than once by developed nations seeking tight national laws on patent protection, giving little room for justiciability in national courts. Even competition in trade appears to be downplayed where there are greater gains to be made from reducing rather than increasing the flow of goods and commodities, through secure legal protection. Indications of a rise in the share of trade of developing countries give rise to accusations of price-cutting and dumping of goods in markets of developed countries.

Dumping is not a criminal offence, unlike the infringement of intellectual property rights. Temporary import restrictions are regarded as a safeguard that could operate as a short-term measure against unilateral dumping action. The understandings of standards between countries, that emerged before the Appellate Council of the WTO in the Beef Hormones case raises doubts about whether the WTO has a sufficient and well-rounded understanding of the manner in which standards for trade should be set out and negotiated.

Taxation is the true measure of the legitimacy of a government, and if a subsidy is viewed as the flip side of a tax, it is a legitimate and universally recognised tool of government policy. As a negative tax is the true character of a subsidy, it achieves the task of affecting the incidence of economic activity and should not be hastily discarded from poor-country governments. Developing countries have also increasingly become pro-active in taking developed countries to task where they have found trade barriers raised against their agricultural commodities. Complaints against subsidies on cotton and sugar to US farmers were upheld by the WTO in dispute settlement, with widespread implications for other major traded food crops, particularly rice and wheat, since farmers receive considerable subsidies for these major cereal crops from their governments in many developed countries.

Dissonances and discordances

The needs of people, nation states and international agencies fundamentally oppose one another, and the academic disciplines also display this loggerhead approach as they battle for intellectual supremacy in conceptualising international development. The scramble to claim a disciplinary advantage has also become visible in the answers given to how and why countries grow economically, socially or politically, even as many answers fall by the wayside, and the answers continue to trouble those engaged in the world of international development. The preponderance of the textual over the oral is reflected in the manner in which the social is regarded as softer and less reliable than the written and readable within neoclassical economics. The bias for the text over the oral also manifests itself strongly in the legal system, e.g. written contracts. This biased rubric projects a partial reality based on the letter of the law rather than on listening to the voices of those affected by inequity and immorality.

The rubric of unfettered capitalism that had come to reign in the last two decades of the last century generated rules that gave primacy to the creation rather than the distribution of riches. The discordant forms of development that have been produced by the structures that support capitalist accumulation have become accepted forms of exclusion and inequity, and given vent to systemic dissonances between the words and agendas imposed by the major capitalist players and the demands of excluded groups and communities for acknowledgement and remedy of their unmet needs. Exclusion occurs within this dominant rubric as it denies differences in ideas and understandings.

The use of a universal rubric of economic development that is based on a single set of principles cannot hear the growing cacophony of discordant voices, for the prevailing rubric denies the possibility of disagreement in the ideas that are lodged in individual minds. Inability to create concordance is a telling consequence of the growing insularity of those amassing riches but using rules that alienate many groups and communities in a late twentieth-century rubric of capitalism.

Where the form of independence is based on the rights of the individual there is a preference for personal gain, with little regard for community or nation. The rules of the nation are formally set out to protect and uphold the rights of the individual, sometimes even against the interference of the State. Yet there are also tendencies to use the State's own resources to assist the wealth-creation activities of private individuals. Traditional forms of redistribution have now been phased out, if not made completely obsolete, by the new and fast-growing strata of elite. Also, traditional forms of organised protest, such as by trade union actions, have been replaced by new forms, which manifest either as extreme violence in local movements using armed struggle and guerrilla tactics, or as organised protests that are inspired by new international legal movements and a new shared language of global rights. There is now an increasing divergence between the forms and vocabulary of dissent and protest in the local and the global spheres, though these struggles do both meld and mar in the twenty-first century.[12]

Conflict is a characteristic of a pluralist market society, a natural counterpart of technical progress and creation of new wealth, for which the market society is rightly famous. Emerging inequalities and sectoral or regional declines are the counterpart of the ability of various dynamic groups and regions that avail themselves of new economic opportunities and align themselves with new hierarchies and rules. Rules that support wealth-creating methods with legitimacy come from the legislature, while the remedies for justice denied to the languishing victims of development come from judicial decisions. Justice as ethical fair play or equity, and not interpretation of law, is not restricted to particular political systems or levels of economic development, and the ability to draw on

[12] See Caporaso and Tarrow (2008) for the vagaries of domestic movements, while Appadurai (2002) focuses on the abilities that lie within deep processes of change in the local sphere.

notions of duty and obligation opens the way to bringing the reciprocal and interpersonal aspects of exchange back into a new rubric of capitalism.

The power of property rights regimes and the ways to reduce uncertainty and management of risk have become the touchstone of the existing pattern of human development. While technology does hold the key to new opportunities, the creation of wealth occurs within particular forms of organisation which are based on skills, knowledge and enterprise that reside in that society. The ability to hear other voices, to refashion social structures, also empowers individuals, as their greater and more nuanced understanding crafts new incentives to access pathways to wealth and power, and raises more demands to reorder laws and norms in order to reduce conflicting motivations in numerous persons, disorder and suffering. Motivations to use laws as the weapon of political power, and economic motivations as the weapons of wealth, cause discordances such as the hardening of hearts against historical injustices and the loss of morality.

The use of the market and the contract as the only two instruments available to design international development trajectories without any acknowledgement of the role of communities, sub-national administration and the government, impoverishes our thinking and makes for very shallow intellectual analysis. The power of capitalism lies in its ability to transform the realm of social hierarchies, to create a new set of ethical principles and thereby transform both state and societal processes as it creates new waves of capitalist accumulation. It is this expanded rubric of international development that will permit a larger and more reflexive set of rules across a range of levels, from local, sub-national and national to global, and will be a valuable tool in understanding the full power of capitalist accumulation. It will also have the capacity, to bring in new and equitable remedies that draw social norms, morality and reciprocity out of the cold and into the heart of an expanded framework where socially embedded practices of regulation provide a way forward to reformulate the relationship between riches and redistribution, ensuring that dissenting voices are heard, and that the discordances do not turn into a harbinger of financial collapse or violent upheaval.

Bibliography

Acemoglu, Darn (2003) 'Why Not a Political Coase Theorem? Social Conflict, Commitment and Politics', *Journal of Comparative Economics*, 31 (4, December), 620–52.

Adams, W.M., Brockington, Dan, Dyson, Jane and Vira, Bhaskar (2002) 'Analytical Framework for Dialogue on Common Property Resources', lead paper for Round Table on 'Promoting Policy Dialogue for Common Pool Resource Management', 9th Biennial Conference of the International Association for the Study of Common Property, Victoria Falls, Zimbabwe, 17–21 June.

Agarwal, Bina (1992) *A Field of One's Own*, Cambridge: Cambridge University Press.

Akerlof, George A. and Kranton, Rachel E. (2000) 'Economics and Identity', *Quarterly Journal of Economics*, 115 (3), 715–53.

—— (2005) 'Identity and Economics of Organizations', *Journal of Economic Perspectives*, 19 (1), 9–32.

Alexander, J.M. and Talpade Mohanty, C. (eds) (1997) *Feminist Genealogies, Colonial Legacies and Democratic Futures*, London: Routledge.

Alt, J.E. and Shepsle, K.A. (eds) (1990) *Perspectives on Positive Political Economy*, Cambridge: Cambridge University Press.

Amsden, A. (1989) *Asia's Next Giant: South Korea and Late Industrialization*, Oxford: Oxford University Press.

—— 2001 *The Rise of 'the Rest': Challenges to the West from Late-Industrializing Countries*, Oxford: Oxford University Press,

Amsden, Alice and Hikino, Takashi (2002) 'The Bark is Worse than the Bite: New WTO Law and Late Industrializers', *Annals of the American Academy of Political and Social Science*, 570, 104–14.

Anderson, B. (1991) *Imagined Communities: Reflections on the Origin and Spread of Nationalism*, London: Verso.

Anderson, W. and Martin, K. (2006) *Agricultural Trade Reform and Doha Development Agenda*, Washington, DC: World Bank Publications.

Anghie, A. (2000) 'Time Present and Time Past: Globalization, International Financial Institutions and the Third World', *New York University Journal of International Law and Politics*, 32 (2), 243.

—— (2002) 'Colonialism and the Birth of International Institutions: Sovereignty, Economy and the Mandate System of the League of Nations', *New York University Journal of International Law and Politics*, 34 (3), 513.

—— (2005) *Imperialism, Sovereignty and the Making of International Law*, Cambridge: Cambridge University Press.

Ankarloo, Daniel (2002a) 'New Institutional Economics and Economic History', *Capital and Class*, 78, 9–36.

—— (2002b) 'Using Karl Polanyi as a Stepping-Stone for a Critique of the New Institutionalist Orthodoxy', paper presented at the CRIC workshop, 'Polanyi Perspectives on Instituted Economic Processes: Development and Transformation', University of Manchester, 23–25 October,

Anwar, Zainah (2006) *New Straits Times*, 7 April, Singapore.

Appadurai, Arjun (2002) 'Deep Democracy: Urban Governmentality and the Horizon of Politics', *Public Culture*, 14 (1, Winter), 21–47.

Arrow, K. (1959) 'Functions of a Theory of Behaviour under Uncertainty', *Metroeconomica*, 11, 12–20.

Athukorala, P. (ed.) (2002a) *The Economic Development of South Asia*, Cheltenham: Edward Elgar.

—— (2002b) 'Malaysian Trade Policy and 2001 World Trade Policy Review', *World Economy*, 25 (9), 1299–317.

Atkinson, Anthony B. (1999) 'Is Rising Income Inequality Inevitable? A Critique of the Transatlantic Consensus', UNU/World Institute for Development Economic Research (UNU/WIDER), Annual Lectures 3.

Avvaiyar (2008 [13th century CE]) 'Tamil verse 12' http://www.tamilnation.org/literature/auvaiyar/nalvazhi.htm (accessed 25 August).

Bail, C., Faulkner, R. and Marquand, H. (eds) (2002) *The Cartagena Protocol on Biosafety: Reconciling Trade in Biotechnology with Environment and Development?* London: Earthscan.

Baland, Jean-Marie, Dreze, Jean and Leruth, Luc (1998) 'Daily Wages and Piece Rates in Agrarian Economies', *Journal of Development Economics*, 59 (2, August), 445–61.

Bao, M. (2006) 'The Evolution of Environmental Policy and its Impact in the People's Republic of China', *Conservation and Society*, 4 (1), 36–54

Baqir, R., Alesina, A.and Hoxby, C. (2004) 'Political Jurisdictions in Heterogeneous Communities', *Journal of Political Economy*, 112, 348–96.

Baran, P. (1957) *The Political Economy of Growth*, New York: Monthly Review Press.

Bardhan, P. (2008) 'Law and Development', in A.K. Dutt and J. Ros (eds) *International Handbook of Development Economics*, vol. II, Cheltenham: Edward Elgar. Available at emlab.berkeley.edu/users/webfac/bardhan/papers/BardhanLaw&Development.pdf

Bardhan, P. and Mookherjee, D. (1999) 'Decentralization and Accountability in Infrastructure Delivery in Developing Countries', *The Economic Journal*, 116, 101–27.

—— (2007a) 'Decentralization, Corruption and Accountability: An Overview', in S. Rose-Ackerman (ed.) *Handbook of Economic Corruption*, London: Edward Elgar.

—— (2007b [1999]) 'Decentralization and Accountability in Infrastructure Delivery in Developing Countries', *Economic Journal*, 116, 101–27. (Updating of paper: P. Bardhan and D. Mookherjee (2000) 'Corruption and Decentralization of Infrastructure Delivery in Developing Countries', Working Paper, Institute for Economic Development, Boston University.)

Basu, A and Kohli, A. (2000) *Community Conflicts and the State in India*, New Delhi: Oxford University Press.

Basu, K. (2006) 'Participatory Equity, Identity and Productivity: Policy Implications for Promoting Development', BREAD working paper 119, available at ipl.econ.duke.edu/bread/abstract.php?paper = 119

Bates, R. (1986) 'The Politics of Agricultural Policy – a Reply. Developmental States and African Agriculture', *IDS Bulletin*, 17 (1), 12 – 15.

—— 2005 'Ethnicity', in D. Clark, (ed.) *Companion to Development Studies*, London: Edward Elgar.

Becker, Gary S. (1973) 'A Theory of Marriage', *Journal of Political Economy*, 82 (2), S11–26.

—— (1981a) *A Treatise on the Family*, Harvard: Harvard University Press.

—— (1981b) 'Altruism in the Family and Selfishness in the Marketplace', *Economica*, 48 (149), 1–15.

Ben-Porath, Yoram (1980) 'The F Connection: Families, Friends and Firms and the Organization of Exchange', *Population and Development Review*, 6 (1), 1–30.

Benda-Beckmann, F. von (2002) 'Who's Afraid of Legal Pluralism?' *Journal of Legal Pluralism*, 47, 37–82.

Benda-Beckmann, K. von (2006) 'How Communal is Communal and Whose Communal is it? Lessons from Minangkabau', in F. von Benda-Beckmann, K. von Benda-Beckmann and M.G. Wiber (eds) *Changing Properties of Property*, Oxford: Berghahn.

Beneria, L. and Feldman, S. (1992) (eds) *Unequal Burden: Economic Crises, Persistent Poverty and Women's Work*, Boulder: Westview Press.

Beneria, L. and Roldan, M. (1987) *The Crossroads of Class and Gender: Industrial Homework, Subcontracting, and Household Dynamics in Mexico City*, Chicago: University of Chicago Press.

Benhabib, Seyla (1992) *Situating the Self, Gender, Community and Postmodernism in Contemporary Ethics*,

Berg, A. and Krueger, A. (2003) 'Trade, Growth and Poverty: A Selective Survey', IMF Working Paper, WP/03/30.

Berg, M. (1982) *The Machinery Question and the Making of Political Economy, 1815–1848*, Cambridge: Cambridge University Press.

Berlin, Isaiah (2002 [1958]) 'Two Concepts of Liberty', in I. Berlin, *Four Essays on Liberty*, London: Oxford University Press.

Berman, H. (1983) *Law and Revolution: The Formation of the Western Legal Tradition*, Harvard: Harvard University Press.

Béteille, A. (1991) *Society and Politics in India: Essays in Comparative Perspective*, London: Athlone Press.

Bhagwati, J. (2002) *Free Trade Today*, Princeton: Princeton University Press,

Bird, Richard M. and Ebel, Robert D. (2006) 'Fiscal Federalism and National Unity', in Ahmad Ehtisham and Giorgio Brosio (eds) *Handbook of Fiscal Federalism*, London: Edward Elgar.

Bird, Richard M. and Rodriguez, Edgard R. (1999) 'Decentralization and Poverty Alleviation: International Experience and the Case of the Philippines', *Public Administration and Development*, 19, 299–319.

Boisvert, V. and Caron, A. (2002) 'The Convention on Biodiversity: An Institutionalist Perspective on the Debates', *Journal of Economic Issues*, 36 (1, March), 151–66.

Boserup, E. (1970) *Women's Role in Economic Development*, London: George Allen & Unwin.

Bouckaert, Boudewijn and De Geest, Gerrit (eds) (2000) *Encyclopedia of Law and Economics, Volume I. The History and Methodology of Law and Economics*, Cheltenham, Edward Elgar.

Bowles, S. and Gintis, H. (1993) 'The Revenge of Homo Economicus: Contested Exchange and the Revival of Political Economy', *Journal of Economic Perspectives*, 7 (1), 83–102.

Brass, T. (1995) *New Farmer's Movements in India*, London: Routledge.

Brown, G.K., Ali, S.H. and Muda, W.M.W. (2004) 'Power Levers in Malaysia', CRISE Policy Context Paper 4, Queen Elizabeth House, University of Oxford.

Bruni, L. and Porta, P. Luigi (eds) (2005) *Economics and Happiness: Framing the Analysis*, New York: Oxford University Press.

Bryan, D. and Rafferty J. (2005) *Capitalism with Derivatives: A Political Economy of Financial Derivatives, Capital, and Class*, London: Palgrave Macmillan.

Buchanan, J. and Tullock, G. (1962) *The Calculus of Consent: Logical Foundations of Constitutional Democracy*, Ann Arbor, MI: University of Michigan Press.

Buscaglia, E. (2000) 'Law and Economics of Development', in B. Bouckaert and G. De Geest (eds) *Encyclopedia of Law and Economics*, 0580, Cheltenham: Edward Elgar.

Busch, M.L. and Reinhardt, E. (2000) 'Bargaining in the Shadow of the Law: Early Settlement in GATT/WTO Disputes', *Fordham International Law Journal*, 24 (1–2, November–December), 158–72.

Calabresi, Guido, and Melamed, A. Douglas (1972) 'Property Rules, Liability Rules and Inalienability: One View of the Cathedral', *Harvard Law Review* 85 (6, April), 1089–128.

Caporaso, James A. and Tarrow, Sidney (2008) 'Brussels: Supranational Institutions and the Transnational Embedding of Markets', paper presented 28 October, Cambridge University (referring to Sydney Tarrow (2005) *The New Transnational Activism*, Cambridge: Cambridge University Press).

Cárdenas, Juan-Camilo and Ostrom, Elinor (2006) 'How Norms Help Reduce the Tragedy of the Commons: A Multi-Layer Framework for Analyzing Field Experiments', in J. Drobak (ed.) *Norms and the Law*, Cambridge: Cambridge University Press.

The Cartagena Protocol on Biosafety to the Convention on Biological Diversity (CBD) was adopted by the Conference of the Parties to the Convention on 29 January 2000. Information on Protocol and Convention are available at the website of the Secretariat of CBD at http://www.cbd.int/ (accessed 20 January 2009). CBD Joint Agreements entered into by CBD referred to as Partnership Agreements are also available at this website.

CEDAW (1979) *The Convention on Elimination of Discrimination against Women (CEDAW) 1979*, available at http://www.un.org/womenwatch/daw/cedaw/text/econvention.htm (accessed 25 August 2008).

Chakravartty, P. and Zhao, Y. (2008) *Global Communications: Towards a Transcultural Political Economy*, New York: Rowman and Littlefield.

Chambers, R. (1997) *Whose Reality Counts: When First Comes Last*, Bourton-on-Dunsmore, UK: ITDG Publishing.

Chang, H.J. (1993) 'The Political Economy of Industrial Policy in Korea', *Cambridge Journal of Economics*, 17 (2), 131–57.

—— (1994) *The Political Economy of Industrial Policy*, London: Macmillan.

—— (2000) 'The Hazard of Moral Hazard – Untangling the Asian Crisis', *World Development*, 28 (4), 775–788.

—— (2001) 'Intellectual Property Rights and Economic Development – Historical Lessons and Emerging Issues', *Journal of Human Development*, July, 2 (2), 287–309.

—— (2002) 'Breaking the Mould – An Institutionalist Alternative to Neo-Liberal Theory of the Market and the State', *Cambridge Journal of Economics*, 28 (5), 413–29.

—— (2004) 'Regulation of Foreign Investment in Historical Perspective', *European Journal of Development Research*, 16 (3), 687–715.

—— (2005) 'Kicking Away the Ladder: "Good Policies" and "Good Institutions" in Historical Perspective', in K. Gallagher (ed.) *Putting Development First: The Importance of Policy Space in the* WTO *and IFIs*, London: Zed Books.

—— (2006) 'Policy Space in Historical Perspective – with Special Reference to Trade and Industrial Policies', *Economic and Political Weekly*, 41 (7, 18 February), 627–33.

Chang, H.J. and Grabel, Ilene (2004a) *Reclaiming Development: An Alternative Economic Policy Manual*, London: Zed Books.

—— (2004b) 'Reclaiming Development from the Washington Consensus', *Journal of Post-Keynesian Economics*, 27 (2), 273–91.

Chang, H.-J. and Rowthorn, B. (1995) 'Introduction' (Chapter 1), in H.-J. Chang and B. Rowthorn (eds) *The Role of the State in Economic Change*, Oxford: Oxford University Press.

Chatterjee, P. (1993) *The Nation and its Fragments*, Princeton: Princeton University Press.

—— (2003) 'Beyond the Nation or Within?' in Carolyn M. Elliott (ed.) *Civil Society and Democracy: A Reader*, New Delhi: Oxford University Press, pp. 134–44.

Cheah, W.L. (2004) 'Sagong Tasi and Orang Asli Land Rights in Malaysia: Victory, Milestone of False Start? Law, Social Justice and Global Development', available at http://www/go.warwick.ac.uk/elj/lgd/2004_2/cheah

Chouchena-Rojas, M., Muller, M., Vivas, D. and Winkler, S. (eds) (2005) *Disclosure Requirements: Ensuring Mutual Supportiveness between WTO TRIPS Agreement and CBD*, Gland, Switzerland, and Cambridge, UK: IUCN; and Geneva: ICTSD.

Chua, A. (2003) *World on Fire: How Exporting Free Market Democracy Breeds Ethnic Hatred and Global Instability*, London: Doubleday.

Clarke, J.J. (2000) *The Tao of the West*, London: Routledge.

Coase, R.H. (1937) 'The Nature of the Firm', *Economica*, 4 (16), 386–405.

—— (1960) 'The Problem of Social Cost', *Journal of Law and Economics*, 3, 1–44.

—— (1976) 'Adam Smith's View of Man', *Journal of Law and Economics*, 19 (3), 529–46.

—— (1990 [1932])) 'The Nature of the Firm', in R.H. Coase, *The Firm, the Market and the Law*, Chicago: University of Chicago Press.

—— (1995a [1937]) 'The Institutional Nature of Production', in R.H. Coase, *The Firm, the Market and the Law*, Chicago: University of Chicago Press.

—— (1995b) *Eight Essays on Economics and Economists*, Chicago: University of Chicago Press.

Cole, Daniel H. (1999) 'An Unqualified Human Good: E.P. Thompson and the Rule of Law', available at http://ssrn.com/abstract = 169264, ://papers.ssrn.com/sol3/papers.cfm?abstract_id = 169264 (accessed 25 August 2008).

Collier, J. and Yanagisako, S. (1987) *Gender and Kinship: Essays Toward a United Analysis*, Stanford: Stanford University Press.

Connell, R. (1987) *Gender and Power: Society, the Person, and Sexual Politics*, Stanford: Stanford University Press.

—— (2007) *Southern Theory: the Global Dynamics of Knowledge in Social Science*, Cambridge: Polity Press.

Consumer Unity and Trust Society International (CUTS) (2007) at site www.cuts-international.org/ (accessed 20 January 2009).

Cooke, B. and Kothari, U. (2001) 'The Case for Participation as Tyranny', in B. Cooke and U. Kothari (eds) *Participation: The New Tyranny?* London: Zed Books.

Cooter, R. and Ulen, T. (1988) *Law and Economics*, New York: HarperCollins; London: Scott, Foresman.

—— (1995) *Law and Economics* (second edition), Boston: Addison-Wesley.

—— (1999) *Law and Economics* (third edition), Boston: Addison-Wesley.

—— (2004) *Law and Economics* (fourth edition), Boston: Addison-Wesley.

—— (2007) *Law and Economics* (fifth edition), Boston: Addison-Wesley.

Crawford, James (2002) *International Law as an Open System: Selected Essays*, London: Cameron May. Containing 'The International Law Commission's Articles on State Responsibility: Introduction, Text, and Commentaries'.

Dahl, R. and Linblom, C. (1992 [1953]) *Economics, Politics and Welfare*, London: Transaction.

Das, K. (2006) 'GATS Negotiations and India, Evolution and State of Play', Centad Working Paper, No. 7.

Davies, A. (2006) 'Reviewing Dispute Settlement at the World Trade Organization: A Time to Consider the Role/s of Compensation', *World Trade Review*, 5 (1), 31–67.

De, A. and Dreze, J. (1999) *Public Report on Education in India (PROBE)*, Oxford: Oxford University Press.

De Soto, Hernando (2000) *The Mystery of Capital – Why Capitalism Triumphs in the West and Fails Everywhere Else*, London: Bantam.

—— (2002) *The Other Path: The Economic Answer to Terrorism*, New York: Basic Books.

Deakin, S. (2001) 'The Contract of Employment: A Study in Legal Evolution', University of Cambridge Centre for Business Research Working Paper No. 203.

Deakin, S., Lane, C. and Wilkinson, F. (1997) 'Contract Law, Trust Relations and Incentives for Co-operation: A Comparative Study', in S. Deakin and J. Michie (eds) *Contracts, Co-operation and Competition: Studies in Economics, Management and Law*, Oxford: Oxford University Press.

Demsetz, H. (1966) 'Some Aspects of Property Rights', *Journal of Law and Economics*, 9, 61–70.

Denning, Sir Alfred (1949) 'Freedom under the Law', in *The Hamlyn Lectures 1949*, London: Stevens and Sons.

Deshpande, A. (2005) 'Affirmative Action in India and the United States, Background Paper', World Development Report on Equity and Development, available at siteresources.worldbank.org/INTRANETSOCIALDEVELOPMENT/Resources/Affirmative_Action_India_Ashwini.pdf

DFID (UK Department for International Development) (2006) *Eliminating World Poverty: Making Governance Work for the Poor* (White Paper on International Development), London: DFID.

Diamant, Neil (2000) 'Revolutionizing the Family: Politics, Love and Divorce in Urban and Rural China, 1940–68', 42 *Stanford Law Review*, 4, 993–1058.

Dietrich, Michael (2002) 'The Contested Sovereignty of the Firm', *Review of Political Economy*, 14 (2, April), 193–209.

Drobak, John N. (ed.) (2006) *Norms and the Law*, Washington: Washington University, School of Law, and Cambridge University Press.

Duttfield, Graham (2000) *Intellectual Property Rights, Trade and Biodiversity*, London: Earthscan. (Earlier version: G. Duttfield (2003) *Two Globalizations of Law and Legal Thought: 1850–1968*, 36 *Suffolk University Law Review* 631).

Eggertson, T. (1990) *Economic Institutions and Behaviour*, Cambridge: Cambridge University Press.

Einsenstadt, S. and Roninger, L. (1984) *Patrons, Clients, and Friends: Relations and the Structure of Trust in Society*, Cambridge: Cambridge University Press.

Ellickson, Robert (1986) 'Of Coase and Cattle: Dispute Resolution among Neighbors in Shasta County', 38 *Stanford Law Review* 623, 659–67; reprinted in Avery Wiener Katz (ed.) (1998) *Foundations of the Economic Approach to Law*, Oxford: Oxford University Press.

—— (2005) *Order without Law: How Neighbors Settle Disputes*, Cambridge, MA: Harvard University Press.

—— (2006) *Norms and the Law*, ed. John N. Drobak, Washington: Washington University, School of Law, and Cambridge University Press.

Elson, D. (1991) *Male Bias in Macroeconomic Analysis*, Manchester: Manchester University Press.

Engels, F. (1986 [1884]) *The Origins of the Family, Private Property and the State*, Harmondsworth: Penguin.

England, P. (1993) *Beyond Economic Man: Feminist Theory and Economics*, Chicago: University of Chicago Press.

England, P. and Folbre, N. (1999) 'Who Should Pay for the Kids?' *Annals of the American Academy of Political and Social Science*, 563 (1), 194–207.

Enloe, C. (1977) 'Internal Colonialism, Federalism and Alternative Development Strategies', *Publius*, 7 (4), 145–60.

Epstein, R. (1995) *Simple Rules for a Complex World*, Cambridge, MA: Harvard University Press.

Erickson, E. (1950) *Childhood and Society*, New York: W.W. Norton.

Evans, P. (1995) *Embedded Autonomy: States and Industrial Transformation*, Princeton, NJ: Princeton University Press.

—— (2000) 'Fighting Marginalisation with Transnational Networks: Counter-Hegemonic Globalisation', *Contemporary Sociology*, 29 (January), 230–41.

Evans, Peter, Rueschmeyer, Dietrich and Skocpol, Theda (eds) (1985) *Bringing the State Back In*, Cambridge: Cambridge University Press.

Faundez, J. (2000) 'Legal Reform in Developing and Transition Countries – Making Haste Slowly', *Law, Social Justice and Global Development*, available at http://elj.warwick.ac.uk/global/issue/2000–2001/faundez.html. New citation as at 1 April 2004: http://www2.warwick.ac.uk/fac/soc/law/elj/lgd

Fennell, S. (2003) *Long Term Trends in Indian and Chinese Agriculture: a perspective from household, community and national levels*, Ph.D. thesis approved by the University of Cambridge, Cambridge University.

—— (2007a) 'Investigating Social Norms: Towards an Understanding of "Embeddedness"', in J. Singh (ed.) *Understanding Regulation: Legal and Institutional Dimensions*, Oxford: Berghahn Books.

—— (2007b) 'Public–Private Partnerships in Education in India', Working Paper no. 7, RECOUP, University of Cambridge.

—— (2008) 'Contested Gender Frameworks: Economic Models and Provider Perspectives on Education', in S. Fennell and M. Arnot (eds) *Gender Education and Equality in a Global Context: Conceptual Frameworks and Policy Perspectives*, London: Routledge.

Ferber, M. and Nelson, J. (1993) *Beyond Economic Man: Feminist Theory and Economics*, Chicago: University of Chicago Press.

Ferejohn, John and Kramer, Larry (2006) 'Judicial Independence in a Democracy: Institutionalizing Judicial Restraint', John N. Drobak (ed.) *Norms and the Law*, Cambridge: Cambridge University Press.

Fine, B., Lapavitsas, C. and Pincus, J. (eds) (2001) *Development Policy in the 21st Century: Beyond the Post-Washington Consensus*, London: Routledge.

Folbre, Nancy (2001) *The Invisible Heart: Economics and Family Values*, New York: New Press.

—— (2002) 'Disincentives to Care: A Critique of US Family Policy', unpublished manuscript, Department of Economics, University of Massachusetts.

Folbre, Nancy and Abel, M. (1989) 'Women's Work and Women's Households in the US Census', *Social Research*, 56 (3), 545–70.

Frank, Andre Gunder (1998) *ReOrient: Global Economy in the Asian Age*, Berkeley: University of California Press.

Frey, B.S. and Stutzer, A. (2002) *Happiness and Economics: How the Economy and Institutions Affect Well-Being*, Princeton: Princeton University Press,

Geertz, Clifford (1963) *Old Societies and New States: The Quest for Modernity in Asia and Africa*, London: Free Press of Glencoe.

—— (1968 [1963]) *Peddlers and Princes: Social Development and Economic Change in Two Indonesian Towns*, Chicago: University of Chicago Press.

Glaeser, Edward, Johnson, Simon and Shleifer, Andrei (2001) 'Coase versus the Coasians', *Quarterly Journal of Economics*, 116, 853–900.

Glenn, H. Patrick (2004) *Legal Traditions of the World: Sustainable Diversity in Law* (second edition), Oxford: Oxford University Press.

Glyn, A., Hughes, Alan, Lipietz, Alain and Singh, Ajit (1990) 'The Rise and Fall of the Golden Age', in Stephen Marglin and Juliet Schor (eds), *The Golden Age of Capitalism: Reinterpreting Postwar Experience*, Oxford: Clarendon Press.

Goldman, D. (2008) *Globalisation and the Western Legal Tradition: Recurring Patterns of Law and Authority*, Cambridge: Cambridge University Press.

Gomez, E. (2004) *The State of Malaysia: Ethnicity, Equity, Reform*, London: Routledge Curzon.

Gomez, Terrence and Jomo, K.S. (1997) *Malaysia's Political Economy: Politics, Patronage and Profits*, Cambridge: Cambridge University Press.

Goody, J. (1962) *Death, Property and the Ancestors*, Stanford: Stanford University Press.

Grade, Michael (2005) 'The Future of Impartiality', Goodman Media Lecture, given at the Institute of Mechanical Engineers, 11 May 2005, available at granovet_embed.html (accessed 24 August 2008).

Granovetter, Mark (1974) 'Economic Action and Social Structure: The Problem of Embeddedness', available at http://faculty.babson.edu/krollag/org_site/org_theory/Scott_articles/ (accessed 26 August 2008).

Greif, Avner (1992) 'Institutions and International Trade: Lessons from the Commercial Revolution', *American Economic Review*, 82, (2, May), 128–33.

Grout, P., Jewitt, I. and Sonderegger, S. (2007) 'Reputational Self-Governance and the Reform of Legal Services', Paper 07/170, Department of Economics, University of Bristol.

Guha, R. (1989) *The Unquiet Woods: Ecological Change and Peasant Resistance in the Himalaya*, Berkeley: California University Press.

Hadden, Jennifer and Tarrow, Sidney (2006) 'When Barking Dogs Wimper: The Sad Story of the Global Justice Movement in the United States after Seattle', paper presented at the Workshop on Contentious Politics, Columbia University, 4 December.

Hajjar, Lisa (2006) 'Religion, State Power, and Domestic Violence: A Framework for Comparative Analysis', *Law and Social Inquiry*, 29 (1), 1–38.

Hak, Nora A. (2005) 'Reconciliation and Conciliation in Malaysia: A Review of the Relevant Provisions of the Law Reform (Marriage and Divorce) Act 1976', paper presented at 9th Australian Institute of Family Studies Conference, Melbourne, 9–11 February.

Hall, P. and Soskice, D. (2001) *Varieties of Capitalism: The Institutional Foundations of Comparative Advantage*, New York: Oxford University Press.

Hamayotsu, Kikue (2002) 'Islam and Nation Building in Southeast Asia: Malaysia and Indonesia in Comparative Perspective', *Pacific Affairs*, 75 (3, Fall), 353–75.

—— (2003) 'Politics of Syariah Reform: The Making of the State Religio-Legal Apparatus', in V. Hooker and N. Othman (eds) *Malaysia: Islam, Society and Politics*, Singapore: Institute of Southeast Asian Studies.

Harper, T. (1999) *The End of Empire and the Making of Malaya*, Cambridge: Cambridge University Press.

Hart, Gillian (1991) 'Engendering Everyday Resistance: Gender, Patronage, and Production Politics in Rural Malaysia', *Journal of Peasant Studies*, 19 (1), 93–121.

—— (1992) 'Household Production Reconsidered: Gender, Labor Conflict, and Technological Change in Malaysia's Muda Region', *World Development*, 20 (6), 809–23.

—— (1995) 'Gender and Household Dynamics: Recent Theories and their Implications', in M. Quirbir (ed.) *Critical Issues in Asian Development: Theories and Policies*, Oxford: Oxford University Press.

—— (1997) 'From "Rotten Wives" to "Good Mothers": Household Models and the Limits of Economism', *Bulletin of the Institute of Development Studies*, 28 (3), 14–25.

Hart, Keith (1971) 'Migration and Tribal Identity among the Frafras of Ghana', *Journal of Asian and African Studies*, 6, 21–36.

Hatch, Elvin (1989) 'Theories of Social Honor', *American Anthropologist*, 91 (2), 341–53.

Hatchard, J. and Kessaris, A. (eds) (2003) *Law and Development: Facing Complexity in the 21st Century*, Manchester: Cavendish.

He, Liping (2008) 'Has Fiscal Federalism Worked for Macroeconomic Purposes? The Chinese Experience, 1994–2003', *China and World Economy*, 16 (1), 17–33.

Heckman, James J. (1997) 'The Intellectual Roots of the Law and Economics Movement', *Law and History Review*, 15 (2), 327–32.

Henderson, J. and Phillips, R. (2007) 'Unintended Consequences: Social Policy, State Institutions, and the Stalling of the Malaysian "Industrialization" Project', *Economy and Society*, 36 (1, February), 78–102.

Heremans, Dirk (2000) 'Regulation of Banking and Financial Markets', in B. Bouckaert and G. De Geest (eds) *Encyclopedia of Law and Economics: Volume III, The Regulation of Contracts*, Cheltenham: Edward Elgar.

Heyer, Amrik, Stewart, Frances and Thorp, Rosemary (eds) (2002) *Group Motivation and Development: Is the Market Destroying Cooperation?* Oxford: Oxford University Press.

—— (2003) 'When and How Far is Group Formation a Route out of Chronic Poverty?' paper presented at conference 'Staying Poor: Chronic Poverty and Development Policy', University of Manchester, 7–9 April

Higgins, Rosalyn J. (2003) 'Reflections from the International Court', in Malcolm D. Evans (ed.) *International Law*, Oxford: Oxford University Press.

Hilf, Meinhard (2003) 'Powers, Rules and Principles: Which Orientation for WTO/GATT Law?' *Journal of International Economic Law*, 1, 111–30.

Hill, M. and Kwen Fee, L. (1995) *The Politics of Nation Building and Citizenship in Singapore*, London: Routledge,

Hines, James (1999) 'Three Sides of Harberger Triangles', *Journal of Economic Perspectives*, 13 (2), 167–88.

Hirschman, Albert, O. (1970) 'The Search of Paradigms as a Hindrance to Understanding', *World Politics*, 22 (3), 329–43.

—— (1991) *The Rhetoric of Reaction, Perversity, Futility, Jeopardy*, Cambridge, MA: Belknap Press.

Hobsbawm, E. (1968) *Industry and Empire: From 1750 to the Present*, Harmondsworth: Penguin.

—— (1987) *The Age of Empire: 1815–1914*, New York: Vintage.

—— (1990) *Nations and Nationalism since 1780: Programme, Myth, Reality*, Cambridge: Cambridge University Press.

Hodgson, Geoffrey Martin (1993) *Economics and Evolution: Bring Life Back into Economics*, Cambridge: Polity Press.

—— (2001) *How Economics Forgot History: The Problem of Historical Specificity in Social Science*, London: Routledge.

Hoff, Karla and Stiglitz, Joseph, E. (2001) 'Modern Economic Theory and Development', in G.M. Meier and J.E. Stiglitz (eds) *Frontiers of Development Economics*, New York and Oxford: Oxford University Press for the World Bank.

Hogg, M.A. and Vaughan, G.M. (2002) *Social Psychology* (third edition), London: Prentice Hall.

Hooker, M.B. (1968) 'The Interaction of Legislation and Customary Law in a Malay State', *American Journal of Comparative Law*, 16 (3, Summer), 415–430.

—— (1971) *Adat Laws in Modern Malaya*, Kuala Lumpur: Oxford University Press.

Hovenkamp, Herbert (1990) 'The First Great Law and Economics Movement', 42 *Stanford Law Review*, 993, 996–7.

Howse, R.L. (2005) 'Back to Court after *Shrimp/Turtle*: India's Challenge to Labour and Environmental Linkages in the EC Generalized System of Preferences', in M. Andenas and F. Ortino (eds) *WTO: Law and Process*, London: British Institute of International and Comparative Law.

Hoxby, C. (ed.) (2003) *The Economics of School Choice*, Chicago: University of Chicago Press.

Hudec, R. (1970) 'The GATT Legal System: A Diplomat's Jurisprudence', 4 *Journal of World Trade Law*, 615–65.

—— (1980) 'GATT Dispute Settlement after the Tokyo Round: An Unfinished Business', 13 *Cornell International Law Journal*, 2, 145–203.

Humphries, J. (1990) 'Enclosures, Common Rights and Women: The Proletarianization of Families in Late Eighteenth and Early Nineteenth Century Britain', *Journal of Economic History*, 50 (1), 17–42.

Huntingdon, S. (1968) *Political Order in Changing Societies*, New Haven: Yale University Press.

ICTSD (International Centre for Trade and Sustainable Development) (2007) 'China Programme', *Bridges Weekly Trade News Digest*, 11 (6).

—— (2008a) *News and Analysis*, 12 (1, February).

—— (2008b) 'WTO Panel Rejects US Appeal, Upholding Brazil's Victory in Cotton Dispute', reported on 11 June 2008, citing BBC News, 27 July 2007; 'US Loses in Cotton Dispute at WTO', and BBC News, 2 June 2008; 'US Loses WTO Brazil Cotton Appeal'; available at ictsd.net/i/news (accessed 20 January 2009).

IUCN (International Union for the Conservation of Nature) (2005) *Disclosure Requirements: Ensuring Mutual Supportiveness between the WTO TRIPS Agreement and the CBD*, Switzerland: IUCN.

Iyer, Justice V.R. Krishna (1991) *Justice at Crossroads*, New Delhi: Deep and Deep.

Jacka, T. (1997) *Women's Work in Rural China: Change and Continuity in an Era of Reform*, Cambridge: Cambridge University Press.

Jayasuriya, Kanishka (2000) 'The Rule of Law and the Regimes of Exception in East Asia' Working Paper No. 96, National Library of Australia.

Jennings, Mark (2004) 'The WTO and International Law', paper presented at ANZSIL Conference, 18–20 June, Canberra.

Jensen, M. and Meckling, W. (1976) 'Theory of the Firm: Managerial Behavior, Agency Costs and Ownership Structure', *Journal of Financial Economics*, 39, 1021–39.

Jepperson, Ronald (2002) 'Political Modernities: Disentangling Two Underlying Dimensions of Institutional Differentiation', *Sociological Theory*, 20 (1), 65–80.

Jesudasan, J. (1989) *Ethnicity and the Economy: The State, Chinese Business and Multinationals in Malaysia*, Kuala Lumpur: Oxford University Press.

Jolly, R. (2005) 'The UN and Development Thinking and Practice', *Forum for Development Studies*, 1 (June), available at http://www.unhistory.org/reviews/FDS_Jolly.pdf (accessed 21 April 2009).

Jolly, R., Emerij, L. and Ghai, D. (2004) *UN Contributions to Development Thinking and Practice*, Bloomington: Indiana University Press.

Jomo, K.S. (ed.) (1999) *Rethinking Malaysia*, Kuala Lumpur: Malaysian Social Science Association.

Josling, T., Zhao, Longyue, Carcelen, Jeronimo and Arha, Kaush (2006) *Implications of WTO Litigation for the WTO Agricultural Negotiations*, IPC Issue Brief, Washington.

Kabeer (15th century CE) 'Illusion and Reality', available at http://www.poemhunter.com/poem/illusion-and-reality/ (accessed 25 August 2008).

Kabeer, N. (1994) *Reversed Realities: Gender Hierarchies in Development Theory*, London: Verso.

Kandiyoti, Deniz (1998) 'Bargaining with Patriarchy', *Gender and Society*, 2 (3), 274–90.

Kannabiran, K.G. (2003) *The Wages of Impunity, Power, Justice and Human Rights*, Hyderabad: Orient Longman.

Kautilya (1915) *Arthashastra*, trans. R. Shamasastry, Book III, Chapter 1; available at http://www.mssu.edu/projectsouthasia/history/primarydocs/Arthashastra/BookIII.htm (accessed 25 August 2008).

Kee, James Edwin (2004) 'Fiscal Decentralization: Theory as Reform', in A. Khan and W. Hildreth (eds) *Financial Management Theory in the Public Sector*, Westport CT: Praeger.

Keith, R. and Lin, Y. (2001) *Law and Justice in China's New Marketplace*. New York: Palgrave.

Kennedy, David W. (2003) 'The Politics and Methods of Comparative Law', in Pierre Legrand and Roderick Munday (eds) *Comparative Legal Studies: Traditions and Transitions*, Cambridge: Cambridge University Press.

Kennedy, Duncan (2006) 'Three Globalizations of Law and Legal Thought: 1850–2000', in D.M. Trubek and A. Santos (eds) *The New Law and Economic Development, A Critical Appraisal*, Cambridge: Cambridge University Press.

Khan, M. (1996) 'State Failure in Weak States', in J. Harriss, J. Hunter and C.M. Lewis (eds) *New Institutional Economics and Third World Development*, London: Routledge.

—— (2003) 'State Failure in Developing Countries and Institutional Reform Strategies', in B. Tungodden, N. Stern and I. Kolstad (eds) *Toward Pro-Poor Policies. Aid, Institutions, and Globalization. Annual World Bank Conference on Development Economics, Europe (2003)*, Oxford: Oxford University Press and World Bank.

Khor, Martin (2002) 'The WTO, the Post-Doha Agenda and the Future of the Trade Agenda: A Development Perspective', paper presented at ADB Annual Conference on 'Doha Development Agenda: Implications for Developing Asia', 10 May, Shanghai, People's Republic of China.

Kindleberger, C. and Aliber, R. (2005) *Manias, Panics and Crashes: A History of Financial Crises*, New York: Palgrave Macmillan.

Kingdon, G. and Muzzamil, M. (2003) *The Political Economy of Education in India: Teacher Politics in Uttar Pradesh*, Oxford: Oxford University Press.

Kivel, Paul (2004) *You Call This a Democracy? Who Benefits, Who Pays, and Who Really Decides*, Oman: Apex Press.

Knight, J. (1991) *Institutions and Social Conflict*, Cambridge: Cambridge University Press.

Kohli, A. (2004) *State-Directed Development: Political Power and Industrialization in the Global Periphery*, Cambridge: Cambridge University Press.

Krueger, A. (1974) 'The Political Economy of Rent Seeking', *American Economic Review*, 3, 291–303.

Krugman, P. (2007) *The Conscience of a Liberal*, New York: W.W. Norton.

Lal, Deepak (1988) *The Hindu Equilibrium: Volume 1, Cultural Stability and Economic Stagnation*, Oxford: Clarendon Press.

—— (2000) *The Poverty of 'Development Economics'* (second revised and expanded US edition), Cambridge, MA: MIT Press.

Lambach, D. (2004) 'State in Society: Joel Migdal and Limits of State Authority', paper presented at the Danish Political Theory Network Conference 'Political Concepts Beyond the Nation State: Cosmopolitanism, Territoriality, Democracy', 27–30 October, University of Copenhagen.

Lao Tse (2007) *Dao De Jing*, trans. James Legge, New York: BN Publications.

Lewis, W.A. (1954) 'Economic Development with Unlimited Supplies of Labour', *Manchester School of Economic and Social Studies*, 22 (2), 139–91.

Li Guo (2005) 'Chongqing Gives Notice that it will Control Local Legislation and Prudently Use Legislative Resources', *Procuratorial Daily*, 10 October, available at www.jcrb.com (taken from *Workers' Daily*).

Libecap, G. (1989) *Contracting for Property Rights*, New York: Cambridge University Press.

—— (2004) 'State Regulation of the Common Pool', in Claude Menard and Mary Shirley (eds) *The Handbook of the New Institutional Economics*, New York: Kluwer Academic Press.

Libecap, G., with Alston, L. and Mueller, B. (1999) *Titles, Conflict and Land Use: The Development of Property Rights and Land Reform on the Brazilian Amazon Frontier*, Ann Arbor, MI: University of Michigan Press.

Liu, J. (2007) 'Contextualizing Forestry Discourses and Normative Frameworks towards Sustainable Forest Management in Contemporary China, *International Forestry Review*, 9 (2), 653–60.

Loibl, Gerhard (2003) 'International Economic Law', in Malcolm D. Evans (ed.) *International Law*, Oxford: Oxford University Press.

Long, Chun-Lin and Zhou, Yilan (2001) 'Indigenous Community Forest Management in Jinuo People's Swidden Agroecosystems', *South West China, Biodiversity and Conservation*, 10, 753–67.

Lubman, S.B. (1999) *Bird in a Cage: Legal Reform in China after Mao*, Stanford: Stanford University Press.

Lundberg, S. and Pollak, R. (1993) 'Separate Spheres Bargaining and the Marriage Market', *Journal of Political Economy*, 101 (6), 988–1010.

McAuslan, P. (2003) *Bringing the Law Back In: Essays in Land, Law and Development*, Farnham, UK: Ashgate.

McChesney, Fred (2006) Coase, Demsetz and the Unending Externality Debate, *Cato Journal*, 26 (1), 179–200.

McCrudden, C. and Gross, S. (2006) 'WTO Government Procurement Rules and the Local Dynamics of Procurement Policy: A Malaysian Case Study', *European Journal of International Law*, 17, 151.

Maki, U. (1998) 'Against Posner, Against Coase, Against Theory', *Cambridge Journal of Economics*, 22 (5), 587–95.

Malinvaud, E. (1977) *The Theory of Unemployment Reconsidered*, Oxford: Blackwell.

Mamdani, M. (1996) *Citizen and Subject: Contemporary Africa and the Legacy of Late Colonialism*, London: James Currey; Princeton: Princeton University Press.

Mandel, R. and Humphrey, C. (eds) (2002) *Markets and Moralities: Ethnographies of Postsocialism*, Oxford: Berg.

Marglin, S. (1974) 'Why Bosses Do What They Do: The Origins and Functions of Hierarchy in Capitalist Production', available at http://www.economics.harvard.edu/faculty/marglin/files/

Marx, K. (1867) *Capital*, available at http://www.marxists.org/archive/marx/works/1867-c1/ (accessed 19 January 2009).

Marx, Karl and Engels, F. (1848) *The Communist Manifesto*, available at www.anu.edu.au/polsci/marx/classics/manifesto.html (accessed 19 January 2009).

Maskus, K.E. and Wilson, J.S. (2001) *Quantifying the Impact of Technical Barriers to Trade: Can it be Done?* Ann Arbor, MI: University of Michigan Press.

Means, Gordon P. (1985) 'The Orang Asli: Aboriginal Policies in Malaysia', *Pacific Affairs*, 58 (4), 637–52.

Medema, Steven G. and Samuels, Warren, J. (2001) 'The Economic Role of Government, as, in Part, a Matter of Selective Perception, Sentiment and Valuation: The Case of Pigovian and Paretian Welfare Economics', *American Journal of Economics and Sociology*, 59 (1), 87–108

Medema, Steven G. and Zerbe, Richard O. (2000) 'The Coase Theorem', entry 0730 in B. Bouckaert and G. De Geest (eds) *Encyclopedia of Law and Economics: Volume I, The History and Methodology of Law and Economics*, Cheltenham, Edward Elgar.

Meng Wancheng *et al.* (2007) *Xiandai jinbao* (Modern Golden Newspaper) 23 March, available at http://paper.lifeningbo.com.cn/html/2007-03/23/content_52427724.htm

Michael, Robert T., Hartmann, Heidi I. and O'Farrell, Brigid (1989) *Pay Equity: Empirical Inquiries*, US National Research Council, Committee on Women's Employment and Related Social Issues, Panel on Pay Equity Research, New York: National Academies Press.

Migdal, J. (1998) *Strong Societies and Weak States: State–Society Relations and State Capabilities in the Third World*, Princeton: Princeton University Press.

—— (2001) *State in Society: Studying How States and Societies Transform and Constitute One Another*, Cambridge: Cambridge University Press.

Migdal, J., Kohli, A. and Shue, V. (1994) *State Power and Social Forces: Domination and Transformation in the Third World*, Cambridge: Cambridge University Press.

Mill, John S. (1970 [1869]) *The Subjection of Women*, Cambridge, MA: MIT Press.

Mills, C. Wright (1956) *The Power Elite*, New York: Oxford University Press.

Mitlin, D. and Satterwaite, D. (eds) (2002) *Empowering Squatter Citizens*, London: Earthscan.

Mongia, R. (2007) 'Historicizing State Sovereignty: Inequality and Form of Equivalence', *Comparative Studies in Society and History*, 49 (2), 382–411.

Mosca, Gaetano (1939 [1896]) *Elementi di scienza politica* (The Ruling Class), New York: McGraw-Hill.

Mullally, S. (2004) 'Feminism and Multiculturalism Dilemmas in India: Revisiting the Shah Bano Case', *Oxford Journal of Legal Studies*, 24 (4), 671–92.

Mulvany, Patrick (2002) 'The Perils of Setting a Biodiversity Target' ITDG, available at http://www.ukabc.org/wssd_030902.htm (accessed 27 August 2008).

Murphy, R. (2007) 'Paying for Education in Rural China', in V. Shue and C. Wong (eds) *Paying for Progress in China: Public Finance, Human Welfare and Changing Patterns of Inequality*, London: Routledge.

Nelson, R. and Winters, S.G. (1982) *An Evolutionary Theory of Economic Change*, Cambridge, MA: Harvard University Press.

Nock, S. and Brinig, M. (2002) 'Weak Men and Disorderly Women: Divorce and the Division of Labour', in R. Rowthorn and A. Dnes (eds) *Marriage and Divorce: A Law and Economics Approach*, Cambridge: Cambridge University Press.

North, D.C. (1990) *Institutions, Institutional Change and Economic Performance*, Cambridge: Cambridge University Press.

—— (2005) *Understanding the Process of Economic Change*, Princeton: Princeton University Press.

North, D.C. and Thomas, R.P. (1974) 'The Rise and Fall of the Manorial System: A Theoretical Model', *Review of Radical Political Economy*, 6, 60–112.

—— (1976) *The Rise of the Western World: A New Economic History*, New York: Cambridge University Press.

Nurkse, R. (1953) *Problems of Capital Formation in Underdeveloped Countries*, Oxford: Blackwell.

Offe, Claus and Wisenthal, Helmut (1980) 'Two Logics of Collective Action: On Social Class and Organizational Form', *Political Power and Social Theory*, 1, 67–115.

Offer, A. (1992) *Property and Politics 1870–1914: Landownership, Law Ideology and Urban Development in England*, Oxford: Oxford University Press.

Ogus, A. (1994) *Regulation: Legal Form and Economic Theory*, New York: Oxford University Press.

Oi, J. (1999) *Rural China Takes Off: Institutional Foundations of Economic Reform*, Berkeley: University of California Press.

Okin, Susan Moller (1979) *Women in Western Political Thought*, Princeton: Princeton University Press.

—— (1989) *Justice, Gender and Family*, New York: Basic Books.

Olson, M. (1965) *The Logic of Collective Action: Public Goods and the Theory of Groups*, Cambridge, MA: Harvard University Press.

—— (1982) *The Rise and Decline of Nations: Economic Growth, Stagflation, and Social Rigidities*, New Haven: Yale University Press.

—— (1993) 'Dictatorship, Democracy, and Development', *American Political Science Review*, 87, 567–76.

Ong, Aihwa (1990) 'State versus Islam: Malay Families, Women's Bodies, and the Body Politic in Malaysia', *American Ethnologist*, 17 (2), 258–76.

Ortino, F. and Petersmann, E.-U. (2004) *The WTO Dispute Settlement System 1995–2003: A Consultation Process*, The Hague: WTO.

Ostrom, Elinor (1990) *Governing the Commons*, Cambridge: Cambridge University Press.

—— (2005) *Understanding Institutional Diversity*, Princeton: Princeton University Press.

Otto, J., Polak, M., Chen, J. and Li, Y. (eds) (2000) *Law-Making in the People's Republic of China*, The Hague: Kluwer Law International.

Oxfam (2007) publications available at website http://www.oxfam.org.uk/

Page, Sheila (2001) 'Developing Countries in GATT/WTO Negotiations', Working Paper, Overseas Development Institute.

Palmer, Michael (1995) 'The Re-emergence of Family Law in Post-Mao China: Marriage, Divorce and Reproduction', *China Quarterly*, 141 (March, Special Issue: China's Legal Reforms), 110–34.

—— (2005) 'On China's Slow Boat to Women's Rights: Revisions to the Women's Protection Law, 2005', *International Journal of Human Rights*, 11 (1), 151–77.

Palmeter, David and Mavroidis, Petros (1998) 'The WTO System and Sources of Law', *American Journal of International Law*, 92 (3), 358–413

Pareto, V. (1968 [1901]) *The Rise and Fall of Elites*, New York: Bedminster Press.

Patel, S. and Thorner, A. (eds) (1995) *Bombay: Mosaic of Modern Culture*, Bombay: Oxford University Press.

Pateman, C. (1988) *The Sexual Contract*, Stanford: Stanford University Press.

Patinkin, D. (1987) 'Walras Law', in *The New Palgrave, A Dictionary of Economics*, Volume 4, London: Macmillan, pp. 864–8.

Peerenboom, Randall (2002) *China's Long March Towards the Rule of Law*, Cambridge: Cambridge University Press.

Peletz, Michael G. (1993) 'Sacred Texts and Dangerous Dragons: The Politics of Law and Cultural Rationalisation in Malaysia', *Comparative Studies in History and Society*, 35 (1), 66–109.

People's Union for Democratic Rights (1982) *Undeclared Civil War: A Critique of Forest Policy*, New Delhi: PUDR.

Pildes, Richard H. (1996) 'The Destruction of Social Capital through Law', *University of Pennsylvania Law Review*, 144 (5), 2055–77.

Pollak, Robert, A. (1985) 'A Transaction Cost Approach to Families and Households', *Journal of Economic Literature*, 23, 581–608.

Polyani, K. (1971 [1944]) *The Great Transformation*, Boston: Beacon Press.

Porter, M. (1992) 'Capital Disadvantage: America's Failing Capital Investment System', *Harvard Business Review*, 70, 65–82.

Posner, Richard A. (1987) 'The Law and Economics Movement', *American Economic Review*, 77 (2), 1–13.

—— (1993) 'What Do Judges and Justices Maximize? (The Same Thing Everyone Else Does)', *Supreme Court Economic Review*, 3, 1–41.

—— (1998) *Economic Analysis of the Law* (fifth edition), New York: Aspen Law and Business.

Potter, Pitman B. (1994) 'Riding the Tiger: Legitimacy and Legal Culture in Post-Mao China', *China Quarterly*, 138, 325–58.

—— (1999) 'The Chinese Legal System: Continuing Commitment to the Primacy of State Power', *China Quarterly*, 159, 673–83.

—— (2001) 'The Legal Implications of China's Accession to the WTO', *China Quarterly*, 167, 592–609.

Powell, Robert (2006) 'War as a Commitment Problem', *International Organization*, 60 (1), 169–203

Powell, S. and Schmidt, A. (2005) 'The Cotton and Sugar Subsidies Decisions: WTO's Dispute Settlement System Rebalances the Agreement on Agriculture', No. 15640, Technical Papers from University of Florida, International Agricultural Trade and Policy Center.

Price, R.B. (1967) 'Ideology and Indian Planning', *American Journal of Economics and Sociology*, 26 (1), 47–64.

Prosser, T. (1990) 'The Constitutions and Political Economy: The Privatisation of Public Enterprises in France and Great Britain', 53 *Modern Law Review*, 3, 305–20

—— (1997) *Law and the Regulators*, Oxford: Clarendon Press.

Qin, Julia Ya (2003) 'WTO Plus Obligations and their Legal Implications for the World Legal System', *Journal of World Trade*, 27 (3), 483–522.

—— (2007) 'The Impact of WTO Accession on China's Legal System: Trade, Investment and Beyond' (9 May 2007), Wayne State University Law School Research Paper No. 07–15, available at http://ssrn.com/abstract = 985321 (accessed 25 August 2008).

—— (2008a) 'China, India, and the Law of the World Trade Organization', *Asian Journal of Comparative Law*, 3 (1), Article 8.

—— (2008b) 'The Challenge of Interpreting "WTO-Plus" Provisions', paper presented at the Society of International Economic Law (SIEL) Inaugural Conference, 8 July, Wayne State University Law School, available at http://papers.ssrn.com/sol3/papers.cfm?abstract_id = 1156861 (accessed 26 August 2008).

Raghavan, C. (2003) 'Reviewing the current WTO situation in light of the past developments', Editor Emeritus of SUNS (South North Development Monitor), Geneva, 17 August 2006.

Rajagopal, B. (2000) 'From Resistance to Renewal: The Third World, Social Movements, and the Expansion of International Institutions', *Harvard International Law Journal*, 41 (2), 529–78.

—— (2003) *International Law from Below: Development, Social Movements and Third World Resistance*, Cambridge: Cambridge University Press.

Rajamani, L. (2006) *Differential Treatment in International Environmental Law*, Oxford: Oxford University Press.

Rajan, R. and Zingales, L. (2004) *Saving Capitalism from the Capitalists: Unleashing the Power of Financial Markets to Create Wealth and Spread Opportunity*, Princeton: Princeton University Press

Rehnema, M. and Bawtree, V. (eds) (1997) *The Post-Development Reader*, London: Zed Books.

Rendra, W.S. (1974) 'State of Emergency', in *Ballads and Blues, Poems*, translated from Indonesian by B. Raffel, H. Aveling and D. May, Oxford: Oxford University Press.

Ricardo, David (1821) *On Principles of Political Economy and Taxation*, available at http://books.google.com (accessed 25 August 2008).

Risbud, Neelima (2003) 'Understanding Slums: Case Study', in United Nations (ed.) *The Global Reports on Human Settlements*, New York: United Nations.

Rist, G. (2002) *The Origins of Development: From Western Theory to Global Faith*, London: Zed Books.

Rodrik, D. (2001) *The Global Governance of Trade as if Development Really Mattered*, available at http://www.ksghome.harvard.edu/~drodrik/ (accessed 30 September 2007).

Rose-Ackerman, Susan (1995) *Controlling Environmental Policy: The Limits of Public Law in Germany and the United States*, New Haven: Yale University Press.

Rosenberg, N. and Birdzell, L. (1986) *How the West Grew Rich*, New York: Basic Books.

Rosser, E. (2007) 'Obligations of Privilege', *NYU Review of Law and Social Change*, 31, 1 (American University, WCL Research Paper).

Rothschild, Emma (2001) *Economic Sentiments: Adam Smith, Condorcet, and the Enlightenment*, Harvard: Harvard University Press.

Rowbotham, S. (1976) *Woman's Consciousness, Man's World*, Harmondsworth: Pelican/Penguin.

Rowthorn, R. (2002a) 'Marriage as a Signal', in R. Rowthorn and A. Dnes (eds) *The Law and Economics of Marriage and Divorce*, Cambridge: Cambridge University Press.

Rowthorn, R. and Dnes, A. (eds) (2002b) *The Law and Economics of Marriage and Divorce*, Cambridge: Cambridge University Press.

Said, E. (1978) *Orientalism: Western Concepts of the Orient*, London: Penguin.

Sathe, S.P. (2003) *Judicial Activism in India* (second edition), New Delhi: Oxford University Press.

Scitovsky, Tibor (1954) 'Two Concepts of External Economies', *Journal of Political Economy*, 62 (2), 143–51.

Scott, Joan W. (1988) *Gender and the Politics of History*, New York: Columbia University Press.

Seabright, P. (2005) *The Company of Strangers: A Natural History of Economic Life*, Princeton: Princeton University Press.

Secretariat of the Convention on Biological Diversity (2005) *The Handbook (2005) of the Convention on Biological Diversity, including the Cartagena Protocol of Biosafety* (third edition), Montreal: CBD, available at http://www.cbd.int/ (accessed 20 January 2009).

—— (2007) Communiqué of the Secretariat of the Convention on Biological Diversity, Montreal, 2 July, available at http://www.cbd.int/doc/press/2007/pr-2007-07-02-ifap-en.pdf (accessed 28 August 2008).

Seidman, A. and Seidman, R. (1996) 'Drafting Legislation for Development: Lessons from a Chinese Project', *American Journal of Comparative Law*, 44 (1), 1–44.

Sen, Amartya (1982) *Poverty and Famines: An Essay on Entitlements and Deprivation*, Oxford: Clarendon Press.

—— (1999) *Development as Freedom*, Oxford: Oxford University Press.

Shi Jikai (2005) *Life Daily*, China, 27 November, available at www.lifedaily.cn

Shleifer, A. and Vishny, R. (2002) *The Grabbing Hand: Government Pathologies and Their Cures*, Harvard: Harvard University Press.

Sidanius, Jim and Pratto, Felicia (1999) *Social Dominance*, Cambridge: Cambridge University Press.

Singh, A. (1989) 'Third World Competition and De-industrialisation in Advanced Countries', *Cambridge Journal of Economics*, 13 (1, March), 103–20.

—— (2003) 'Capital Account Liberalization, Free Long-Term Capital Flows, Financial Crises and Economic Development', *Eastern Economic Journal*, 29 (2), 191–216.

Singh, A., Glen, J., Zammit, A., De-Hoyos, R., Singh, A. and Weisse, B. (2005) 'Shareholder Value Maximisation, Stock Market and New Technology: Should the US Corporate Model be the Universal Standard?' *International Review of Applied Economics*, 19 (4), 419–37.

Singh, Nirvikar (2007) 'Fiscal Federalism and Decentralization in India: Competitive, Cooperative or Market Preserving Federalism?' MPRA Paper no. 1447, University Library of Munich, Germany.

Sinha, Aseema (2005) *The Regional Roots of Developmental Politics in India: A Divided Leviathan*, Indiana: Indiana University Press.

Sivaramakrishnan, K. (1995) 'Colonialism and Forestry in India', *Comparative Studies in Society and History*, 37 (1), 3–40.

Smelser, N. and Swedberg, R. (1995) *The Handbook of Economic Sociology*, Princeton: Princeton University Press.

Smith, Adam (1976 [1776]) *An Inquiry into the Nature and Causes of the Wealth of Nations*, ed. Edwin Cannan (second edition), Chicago: University of Chicago Press.

—— (2002 [1761, 1817]) *The Theory of Moral Sentiments*, ed. Knud Haakonssen, New York: Cambridge University Press.
Smith, J.W. (2005) *Economic Democracy: The Political Struggle of the Twenty-First Century* (fourth edition), available at http://www.ied.info/books/economic-democracy (accessed 20 January 2009).
Snyder, Francis G. (1980) 'Law and Development in the Light of Dependency Theory', *Law and Society Review*, 14 (3), 723–804.
Solow, Robert M. (1956) 'A Contribution to the Theory of Economic Growth', *Quarterly Journal of Economics*, 70 (1), 65–94.
Sousa Santos, B. de (1974) 'Social Structure: The Problem of Embeddedness', available at http://faculty.babson.edu/krollag/org_site/org_theory/Scott_articles/granovet_embed.html (accessed 26 August 2008).
—— (2003) 'The World Social Forum: Towards a Counter-Hegemonic Globalisation', available at http://www.ces.fe.ua.pt/bss/fsm.php = A9 (accessed 26 August 2008).
SPARC (1985) *We, the Invisible: A Census of Pavement Dwellers*, Mumbai: SPARC.
Stewart, F. (1990) 'Basic Needs Strategies, Human Rights and the Right to Development', QEH Working Paper Luca D'Angliana 2.
—— (2000) 'Horizontal Inequalities: A Neglected Dimension of Development', CRISE Working Paper 1, Queen Elizabeth House, University of Oxford.
—— (2001) 'Horizontal Inequalities: A Neglected Dimension of Development, UNU/World Institute for Development Economic Research (UNU/WIDER), Annual Lectures 5.
Stigler, G. (1966) *The Theory of Price* (third edition), New York: Macmillan.
Strathern, M. (1999) *Property, Substance and Effect: Anthropological Essays on Persons and Things*, London: Athlone Press.
—— (2003) 'Redescribing Society', *Minerva*, 41 (3), 263–76.
—— (2005) *Kinship, Law and the Unexpected*, Cambridge: Cambridge University Press.
Summer, Lawrence (2007) *Financial Times*, 24 September.
Sun, Xiaoli (2007) 'The Effects of Fiscal Federalism on Compulsory Education in China: For Better or Worse', *Journal of Administration and Governance*, 2, 1.
Sundar, N. and Jeffery, R. (eds) (1999) *A New Moral Economy for India's Forests?* New Delhi: Sage.
Sunstein, C. (2003) *Why Societies Need Dissent*, Harvard: Harvard University Press.
Sweezy, P. (1971 [1941]) *The Theory of Capitalist Development*, New York: Modern Reader Paperbacks.
Sykes, Alan (2003) 'The Economics of WTO Rules on Subsidies and Countervailing Measures', University of Chicago Law and Economics, Olin Working Paper no. 186, available at http://ssrn.com/abstract = 415780 or DOI: 10.2139/ssrn.415780
Talpade Mohanty, Chandra (1988) 'Under Western Eyes: Feminist Scholarship and Colonial Discourses', *Feminist Review*, 30, 61–80.
—— (2003a) '"Under Western Eyes" Revisited: Feminist Solidarity through Anticapitalist Struggles, *Signs: Journal of Women in Culture and Society*, 28, 499–535.
—— (2003b) *Feminism without Borders: Decolonizing Theory, Practicing Solidarity*, Durham: Duke. University Press.
Tambiah, Stanley (1989) 'Ethnic Conflicts in the World Today', *American Ethnologist*, 16, 335–49.
—— (1997) *Levelling Crowds: Ethnonationalist Conflicts and Collective Violence in South Asia*, Berkeley: University of California Press.
Tang, W. and Parish, W. (1996) *Chinese Urban Life under Reform: The Changing Social Contract*, Cambridge: Cambridge University Press.

Tanner, Murray Scott (1999) *Politics of Lawmaking in Post-Mao China: Institutions, Processes and Democratic Prospects*, New York: Oxford University Press.

Tanzi, V. (1995) 'Fiscal Federalism and Decentralization: A Review of Some Efficiency and Macroeconomic Aspects', in *Annual World Bank Conference on Development Economics 1995*, Washington, DC: World Bank.

Tarrow, S. (1998) *Power in Movement: Social Movements and Contentious Politics*, Cambridge: Cambridge University Press.

Thirlway, H. (2003a) 'The International Court of Justice', in Malcolm D. Evans (ed.) *International Law*, Oxford: Oxford University Press.

—— (2003b) 'The Sources of International Law', in Malcolm D. Evans (ed.) *International Law*, Oxford: Oxford University Press.

Thomas, D.Q. and Beasley, M.E. (1993) 'Domestic Violence as a Human Rights Issue', *Human Rights Quarterly*, 15, 36–62.

Thompson, E.P. (1966) *The Making of the English Working Class*, New York: Vintage Books.

Tilly, Charles (1977) 'Major Forms of Collective Action in Western Europe, 1500–1750', *Theory and Society*, 3 (3), 365–75.

Tinker, I. (ed.) (1990) *Persistent Inequalities: Women and World Development*, New York and London: Oxford University Press.

Trachtman, Joel P. (1999) 'The Domain of WTO Dispute Resolution', *Harvard International Law Journal*, 40, 333.

Trubek, David M. and Galanter, M. (1974) 'Scholars in Self-estrangement: Some Reflections on the Crisis in Law and Development Studies in the United States', *Wisconsin Law Review*, 1062–102.

Trubek, David M. and Santos, Alvaro (eds) (2006) *The New Law and Economic Development: A Critical Appraisal*, Cambridge: Cambridge University Press.

UNCTAD (2006) *Commodity and Statistics Year Book*, available at www.unctad.org/infocomm/anglais

Unger, R. (1975) *Knowledge and Politics*, New York: Free Press

—— (2000) *Democracy Realized: The Progressive Alternative*, Verso

Unterhalter, Elaine (2008) 'Global Values and Gender Equality in Education: Needs, Rights and Capabilities', in D. Fennell and M. Arnot (eds) *Gender Education and Equality in a Global Context: Conceptual Frameworks and Policy Perspectives*, London: Routledge.

Van Seters, M. (ed.) (2006) *Communitarianism in Law and Society*, New York: Rowman and Littlefield.

Varavara Rao, P. (1973) 'The Jail', available at http://www.varavararao.org/ (accessed 31 July 2008).

Veblen, T. (1994 [1944]) *The Theory of the Leisure Class*, Harmondsworth: Penguin Classics.

Vira, B. (1993) 'Common Property in Ecosystems under Stress', at 'Local Cooperation for the Care of Forests', the fourth annual conference of the International Association for the Study of Common Property, Manila, Philippines, 16–19 June, available at http://www.indiana.edu/~iascp/abstracts/675.html (accessed 20 January 2009).

Vira, B., Dubois, O. Daniels, S.E. and Walker, G.B. (1998) 'Institutional Pluralism in Forestry: Considerations of Analytical and Operational Tools', *Unasylva*, 49 (194), 35–42.

Vogel, S. (1996) *Freer Markets, More Rules: Regulatory Reform in Advanced Industrial Countries*, Ithaca: Cornell University Press.

Weingast, B. (2005) 'The Performance and Stability of Federalism: An Institutional Perspective', in Claude Menard and Mary Shirley (eds) *Handbook of the New Institutional Economics*, New York: Springer-Verlag.

Weiss, L. (1998) *The Myth of the Powerless State*, Ithaca, Cornell University Press.

What_Do_Bosses_Do.pdf

Williams, Jerre S. (1956) *The Supreme Court Speaks*, Austin: University of Texas Press.

Williamson, J. (1991) 'British Inequality during the Industrial Revolution: Accounting for the Kuznets Curve', in J. Brenner (ed.) *Income Distribution in Historical Perspective*, Cambridge: Cambridge University Press.

Williamson, Oliver (1982) *The Economic Institutions of Capitalism: Firms, Markets, Relations, Contracting*, New York and London: The Free Press.

Wirth, D.A. (2002) 'European Communities: Measures Affecting Asbestos and Asbestos-containing Products', *American Journal of International Law*, 96 (2), 435–9.

Woolcock, M. (1988) 'Social Capital and Economic Development:Towards a Theoretical Synthesis and Policy Framework', *Theory and Society*, 27 (2), 151–208.

Woolley, Frances R. (1985) 'Getting the Better of Becker', *Feminist Economics*, 2 (1, (Spring), 114–20.

—— (1993) 'The Feminist Challenge to Neoclassical Economics', *Cambridge Journal of Economics*, 17, 485–500.

World Bank (1994) *Infrastructure for Development* (World Development Report), New York: Oxford University Press, available at www.worldbank.org/wdr/ (accessed 20 January 2009).

—— (1996a) *Bureaucrats in Business: The Economics and Politics of Government Ownership*, New York: Oxford University Press.

—— (1996b) *From Plan to Market* (World Development Report), New York: Oxford University Press, available at www.worldbank.org/wdr/ (accessed 20 January 2009).

—— (2003) *Sustainable Development in a Dynamic Economy: Transforming Institutions, Growth and Quality of Life* (World Development Report), New York: Oxford University Press, available at www.worldbank.org/wdr/ (accessed 20 January 2009).

—— (2004) *Making Services Work for Poor People* (World Development Report), New York: Oxford University Press, available at www.worldbank.org/wdr/ (accessed 20 January 2009).

—— (2005) *A Better Investment Climate for Everyone* (World Development Report), New York: Oxford University Press, available at www.worldbank.org/wdr/ (accessed 20 January 2009).

—— (2006) *Equity and Development* (World Development Report), New York: Oxford University Press, available at www.worldbank.org/wdr/ (accessed 20 January 2009).

—— (2007) *Development and the Next Generation* (World Development Report), New York: Oxford University Press, available at www.worldbank.org/wdr/ (accessed 20 January 2009).

World Economic Forum (2007) *The Shifting Power Equation*, Annual Meeting 2007, 24–28 January, Davos, Switzerland, at www.weforum.org (accessed 20 January 2009).

Xi, W. (1999) *Forest Policy, Law and Local Participation in Forest Management in China*, at http://www.iges.or.jp/en/fc/phase1/ir99/1–3-Wang%20.pdf

Yanagisako, Sylvia, Junko (1979) 'Family and Household: The Analysis of Domestic Groups', in *Annual Review of Anthropology*, 161–205

Zacklin, Ralph (2003) 'A Personal Perspective on International Law', in Malcolm Evans (ed.) *International Law*, Oxford and New York: Oxford University Press.

Zhang, Yan and Fang, Ke (2003) 'Politics of Housing Redevelopment in China: The Rise and Fall of Ju'er Hutong Project in Inner-city Beijing', *Journal of Housing and Built Environment*, 18, 75–87.

Zhao, L. and Li, J. (2006) 'China's Hukou system: Multifaceted Changes and Institutional Causes', Discussion Paper 9, China Policy Institute, University of Nottingham.

Zheng, Yongnian (2006) 'Explaining the Sources of de facto Federalism in Reform China: Intergovernment Decentralizaton, Globalization and Central–Local Relations', *Japanese Journal of Political Science*, 7 (2), 101–26.

Cases cited

Romer v. Evans, Scalia, J. dissenting, ROMER v. EVANS, U.S. (1996) ROY ROMER, GOVERNOR OF COLORADO, ET AL. PETITIONERS v. RICHARD G. EVANS ET AL. CERTIORARI TO THE SUPREME COURT OF COLORADO, No. 94–1039, argued 10 October 1995, decided 20 May 1996.

WT/DS 26, DS 39 and DS 48 EC–Hormones cases in WTO dispute settlement case summaries 1995–December 2007, at p. 7, at www.wto.org (accessed 20 January 2009).

WT/DS 50 in WTO dispute settlements: one-page case summaries 1995–December 2007, at p. 17, as WTO dispute (DS 50). INDIA – PATENTS (US), case at www.cuts-international.org (accessed 20 January 2009).

WT/DS 265 in WTO dispute settlement case summaries 1995–December 2007, at p. 98, as EC – Export Subsidies on Sugar, together with cases DS 266 and 283, at www.wto.org (accessed 20 January 2009).

WT/DS 267 in WTO dispute settlement case summaries 1995–December 2007, at p. 99, on US–Upland Cotton, as Case DS 267, at www.wto.org (accessed 20 January 2009).

WT/DS 291 is WTO dispute DS291 together with DS 292 and 293 in WTO dispute settlement case summaries 1995–December 2007, at p 109, on EC – Approval and Marketing of Biotech Products, at www.wto.org (accessed 20 Jan 2009).

WT/DS 320 is US-Continued Suspension of Obligations in the EC-Hormones Dispute, WTO Doc. at www.wto.org

WT/DS 321 is Canada-Continued Suspension of Obligations in the EC-Hormones Dispute, WTO Doc. at www.wto.org

WT/DS 362, WTO dispute; China – Measures Affecting the Protection and Enforcement of Intellectual Property Rights. First submission of US on 30 January 2008 at www.wto.org (accessed 20 January 2009).

Websites consulted

http://cssh.unipune.ernet.in/HumanRights/05%20STATE%20AGRICULTURE%20FOREST%20DALITS%20AND%20TRIBALS/04.pdf

http://ebooks.adelaide.edu.au/m/mill/john_stuart/m645s/

http://ebooks.adelaide.edu.au/m/mill/john_stuart/m645s/chapter4.html (accessed 25 Aug 2008)

http://falcon.arts.cornell.edu/Govt/faculty/Tarrow%20docs/polanyi%20in%20brussels.pdf

http://ictsd.net/i/news/bridgesweekly/12287/

http://paper.lifeningbo.com.cn/html/2007–03/23/content_52427724.htm.

http://papers.ssrn.com/sol3/papers.cfm?abstract_id=1156861

http://www.bbc.co.uk/pressoffice/speeches/stories/grade_goodman.shtml

http://www.cbd.int/doc/press/2007/pr-2007-10-12-8j-en.pdf

http://www.ifta-online.org/Uploads/Issues/58.pdf

http://www.indiana.edu/~iascp/abstracts/675.html
http://www.wto.org/english/res_e/booksp_e/dispu_summary08_e.pdf
http://www.wto.org/english/res_e/booksp_e/dispu_summary08_e.pdf
http://www.wto.org/english/res_e/booksp_e/dispu_summary08_e.pdf
http://www.wto.org/english/res_e/booksp_e/dispu_summary08_e.pdf
http://www.wto.org/english/res_e/booksp_e/dispu_summary08_e.pdf.
https://practicalaction.org/docs/advocacy/eco3_extracts.doc

Index

Lightning Source UK Ltd.
Milton Keynes UK
UKOW040726140612

194381UK00003B/26/P

9 780415 420358